PRACTICAL GUIDES

HISTORY

IN THE
ULUM

COLIN HILL AND JANET MORRIS

Published by Scholastic Publications Ltd,
Villiers House, Clarendon Avenue,
Leamington Spa, Warwickshire CV32 5PR.

Reprinted 1992 , 1992
Written by Colin Hill and Janet Morris
Edited by Christine Lee
Sub-edited by Catherine Baker
Designed by Sue Limb
Illustrated by Jane Bottomley
Photographs by:
John Twinning pages 5, 11, 157, 175
Sue Limb pages 7, 167, 181
Avoncroft Museum pages 59, 115, 185

Artwork by Liz Preece, Castle Graphics,
Kenilworth.
Printed by Ebenezer Baylis, Worcester

Front cover designed by Joy White and Sue Limb.
Front cover illustrated by Jovan Djordjevic.

The publishers wish to thank Edward Law for his help in the preparation of this book.

The publishers wish to thank the Controller of Her Majesty's Stationery Office for permission to quote from *History in the National Curriculum* (DES/WO, HMSO 1991) on pages 14, 19, 22, 28, 38, 44, 47, 62, 75, 84 and 107, and from the *National Curriculum History Working Group Final Report* (DES/WO, HMSO (1990) on page 182.

British Library Cataloguing in Publication Data
Hill, Colin
A practical guide to teaching history within the National Curriculum.
1. Primary Schools. Curriculum. History. Teaching
I. Title II.Morris, Janet
372.8900942

ISBN 0-590-76562-0

Contents

Introduction

If you are one of those teachers for whom every new educational initiative is a professional challenge and a spur to creativity, for whom the appearance of each new National Curriculum ring binder is exciting and stimulating – this may not be the book for you! If, on the other hand, you are one of the many teachers who want to do their very best for the children, but wonder how to cope with history on top of mathematics, science, English, technology and geography – and still teach the children to read – then read on! Our aim in this book is to suggest what you can do and how you might set about it, give information about where you can get help, provide advice on resources, and, not least, help to establish a rationale for teaching primary history.

There are many teachers who will say that the only reason for teaching history at primary level is the National Curriculum. This is more likely to be the view of infant than junior teachers, but in fact many teachers, in both phases, are already teaching some history and enjoying it. Others appreciate the need for history, but find it hard to make a start. Most report a need for new ideas, fresh starting points and help with planning work in an integrated curriculum over a school year.

If we want to give our work real quality, relating it to children's genuine needs, we need to be convinced of its educational value. The value of early history teaching lies firstly in helping children to develop concepts of time (before, after, sooner, later, now, then) and in enabling them to understand sequences of events taking place in time. We also need to encourage understanding of change and stability, similarities and differences and growth and decay. Finally, children need to be aware of their own origins in the past, and of the background to what we regard as the present.

The current debate on whether knowledge or understanding should be stressed more strongly is a pointless one in primary history teaching, since one cannot exist without the other. Children can acquire knowledge through understanding, and can understand if they have sufficient knowledge. Young children need to be actively engaged in their learning.

Aims and objectives

We aim in this book to help you create a framework for learning in which children can develop through talking, listening, writing, reading, painting, drawing, modelling, singing, role-playing, dancing and visiting. The following list sums up our objectives.

- To design themes and topics which satisfy the needs of the National Curriculum in history, simultaneously covering attainment targets in the three core subjects, geography and technology. Some of the topics will use history as the starting point, and others will seek to extract the potential for history from within topics based mainly on mathematics, English or science. The potential for work in history will be discussed in a further section dealing with the basic recurring themes in the infant curriculum, along with work using parish churches and botanic gardens. Suggestions for school assemblies will also be included.
- To address the question of available time and overall structure in planning for a whole-school policy, offering suggestions for reducing curriculum overload.
- To make our plans sufficiently open-ended to enable teachers to adopt them either as a whole or in part, and to be adaptable to individual needs.
- To provide a simplified chart showing attainment targets and programmes of study in the National Curriculum for History at Key Stages 1 and 2.
- To offer advice on using museums effectively, on setting up a school resource bank and on assessment.
- To give lists of addresses and details of various services to teachers of history.

Good reading!

Chapter 1
An outline of Key Stages 1 and 2

Planning ahead

The key to successfully undertaking the Programme of Study for history in the National Curriculum is forward planning, concentrating on the efficient use of pupils' time. At the time of writing, it is suggested that ten per cent of the timetable should be devoted to history teaching. We cannot anticipate schools being able to allocate this amount of time to history teaching if the tasks do not fulfil the requirements of some other curriculum areas. For example, pupils writing a story based upon historical fact, such as an account of life as a sailor on board Columbus' *Santa Maria*, could be working towards Attainment Target 3, Level 4b of the English National Curriculum ('Write stories which have an opening, a setting, characters, a series of events and a resolution which engages the interest of the reader').

Many schools have a whole-school policy for all aspects of the curriculum, which helps teachers plan their lessons within the context of what has gone before and what will follow, and it is this approach that we recommend.

History Study Units

The Programme of Study for history comprises History Study Units (HSUs). HSUs form a coherent series of topics which can be linked to aspects of the core curriculum, other foundation subjects and RE. While this Programme of Study may

Figure 1

PROGRAMME OF STUDY KS1	Key Elements		Pupils should be helped to develop an awareness of the past through stories from different periods and cultures including: well known myths and legends; stories about historical events; eyewitness accounts of historical events and fictional stories set in the past. Pupils should have opportunities to learn about the past from a range of historical sources, including: artefacts; pictures and photographs; music; adults talking about their own past; written sources; buildings and sites and computer based material. Pupils should be taught about the everyday life, work, leisure and culture of men, women and children in the past. They should have the opportunity to investigate: changes in their own lives and those of their family or adults around them; changes in the way of life of British people since WWII; and the way of life of people in a period of the past beyond living memory. Pupils should be taught about the lives of different kinds of men and women and about past events of different types, including local, national and international events and events commemorated by succeeding generations.					
PROGRAMME OF STUDY KS2	Core Study Units		CSU 1 Invaders and settlers	CSU 2 Tudors and Stuarts	CSU 3 Victorian Britain (and/or)	CSU 4 Britain since 1930	CSU 5 Ancient Greece	CSU 6 Exploration and encounters
	Supplementary Study Units, 3 or 4	A Choose 1 or 2	Ships and seafarers	Food and farming	Houses and places of worship	Writing and printing	Land transport	Domestic life, families and childhood
		B Choose 1 or 2	A Unit based on local history	A different type of local history				
		C Choose 1 or 2	Ancient Egypt	Mesopotamia	Assyria	The Indus Valley	The Maya	Benin

take away some of the free choice that teachers have been used to, it does make forward planning of history teaching a relatively uncluttered task, and should go some way to eliminating the problem of pupils studying canals or dinosaurs several times during their primary school careers.

Key Stage 1

Infant school pupils and pupils in the equivalent years of first school (Y1 and Y2, Key Stage 1) have a straightforward programme of study to follow. The programme of study for KS1 consists of one study unit which has to be taught throughout the stage (see Figure 1). Well-known myths and legends, stories about historical events, eyewitness accounts of historical events and fictional stories set in the past should be used to develop an awareness of the past. Pupils should be introduced to the concept of the past through the use of artefacts, pictures and photographs, music, adults talking about the past, buildings and sites, and computer-based material.

Pupils should be taught about the everyday lives of people and should investigate changes in their own family lives and those of adults known to them, changes in the British way of life since 1945 and the way of life of people beyond living memory. The lives of famous men and women should also be studied and pupils should be taught about local, national and international events, as well as events that are commemorated by succeeding generations. Key Stage 1 pupils should work towards the fourteen statements of attainment at Levels 1 to 3 (see Figure 2, page 9).

Key Stage 2

Pupils in year groups 3, 4, 5 and 6 (Key Stage 2) have a mixture of compulsory units and optional units. Nine units in all have to be undertaken during this stage. Five or six Core Study Units have to be selected, with the option of dropping CSU3 (Victorian Britain) or CSU4 (Life in Britain since 1930). All junior pupils, therefore, will undertake Core Study Units 1, 2, 5 and 6, plus 3 and/or 4. At least one unit must be selected from each of the Supplementary Study Units A, B and C. If CSU3 or 4 is dropped, then an additional SSU must be taken to bring the total to nine (Figure 1, page 8).

The Supplementary Study Units are grouped as follows:

- A: units involving the study of a theme over a long period of time;
- B: units based on local history;
- C: units based on the study of a non-European society.

If a second local history Supplementary Study Unit is chosen from Category B, it should be based on a different type of local history from the first.

The school then needs to plan how each unit will introduce pupils to political, economic, technological, scientific, social, religious, cultural and aesthetic perspectives.

Key Stage 2 pupils should work towards the 20 statements of attainment at Levels 2 to 5. Note that the levels overlap those of Key Stage 1, Levels 1 to 3 (Figure 2).

A basis for planning

In following the history Programme of Study, class teachers can no longer make an individual choice about the historical content of their topic or project work, and year groups can no longer agree within the group what they will teach. Three-year and four-year programmes will have to be planned for Key Stages 1 and 2, with teachers co-operating on a school-wide basis.

Key Stage	Level	Attainment Target 1: Knowledge and Understanding of History	Attainment Target 2: Interpretations of History	Attainment Target 3: The Use of Historical Sources
KEY STAGE ONE	Level 1	a) Place in sequence events in a story about the past. b) Give reasons for their own actions.	Understand that stories may be about real people or fictional characters.	Communicate information acquired from a historical source.
KEY STAGE ONE / KEY STAGE TWO	Level 2	a) Place familiar objects in chronological order. b) Suggest reasons why people in the past acted as they did. c) Identify differences between past and present time.	Show an awareness that different stories about the past can give different versions of what happened.	Recognise that historical sources can stimulate and help answer questions about the past.
KEY STAGE ONE / KEY STAGE TWO	Level 3	a) Describe changes over a period of time. b) Give reasons for a historical event or development. c) Identify differences between times in the past.	Distinguish between a fact and a point of view.	Make deductions from historical sources.
KEY STAGE TWO	Level 4	a) Recognise that over time some things changed and others stayed the same. b) Show an awareness that historical events usually have more than one cause and consequence. c) Describe different features of a historical period.	Show an understanding that deficiencies in evidence may lead to different interpretations of the past.	Put together information drawn from different historical sources.
KEY STAGE TWO	Level 5	a) Distinguish between different kinds of historical change. b) Identify different types of cause and consequence. c) Show how different features in a historical situation relate to each other.	Recognise that interpretations of the past, including popular accounts, may differ from what is known to have happened.	Comment on the usefulness of a historical source by reference to its content, as evidence for a particular enquiry.

Figure 2

The work should not be planned around the attainment targets (see Figure 2, page 9) but around the History Study Units in the Programme of Study. In fact, it would be hard to plan around the history attainment targets as they are concerned with awareness, understanding, interpretation, ways of carrying out tasks and ways of communicating information. However, teachers would be wise to acknowledge the attainment targets in their plans. For example, children are expected to be able to comment on the fact that historical events can be seen from more than one point of view. It follows that they must have an opportunity to research the information using a variety of sources that give different points of view about a historical event. The attainment targets can help schools plan a history curriculum that is matched to all pupils' needs. They progress from Level 1 to Level 5 and show how each pupil can be helped to develop knowledge, understanding and skills.

Pupils are expected to communicate the results of their work through oral and visual presentations as well as written results. This will be in line with existing practice in many classrooms, but some teachers may have to reconsider how they ask pupils to present results. Having an interested audience for their work is a great motivator for children. This is an idea we will return to in more detail when we consider using assemblies to present historical work. Individual or group presentations of work can be fun, whilst also giving a sense of achievement.

We advocate the excellent topic-based approach that is already used to teach much history in primary schools. A great deal of the content has been laid down within the National Curriculum, but the advantage of this is that pupils will have history teaching that is planned on a school-wide basis and linked to other areas of the curriculum. A good source of suggestions for planning topic work is *Project Teaching* by David Wray (Scholastic Publications).

Chapter 2
Key Stage 1

In this book, the pattern of work for Key Stage 1 has been organised into three main topics and six themes (see page 13 for definitions of topic and theme). These can be used exactly as they appear in the book or taken apart and used as the basis for other ideas. The history component in each section could be used separately or linked into a differently organised cross-curricular module. In addition to this, we have looked at some of the recurring curriculum themes (such as Christmas) and attempted to show how the historical aspects of these can be harnessed to enrich the children's overall understanding.

Finally, we have suggested a particular local study which encompasses much of the knowledge and understanding needed for Y2.

This book does not attempt to lay down rules for teaching primary history, but does (as the series title promises) offer a practical guide to the National Curriculum. Any school wishing to use the topics and themes as they are presented here might like to consider the format shown in Figure 1 on page 12.

Y1	Term 1	My story
	Term 2	Toys Food
	Term 3	Houses and homes Stories, myths and legends – 1
Y2	Term 1	Suitcase in the attic
	Term 2	Keeping ourselves healthy Stories, myths and legends – 2
	Term 3	Materials Going to school in Great-Grandma's day

Figure 1

In addition to these themes and topics, this chapter will also show how history can be integrated into seasonal topics such as 'Harvest', 'Bonfire night', 'Christmas', 'Easter', 'Diwali' and 'Summer holidays'. Teachers who have appropriate local resources may also wish to use the sections on the parish church and using local botanic gardens. Topics would generally need to be worked on for about a month, of which approximately two weeks should be spent on the history components. However, final decisions about timing would have to be flexible, depending on a whole range of factors.

Chronology

There should be a gradual move towards chronology in Y2, laying foundations for work in Key Stage 2. For this reason, we have designed work on the local parish church, looking at it not from the religious but from the historical point of view. Historically-based comparisons could be made with a mosque or temple.

The need for an appreciation of chronology does not preclude starting from the present and gradually working back. Most experienced infant teachers would agree with the need, when introducing young children to history, to help them understand what 'before' and 'in the past' actually mean. Starting with 'now' is a way in! In their Final Report, the History Working Group say 'chronological teaching could move backwards along the time line, starting from the present. It may be appropriate for example in the early years of pupils' schooling – to start at both ends simultaneously' (3.19).

INSET

Staff INSET in history is essential, and a coherent whole-school policy, which is written down and used by every member of staff, is the only way to ensure work of any quality in history as in any other curriculum area. INSET should begin with every teacher reading the National Curriculum documents for history and *History 5-13* in the HMI 'Curriculum Matters' series.

An INSET day could start with a brainstorming session on 'What should we teach in history?'. The elements suggested could be discussed, sifted, added to and subtracted from until a workable set of principles has been agreed upon. At this point, this book could be used to help organise the content of each year's work. Year group teachers might then find it helpful to work in their groups, with the whole staff coming together at the end for a final analysis. A member of staff who has a particular interest in history (and that need not imply specialist knowledge) should act as overall co-ordinator.

The question of a school history resource bank should be addressed, perhaps using Chapter 7 as a guide and referring to the suggestions given at the end of each topic and theme in this chapter. Methods of assessment will need careful thought, and suggestions to help with this have been included in a separate chapter on Assessment on page 167.

Topics and themes for Key Stage 1

For the purposes of this book, a topic is defined as a particular area of history to be taught and learned, with history as the main element, but using and developing other curriculum areas, especially the core subjects.

A theme will be defined as work designed to teach one or more of the core subjects but where there is much potential for teaching aspects of history. These definitions are purely for convenience and do not apply to history teaching in general.

Art, craft, music and drama will be seen as the media through which learning takes place rather than as 'subjects', although technology will obviously be recognised as a National Curriculum subject and included accordingly.

Each topic and theme will be described and explored in the following format:

- a description of the topic or theme;
- starting points and ways into the theme or topic;
- clear suggestions for developing each aspect of the web, with examples of the type of questions to be asked of the children and the questions the children will be encouraged to raise themselves;
- a list of resources, by no means either complete or prescriptive, which is intended to be added to by individual teachers;
- a topic web outlining the main elements of each topic and theme, with the title as the 'hub', the core curriculum areas branching from it, and all the related activities listed round the perimeter.

Topic A: My story

Links with Attainment Targets

AT1 • use common words and phrases relating to the passing of time, *for example: old, new, before, after, long ago, days of the week, months, years;*
• identify a sequence of events and talk about why they happened, *for example: changes in the pupil's family;*

AT2 • distinguish between different versions of events, *for example: different accounts by pupils of events which happened in the school a week, month or year ago;*

Cross-curricular links

English:
AT1, AT2, AT3, AT4.
Science:
AT1, AT2, AT3, AT4
Maths:
AT1, AT3

This is a main history topic, exploring each child's personal history. It introduces concepts of time (now, then, days, months, years) by using stories from children's own lives and those of their parents and grandparents. It also looks at change and stability over children's own lifetimes and those of their parents.

Starting points

• Ask the children to bring in photographs of themselves as babies, together with some recent photographs.
• Let the children do paintings or drawings of themselves, using the recent photographs for reference.
• Encourage the children to talk about the recent past in terms of all the things they did before starting school, then tape these memories on to cassettes.
• Read and discuss the story of *Milly-Molly-Mandy* by Joyce Lankester Brisley, encouraging the children to comment on the differences and similarities between their families and that of Milly-Molly-Mandy in the 1920s.
• Read 'The very first story' from *My Naughty Little Sister* by Dorothy Edwards and ask the children to recall the births of younger brothers and sisters. Ask them to find out about the early weeks of their own lives from parents or older siblings.

Developments

- Let the children make a scrapbook entitled 'My Story'. This could have the child's self-portrait on the front, and contain a simple family tree, along with all the child's work in connection with the topic.
- Various pictorial representations could be used to present data on children's birthdays. This could include the date and days of the week on which various children were born, places of birth and birth weight and length compared with present weight and length.
- Ask a parent with a baby to bring it into school to be bathed, weighed and measured.
- Organise a visit or series of visits to old people's homes, and encourage the children to take gifts, sing favourite songs and ask questions about the old people's childhoods.

These ideas all involve the help of parents and grandparents in a variety of ways, and all the adults in the school could help in contributing childhood photographs and personal memories.

Discussion

The children could be asked questions such as the following:

- In what ways do you think you have changed since you were a baby?
- In what ways do you think you are the same?
- What kinds of things have changed since your mum and dad or gran and grandad were little?
- If we can't remember things about when we were very small, how do we find out?
- How do we find out about things that happened before we were born?

The family tree

The family tree format on photocopiable page 18 has been designed for use with the main history topic 'My story'. The tree image has been chosen to emphasise the connection with growth and, to some extent, to explain why the term 'family tree' is used at all. The tree analogy breaks down in some senses by placing the child herself at the base of the trunk and the older members of the family on the higher

branches, and there is no reason why any teacher who wishes to do so should not redesign the tree in the opposite direction. The reason for planning it the way we have is that this follows the convention normally used for family trees.

We are well aware of the problems associated with family trees in an age when the traditional family is by no means the accepted norm. The difficulty would lie in the case where, for example, a child does not know who her father or grandparents are. In this kind of situation we suggest that teachers help the child to make a tree showing the relationships she does possess and know about. We do not feel that an adopted child presents a problem, since he can make the tree of the family of which he is a legitimate part.

We see various ways in which the tree can be used, apart from helping each child to see her place in the time span of her own family. We have explained how it could be used in the chapter on Assemblies (see page 157), and we see possiblities for using it to record the generations of, for example, Milly-Molly-Mandy's family. Again, the chart would need some adaptation for this purpose, but some valuable oracy work could arise from trying to deduce different relationships and perhaps creating some more characters we do not know about from the story. This would give an opportunity to point out the difference between a story and real events. It is permissible to create relations for Milly-Molly-Mandy as a story book character, but not for ourselves because history is about finding out about what *really* happened.

Some children might be interested in completing a family tree for a group of people whose names they find on tombstones in the church yard. Another possible use for the family tree would be to record the family relationships of Prince William, for example.

We see the long term aims of working on family trees as being to develop a child's sense of time and understanding of sequence.

Resources

Books

Milly-Molly-Mandy Stories, Joyce Lankester Brisley (Puffin).
New Baby, Judith Baskerville (A & C Black).
My Naughty Little Sister, Dorothy Edwards (Mammoth).
The Tinderbox Song Book, compiled by Sylvia Barratt (A & C Black).
The Year I was Born, compiled by Sally Tagholm (Fantail Series, Penguin).
Then and Now, Summer and Winter, Day and Night ('What's the Difference?' series, Usborne).

Pictures

Make collections of pictures of babies, children of various ages and adults ranging from young to old. These can be cut from magazines and newspapers, and the children can contribute to the collections.

Try to find pictures of hospitals, including if possible a picture of the local maternity unit where some of the children and their siblings may have been born. Pictures cut from catalogues can be useful, including baby equipment, toddler toys, older children's toys and clothing worn by people of different age groups.

Clothing

Display a set of clothing graded in size from the smallest child to adult; for example, a set of shoes or gloves.

Film strips

The following film strips are available from Philip Green Educational Ltd:
F17: *The Baby*.
F15: *Me*.

Pictures and poems

Philip Green Educational Ltd supply the following useful packs of pictures and poems:
AO5: *Families 1*.
AO6: *Families 2*.

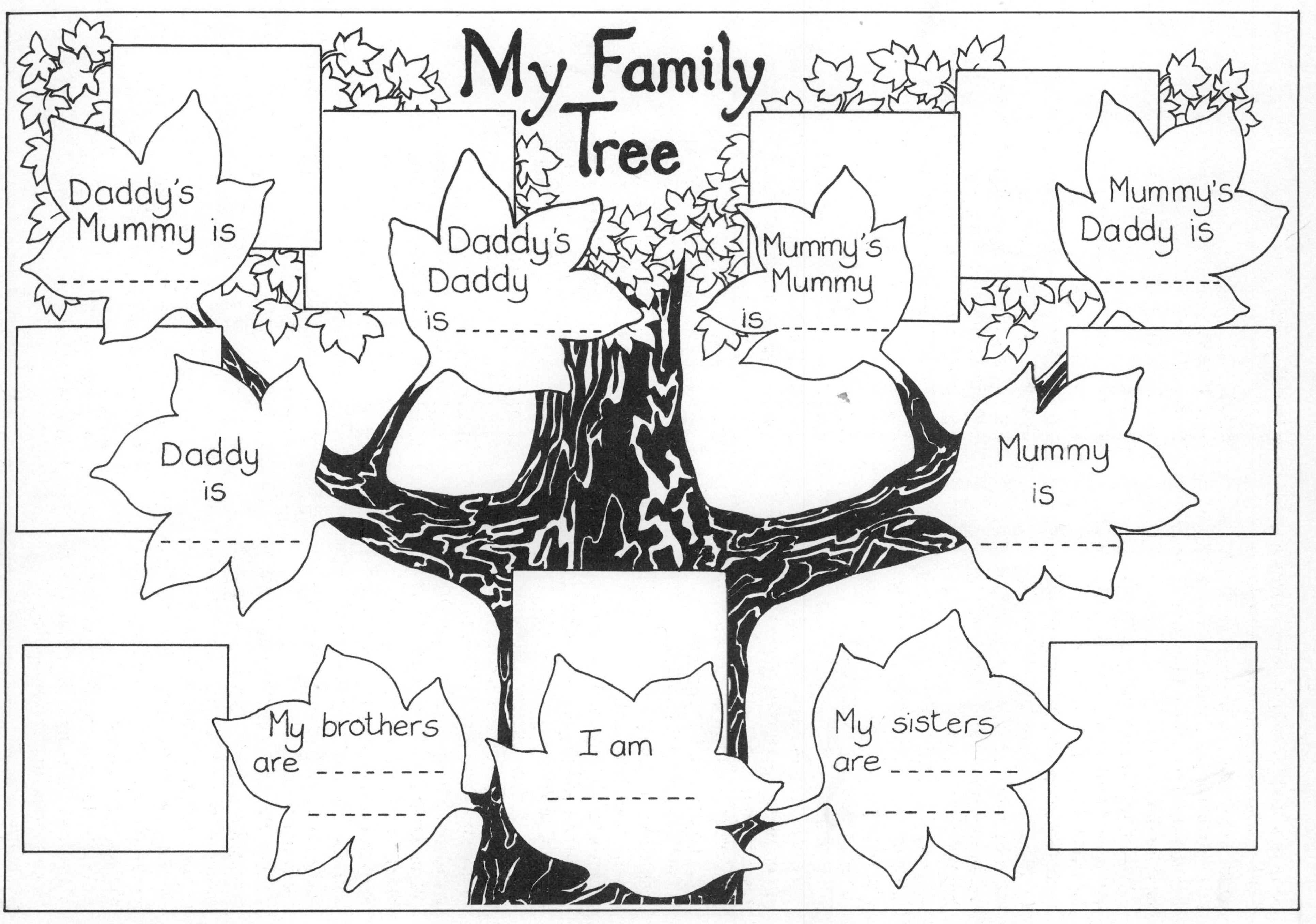

My Family Tree
Daddy's Mummy is
Daddy's Daddy is
Mummy's Mummy is
Mummy's Daddy is
Daddy is
Mummy is
My brothers are
I am
My sisters are

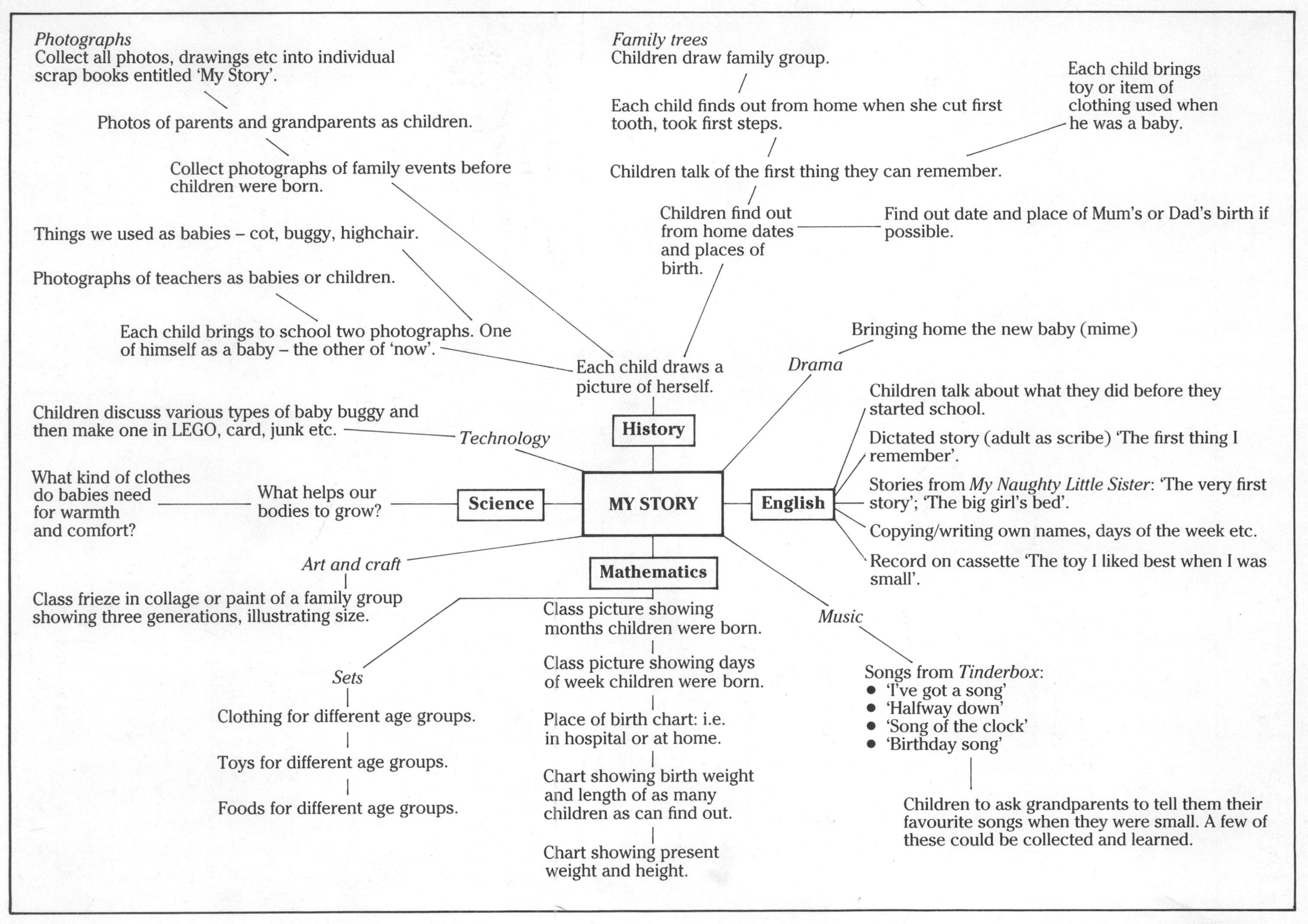
MY STORY
History
Photographs
Collect all photos, drawings etc into individual scrap books entitled 'My Story'.
Photos of parents and grandparents as children.
Collect photographs of family events before children were born.
Things we used as babies – cot, buggy, highchair.
Photographs of teachers as babies or children.
Each child brings to school two photographs. One of himself as a baby – the other of 'now'.
Each child draws a picture of herself.
Family trees
Children draw family group.
Each child finds out from home when she cut first tooth, took first steps.
Children talk of the first thing they can remember.
Each child brings toy or item of clothing used when he was a baby.
Children find out from home dates and places of birth.
Find out date and place of Mum's or Dad's birth if possible.
Drama
Bringing home the new baby (mime)
English
Children talk about what they did before they started school.
Dictated story (adult as scribe) 'The first thing I remember'.
Stories from My Naughty Little Sister: 'The very first story'; 'The big girl's bed'.
Copying/writing own names, days of the week etc.
Record on cassette 'The toy I liked best when I was small'.
Music
Songs from Tinderbox:
• 'I've got a song'
• 'Halfway down'
• 'Song of the clock'
• 'Birthday song'
Children to ask grandparents to tell them their favourite songs when they were small. A few of these could be collected and learned.
Technology
Children discuss various types of baby buggy and then make one in LEGO, card, junk etc.
Science
What helps our bodies to grow?
What kind of clothes do babies need for warmth and comfort?
Art and craft
Class frieze in collage or paint of a family group showing three generations, illustrating size.
Mathematics
Class picture showing months children were born.
Class picture showing days of week children were born.
Place of birth chart: i.e. in hospital or at home.
Chart showing birth weight and length of as many children as can find out.
Chart showing present weight and height.
Sets
Clothing for different age groups.
Toys for different age groups.
Foods for different age groups.

Theme 1: Toys

Links with Attainment Targets

AT2 • develop an awareness of different ways of representing past events, *for example: pictures, written accounts, films, television programmes, plays, songs, reproductions of objects, museum displays;*

AT3 • find out about the past from different types of historical source, *for example: historic houses, objects in museums, paintings, photographs, coins, newspapers.*

Cross-curricular links

English:
All Attainment Targets
Science:
AT10
Maths:
AT1, AT2, AT12

This is a science and technology project in which toys of long ago form the history element. It involves comparisons between modern toys and those played with by parents, grandparents and even great-grandparents, looking at the materials with which they were made, the kinds of play they gave rise to and the contrast between rich and poor children's toys.

Starting points

• Ask the children each to bring in a favourite toy. These could be described and discussed, examining the materials used to make them, considering where they might have been made, and finding out where they were bought from.
• Organise a visit to the toy department of a big store or to a specialist toy shop.
• Read excerpts from *The Adventures of the Little Wooden Horse* by Ursula Moray Williams. Explain that this is a story about a time when the children's great-grandparents were children. The children could be asked to consider the differences between their own favourite toys and the little wooden horse.

Developments

• Invite parents and grandparents in to school to talk about the toys they loved best, showing the children some of these toys if possible. Ask someone over the age of 70 to talk about their toys. This could, if necessary, be taped and played to the children.
• Set up two small displays, one of modern toys and one of older toys. Let the children draw and paint them.
• Try to borrow a collection of very old toys from a museum loan service. Let the children examine them and try to work out

how old each one is in relation to the two displays. Comparisons could be made between materials, styles of play the toys encouraged and how they were made.

- Try to arrange a visit to a toy museum. The Museum of Childhood at Bethnal Green in London would be ideal, but many museums have excellent toy collections, such as the Pinto Collection at the Birmingham Museum.
- Make a collection of pictures of old toys using books and the visual aids sections of libraries. A collection of stories about toys could also be built up.
- Compare particular types of toys, such as old and new dolls or teddy bears.

Discussion

The children could be asked questions such as the following:

- Would your grannie have had a plastic doll? Why not? What might her doll have been made of?
- What would have happened if your grannie had washed her teddy bear?
- Where do you think your Little Pony was made?
- Where was the little wooden horse made?
- What are your favourite toys?
- What were the favourite toys of your great-grandparents?

Resources

Collections of toys, and pictures of toys, of different kinds, both old and new, brought in by children and/or borrowed from a museum.

Books

Toys, Victoria and Albert Museum of Childhood (HMSO).
Entertainment in 1900, Stephen Attmore ('In the past' series, Longman).
The Adventures of Galldora, Modwena Sedgwick (Puffin).
The Adventures of the Little Wooden Horse, Ursula Moray Williams (Puffin).
The Noah's Ark, Ruth Ainsworth (Beaver).

Music

'The Emperor's Nightingale', Jan Holdstock.
'The Fantastic Toyshop', Rossini.

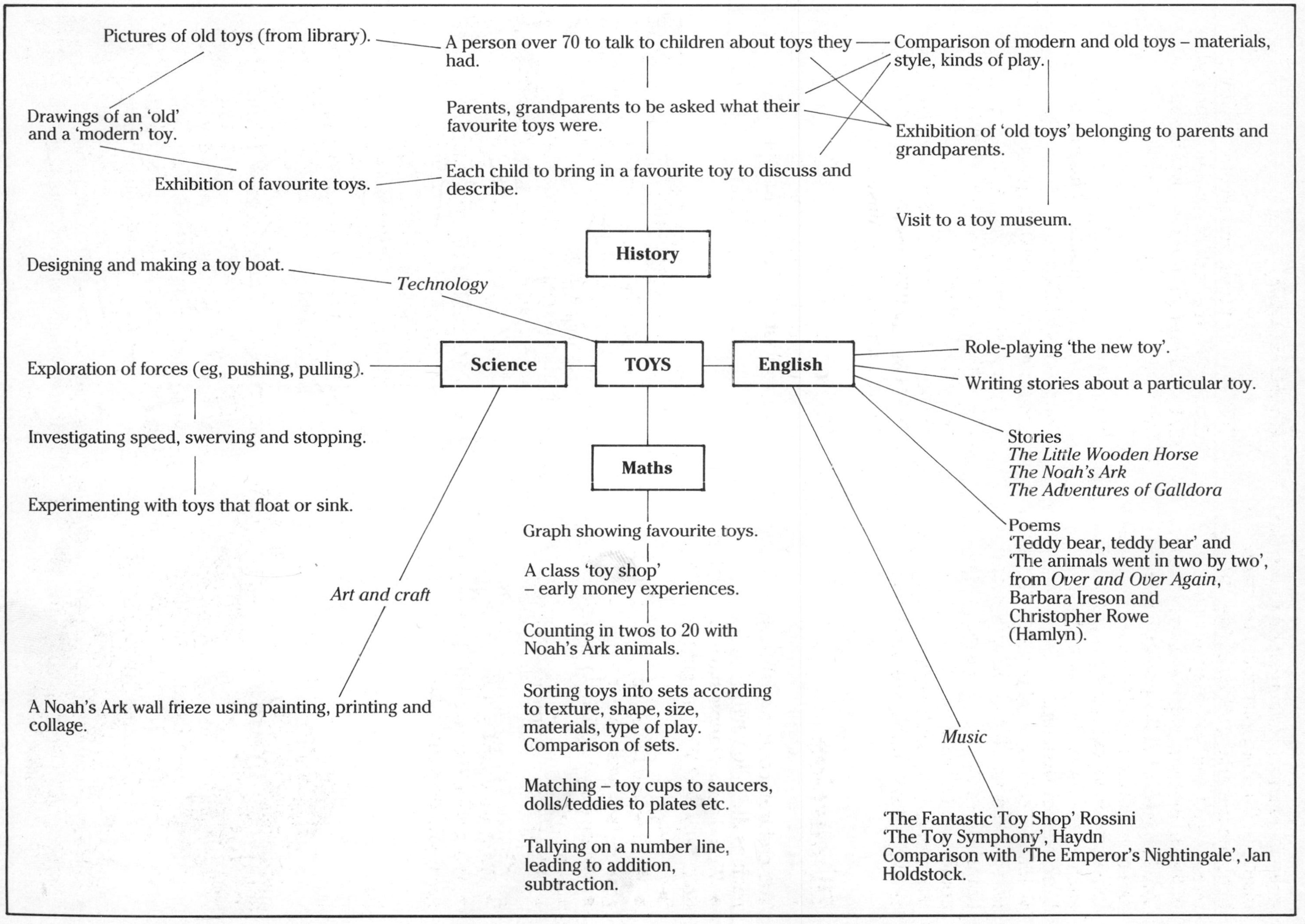
TOYS
History
Pictures of old toys (from library).
Drawings of an 'old' and a 'modern' toy.
Exhibition of favourite toys.
A person over 70 to talk to children about toys they had.
Parents, grandparents to be asked what their favourite toys were.
Each child to bring in a favourite toy to discuss and describe.
Comparison of modern and old toys – materials, style, kinds of play.
Exhibition of 'old toys' belonging to parents and grandparents.
Visit to a toy museum.
Technology
Designing and making a toy boat.
Science
Exploration of forces (eg, pushing, pulling).
Investigating speed, swerving and stopping.
Experimenting with toys that float or sink.
Art and craft
A Noah's Ark wall frieze using painting, printing and collage.
Maths
Graph showing favourite toys.
A class 'toy shop'
– early money experiences.
Counting in twos to 20 with Noah's Ark animals.
Sorting toys into sets according to texture, shape, size, materials, type of play.
Comparison of sets.
Matching – toy cups to saucers, dolls/teddies to plates etc.
Tallying on a number line, leading to addition, subtraction.
English
Role-playing 'the new toy'.
Writing stories about a particular toy.
Stories
The Little Wooden Horse
The Noah's Ark
The Adventures of Galldora
Poems
'Teddy bear, teddy bear' and
'The animals went in two by two',
from Over and Over Again,
Barbara Ireson and
Christopher Rowe
(Hamlyn).
Music
'The Fantastic Toy Shop' Rossini
'The Toy Symphony', Haydn
Comparison with 'The Emperor's Nightingale', Jan Holdstock.

Theme 2: Food

Links with Attainment Targets

AT1 • observe differences between ways of life at different times in the past, *for example: the clothes worn in different periods;*

AT2 • develop an awareness of different ways of representing past events, *for example: pictures, written accounts, films, television programmes, plays, songs, reproductions of objects, museum displays;*

AT3 • find out about the past from different types of historical source, *for example: historic houses, objects in museums, paintings, photographs, coins, newspapers.*

Cross-curricular links

English: All Attainment Targets Science: AT1, AT3, AT13 Maths: AT8, AT9

This is a theme drawing mainly on science, but there are opportunities for children to make comparisons between the food they eat now and the food eaten by their grandparents during the Second World War. There is considerable scope to continue this theme further into the past if the children seem ready and interested. It would also be possible to work on it for some time in Y1 and then return to the theme in Y2. These are decisions teachers can only make for themselves, bearing in mind that the National Curriculum at Key Stage 1 offers scope for flexibility.

Starting points

- The children could discuss and record, through drawing, painting or writing, a typical day's food. This could be followed by an investigation of a typical day's food for a wartime child.
- Ask a grandparent (or possibly an older member of staff) to describe to the children the kind of food they ate and how and why food was rationed. Try to find a ration book to show to the children.
- Organise a class walk to a local supermarket. Follow this up with a visit to an old shop in a 'living museum'. Comparisons could be made and differences noted.

Developments

- Carry out investigations into and comparisons between school dinners now and in the war. It might be possible to involve the school meal service and produce a wartime school dinner.
- Collect old cookery books and compare the recipes with modern ones. Try out some of the recipes.
- Organise a bread-and-jam party in a room which is blacked out, with the children dressed as if prepared for an air raid (wearing track suits renamed 'siren suits'). A cassette recording of an air raid warning siren could be used and the children could role-play 'going to the shelter'.
- Make a collection of food pictures

comparing foods 'then and now'. Wartime posters could be used and a chart made showing the rations a child would have had.

- Arrange a visit to a typical wartime kitchen (many museums have 'pre-fabs' on show). Children could look at the cooker and the larder and be encouraged to make comparisons with methods of food preparation and storage 'then and now'.
- Make collections of pictures of modern cookers and compare them with library pictures of those of the 1940s.
- After some preliminary maths work on money, show the children some pre-decimal coins and explain the kinds and amounts of foods that could be bought with, for example, one shilling.
- After sorting and classifying Smarties, jelly babies and liquorice allsorts, children could be asked to find out from grandparents (or other older relatives) what sweets they ate in the war, how many they had and how they were packaged. A similar investigation could take place with fruit.
- Look at how people grew their own food and link this to science. Children could try growing some food of their own. A visit could be made to local allotments.

For developments in other subject areas see the topic web.

Discussion

Questions the children could be asked include the following:

- Can you thing of something you like to eat that you couldn't have eaten in the war?
- Why do you think food was rationed?
- Do you think children ate the same food as the grown-ups in the war?
- Did soldiers and sailors eat the same as everyone else?
- Can you think of ways that people might have managed to get more food?
- Can you think of some of the differences between shops then and shops now?
- How did your grannie's mum cook the dinner?
- How do your mum and dad cook food?
- What things do we have to help us in our kitchens?
- Could your grannie have had frozen chips for dinner? Why not? Can you find out when ordinary people first had fridges or freezers?

Resources

Books

In the Shops, On the Farm and *In the Garden* ('Zero Books' series, Macdonald).
Young Ideas: Good Food, Edward Ramsbottom (Macmillan).
See How it's Made – The Loaf of Bread, illustrated by Michael Ricketts (Macmillan).
Food and Cooking, Margaret Baker (A & C Black).
First Cookbook (Usborne).
Living Long Ago: Food and Eating (Usborne).
A Very First Poetry Book, compiled by John Foster (Oxford University Press).
Tinderbox Assembly Book and *Tinderbox Song Book*, compiled by Sylvia Barratt (A & C Black).
Make Things that Grandma Made, M Stapleton (Studio Vista).
Wartime cookery books may be obtainable through local libraries and/or borrowed from older people.

Other written resources

Useful pamphlets are available from the Dairy Produce Advisory Service, Milk Marketing Board, Thames Ditton, Surrey.
Child Education, February 1985: 'Project File on Food'.
Ration books may be obtainable from the local Schools Museum Service.
Collections of pictures may be borrowed from local libraries and from personal collections.

Film strips

The following relevant film strips are obtainable from Philip Green Educational Ltd:
F16: Milk.
F11: Bread.

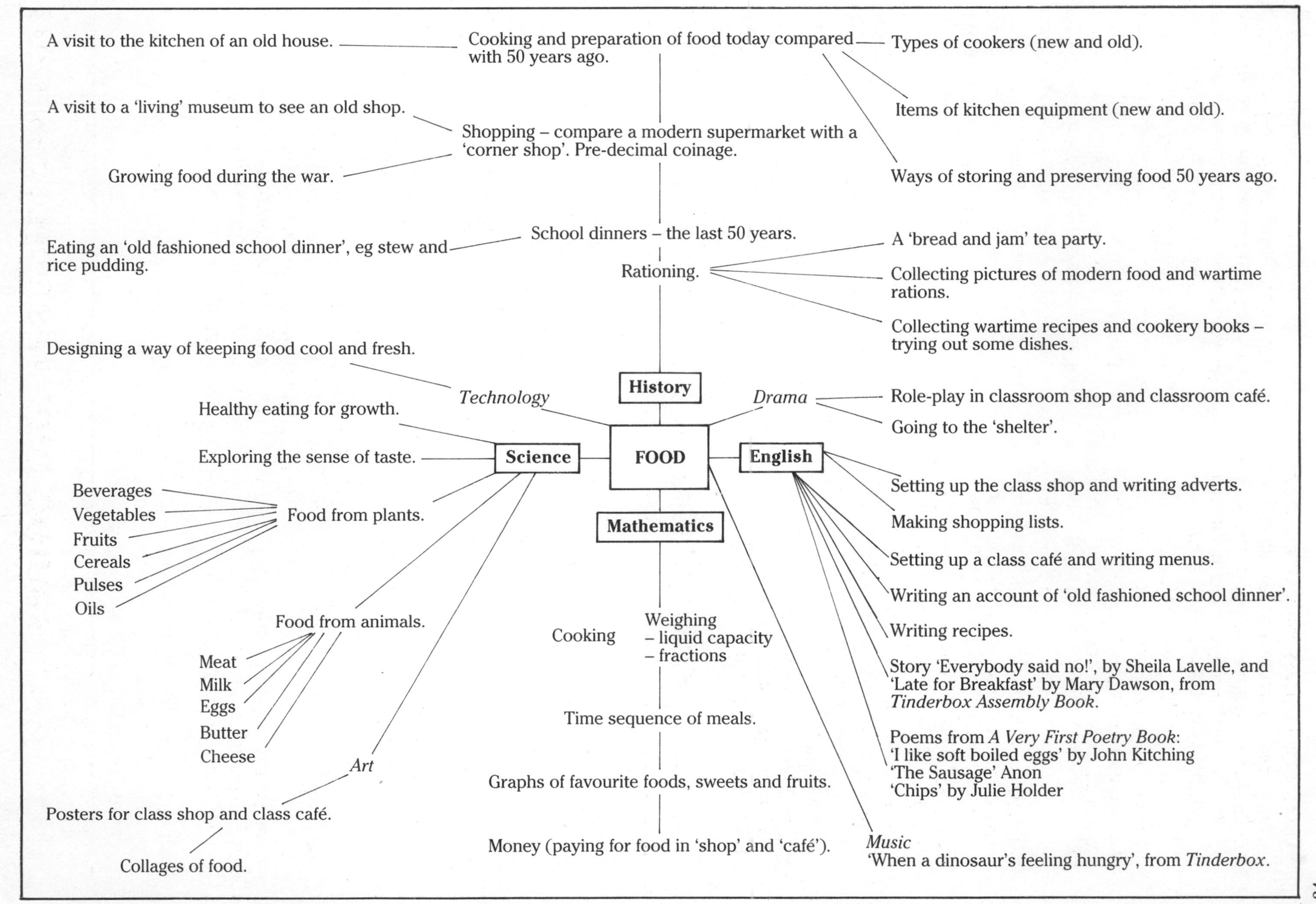
FOOD
History
Cooking and preparation of food today compared with 50 years ago.
A visit to the kitchen of an old house.
Types of cookers (new and old).
Items of kitchen equipment (new and old).
Ways of storing and preserving food 50 years ago.
Shopping – compare a modern supermarket with a 'corner shop'. Pre-decimal coinage.
A visit to a 'living' museum to see an old shop.
Growing food during the war.
School dinners – the last 50 years.
Eating an 'old fashioned school dinner', eg stew and rice pudding.
Rationing.
A 'bread and jam' tea party.
Collecting pictures of modern food and wartime rations.
Collecting wartime recipes and cookery books – trying out some dishes.
Technology
Designing a way of keeping food cool and fresh.
Drama
Role-play in classroom shop and classroom café.
Going to the 'shelter'.
Science
Healthy eating for growth.
Exploring the sense of taste.
Food from plants.
Beverages
Vegetables
Fruits
Cereals
Pulses
Oils
Food from animals.
Meat
Milk
Eggs
Butter
Cheese
Art
Posters for class shop and class café.
Collages of food.
Mathematics
Cooking
Weighing
– liquid capacity
– fractions
Time sequence of meals.
Graphs of favourite foods, sweets and fruits.
Money (paying for food in 'shop' and 'café').
English
Setting up the class shop and writing adverts.
Making shopping lists.
Setting up a class café and writing menus.
Writing an account of 'old fashioned school dinner'.
Writing recipes.
Story 'Everybody said no!', by Sheila Lavelle, and 'Late for Breakfast' by Mary Dawson, from *Tinderbox Assembly Book*.
Poems from *A Very First Poetry Book*:
'I like soft boiled eggs' by John Kitching
'The Sausage' Anon
'Chips' by Julie Holder
Music
'When a dinosaur's feeling hungry', from *Tinderbox*.

Theme 3: Houses and homes

Links with Attainment Targets

AT1 • use common words and phrases relating to the passing of time, *for example: old, new, before, after, long ago, days of the week, months, years;*
• identify a sequence of events and talk about why they happened, *for example: changes in the pupil's family;*
• observe differences between ways of life at different times in the past, *for example: the clothes worn in different periods;*

AT3 • find out about the past from different types of historical source, *for example: historic houses, objects in museums, paintings, photographs, coins, newspapers.*

Cross-curricular links

English: All Attainment Targets
Science: AT1, AT6, AT10
Maths: AT10, AT12

This theme focuses mainly on science, in terms of forces and materials. The history component would be learning about homes through the ages, starting with the children's own homes and then studying a particular old house in the neighbourhood of the school. This would continue with stories and pictures of homes from very long ago, such as caves, huts, Roman villas and castles.

Starting points

• Ask the children to describe and draw their own homes. This could lead to a chart showing the different types of homes people live in.
• Look at an old house in the area and encourage the children to think about how it would have been heated, lit, furnished and decorated. Questions will arise concerning the kind of building materials used (thinking first, perhaps, of the Three Little Pigs!) and about water, electricity and gas supplies.

Developments

• The old house studied could provide a basis for creative writing and drawings about the people who once lived there. Let the children make models of the house using a range of junk materials.
• Make a display of pictures of homes through the ages, and encourage further work on homes that interest the children particularly, such as castles or caves. Use role-play to enrich their appreciation. Castles could be made from various kinds of construction materials such as LEGO or Duplo.

• A walk around the area would allow a comparison of the 'old' homes studied with the way we live today. Look at doors, gates, windows, roofs, chimneys, bricks, decorative features and styles of door handles and letter boxes.
• A visit could be made to a museum of buildings (see Resources on page 181). After this, children could paint pictures of

the different kinds of home they saw, putting them in broad chronological order, starting with the most modern and working backwards, dictating appropriate captions for the teacher to add.

- Convert the home corner into an Edwardian kitchen with fringed table cloth, aspidistra and a 'range' made of large boxes painted black.

Discussion

Questions children might be asked could include the following:

- In what ways is your house different from the old house we have been thinking about?
- Can you think of two things that you have in your living room that would not have been in homes when your great-grandmother was a little girl?
- When do you think houses began to have garages built on to them? What did big houses have instead of a garage? Which people might have owned coaches? Which home of long ago would you have liked to live in?
- Can you think why very few people build or live in castles these days?

Resources

Books

First Stories: Three Little Pigs, illustrated by Stephen Cartwright (Usborne).
Homes ('Starters' series, Macdonald).
Homes, R J Unstead (A & C Black).
Living Long Ago: Houses and Homes ('Explainers' series, Usborne).
Living in Roman Times, Living in Castle Times ('First History' series, Usborne).
Tinderbox Assembly Book, compiled by Sylvia Barratt (A & C Black).
The Tinderbox Song Book, compiled by Sylvia Barratt (A & C Black).
Manors and *Castles*, David Crystal and John Louis Foster (Edward Arnold).
First Ideas: A Place to Live, Edward Ramsbottom and Joan Redmayne (Macmillan).
Young Ideas: Home, Edward Ramsbottom (Macmillan).
The Story of a Castle, John Strickland Goodall (Andre Deutsch).
Castle and Dungeons, Vanessa Miles (Carousel Books, Transworld).
See How it's Made – The House, illustrated by Michael Ricketts (Macmillan).
Castles, Pyramids and Palaces ('Beginners' Knowledge' series, Usborne).
Make this Roman Villa and *Make this Model Castle* (Usborne).

Pictures

Collect a variety of pictures of houses cut from magazines. Pictures of homes through the ages can often be borrowed from the visual aids sections of public libraries.

Film strips

The following film strips are available from Philip Green Educational Ltd:
F25: Castles.
F02: Where do you live?

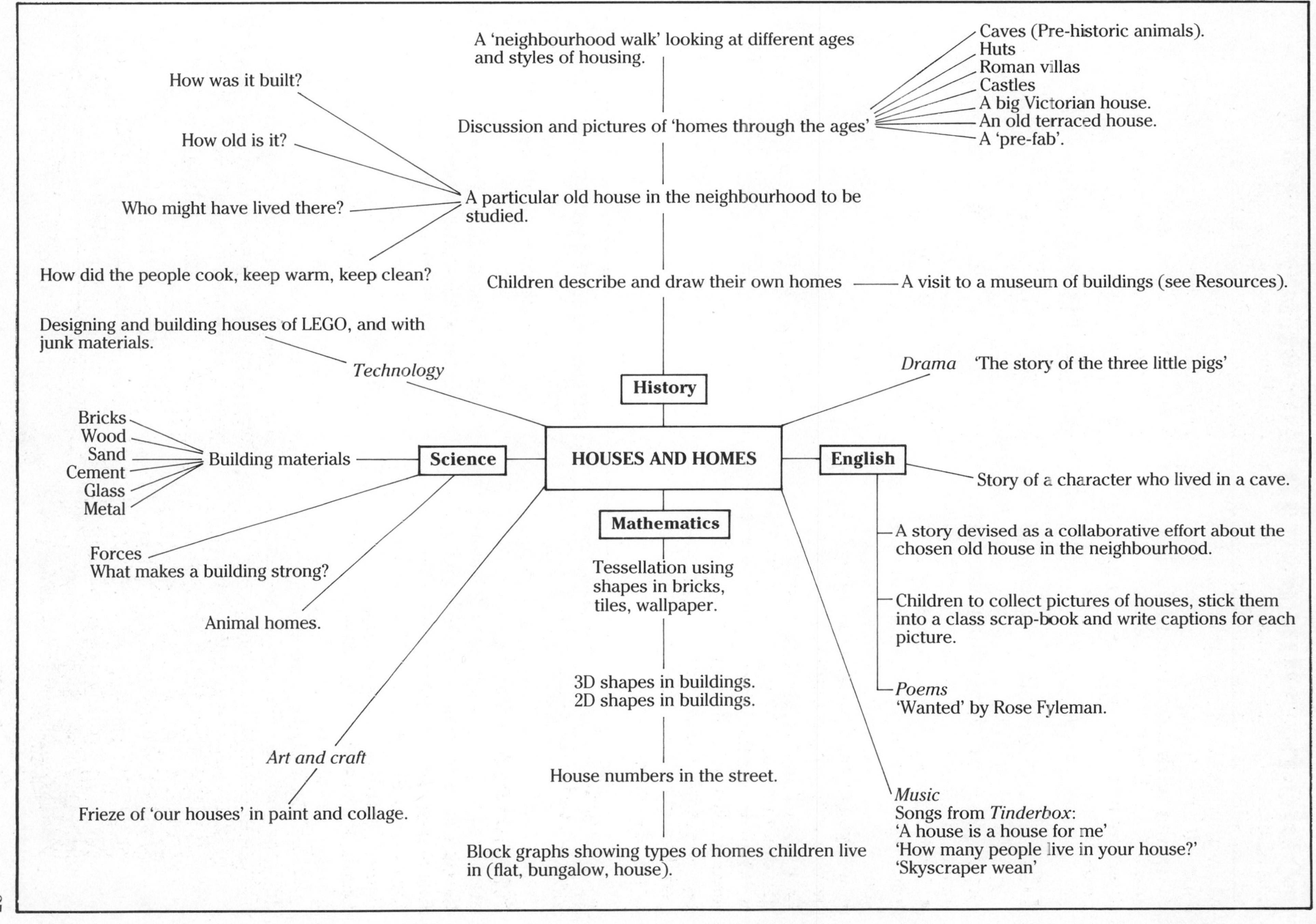
HOUSES AND HOMES
History
A 'neighbourhood walk' looking at different ages and styles of housing.
Discussion and pictures of 'homes through the ages'
Caves (Pre-historic animals).
Huts
Roman villas
Castles
A big Victorian house.
An old terraced house.
A 'pre-fab'.
A particular old house in the neighbourhood to be studied.
How was it built?
How old is it?
Who might have lived there?
How did the people cook, keep warm, keep clean?
Children describe and draw their own homes
A visit to a museum of buildings (see Resources).
Technology
Designing and building houses of LEGO, and with junk materials.
Science
Building materials
Bricks
Wood
Sand
Cement
Glass
Metal
Forces
What makes a building strong?
Animal homes.
Art and craft
Frieze of 'our houses' in paint and collage.
Mathematics
Tessellation using shapes in bricks, tiles, wallpaper.
3D shapes in buildings.
2D shapes in buildings.
House numbers in the street.
Block graphs showing types of homes children live in (flat, bungalow, house).
Drama
'The story of the three little pigs'
English
Story of a character who lived in a cave.
A story devised as a collaborative effort about the chosen old house in the neighbourhood.
Children to collect pictures of houses, stick them into a class scrap-book and write captions for each picture.
Poems
'Wanted' by Rose Fyleman.
Music
Songs from Tinderbox:
'A house is a house for me'
'How many people live in your house?'
'Skyscraper wean'

Topic B: Suitcase in the attic

Links with Attainment Targets

AT1 • use common words and phrases relating to the passing of time, *for example: old, new, before, after, long ago, days of the week, months, years;*
• identify a sequence of events and talk about why they happened, *for example: changes in the pupil's family;*
• observe differences between ways of life at different times in the past, *for example: the clothes worn in different periods;*

AT3 • find out about the past from different types of historical source, *for example: historic houses, objects in museums, paintings, photographs, coins, newspapers.*

Cross-curricular links

English: All Attainment Targets
Science: AT1, AT2, AT3, AT4
Maths: AT2, AT3, AT8, AT12

This is a main history topic in which children are introduced to the question 'What is history?'. In exploring the contents of an old suitcase containing various artefacts from different periods of history, the question of how we find out about the past is considered in some depth. The topic ends with the case history of a visit to the City of Birmingham Museum. Ways and means of setting up a class or school museum will also be suggested.

The children will be introduced to the difference between primary and secondary sources through the questions 'Is this really old or is it a copy?' and 'Was that person really there or is it a made-up story?'. Children will be encouraged to look at an artefact and judge broadly when it originated ('Was this cap worn in the days when my Dad was a little boy or when my Grandad was a little boy?'). Artefacts will be 'set' broadly in chronological order (see topic web).

Preparation for the topic

The suitcase should be set up as a school resource, carefully put together in advance. The contents should have a central core but can be added to and subtracted from at any time. The contents could, if resources in school are not sufficient, be made up from museum loans.

A suggested suitcase would contain artefacts as follows:

- a few old postcards sent from different parts of the country in the Edwardian era, written, stamped and franked;
- several old photographs taken between the wars, for example a school photograph, a wedding photograph and a family group;
- a few articles of clothing such as a Victorian nightdress, an old school cap and a smocked baby dress of the 1940s or 1950s;
- two or three old perfume or medicine bottles;

- old books dating from various periods, including an illustrated children's book;
- an old newspaper reporting an important event;
- a few trinkets or ornaments, such as the little Goss pots brought back from holidays and featuring town crests;
- old birthday and Christmas cards;
- old theatre programmes from pre-Second World War days;
- an old toy such as a 1940s or 1950s Dinky car.

Starting points

- Tell the children that the suitcase was found in an old house, put there long ago by the people who once lived there. The contents of the case could be shown to the children either in groups or as a class, but they should be given opportunities to handle the various artefacts. Discuss the items and encourage the children to consider how they can find out the age of the objects and their original use. Ask them to compare the items with their modern-day counterparts and find out what these things tell us about the past. The point we should be trying to draw out is that all the things in the cases are old and they all tell us something about their original owners.

- Read *The Model Village* by Nicholas Fisk. This is a story about a little girl called Polly who finds a model village in the loft of her house. The illustrations offer accurate examples of Edwardian costume and architecture.

Once the book has been enjoyed and discussed, ask the question, 'How are the objects mentioned in the story in this book different from those in our suitcase?'. The children will need to be led towards the main difference which is that the book is *describing* objects in the past, whilst the things in the suitcase *are* genuine old objects. This is a difficult concept for children to grasp and needs much development.

Developments

- Make a class museum. Artefacts could be contributed by teachers, and by the children themselves with help from older relatives and friends. Each contribution should be discussed and labelled.
- Arrange a table and wall display of things that help us to learn about history, such as books, pictures, photographs and so on. The important differences between the collection of *real* old artefacts and that of secondary source materials should be constantly emphasised.

Discussion

Full and frequent discussions should be encouraged. These should include genuinely open-ended questions, and children's answers should be respectfully considered. For example, if you ask the question, 'How can we find out about what happened in the past?' you could gently lead the children towards the following answers:

- By collecting old things and asking questions about them.
- By reading books and looking at pictures of things from the past.
- By asking older people to tell us about things they remember.
- By watching television programmes, films and videos about the past.
- By listening to radio programmes and cassettes about the past.
- By visiting old buildings.
- By visiting museums.

If you asked the children 'Why is it important for us to know about the past?' the following answers could be encouraged:

- Because it can help us to understand how things began.
- Because it can enable us to understand why things are as they are now.

Further activities

- Ask the children to write postcards from the point of view of a child who has just seen his first motor car.
- Let the children choose an item from the suitcase and make up a story about it, either to be written down or recorded on cassette.

For activities in science, maths and art and craft, see the corresponding topic web on page 37.

Case history: a visit to a museum

A museum visit should be the climax of the topic and should be the means of introducing children to museums as a means of finding out about the past. This topic was used as a basis for work done in history at Acocks Green Infant School, Birmingham, during the autumn term 1990. The headteacher, Gwyneth Higgins, and class teacher, Joan Alexander, agreed to try out some of the activities suggested here and evaluate their success. Closely involved was Rita Smith, Joan's mother, who, working as a regular 'school voluntary helper', told the children about her childhood during and just after the First World War. She also loaned photographs of her mother and grandmother, along with a necklace worn in one of the photographs. Rita demonstrated the enormous value of learning history through the eye-witness accounts of an older person.

The two activities which Joan felt had been of particular value were the setting up of the class museum (in which the children were actively involved by contributing, writing catalogues and conducting other children and parents around) and an excellent visit to the City of Birmingham Museum and Art Gallery. The children spent an enthralling morning working in the museum classroom with Elvin Morris, the museum teacher, learning as much science as history, as well as talking and listening in a thoroughly purposeful way.

A video was made of the visit which later provided a helpful aid to assessing children's progress in history, science and language. Gwyneth and Joan both felt that the topic generated considerable interest in learning about the past, had been the means of involving many parents and pointed the way forward in terms of learning history in the infant school.

Planning a museum visit

Using museums forms an important part of most of the topics and themes in this chapter, and is one of the anchor points of Topic B. This, therefore, seems an appropriate point to look at the planning and carrying out of a museum visit. The visit made by the children from Acocks Green Infant School to the City of Birmingham Museum and Art Gallery will serve as a useful model for discussing the planning of a visit, and can also illustrate the value of good quality museum teaching.

Defining the purpose of a visit
In deciding to take your children to a museum, you will need first to define exactly what your purpose is. There could be a number of purposes, for example:

- looking at a particular subject such as the Romans, Egyptians, paintings (either in general or a particular group), prehistoric animals, costume, toys or transport;
- discovering different aspects of a theme such as colour and light, childhood and old age or food and drink;
- visiting and experiencing a particular exhibition;
- an introduction to the practice of museum visiting, demonstrating its potential for learning about the past.

Whichever purpose is identified can serve as the starting point for the visit and help clarify the planning.

Choosing a date
The next stage is to contact the museum's schools department to discuss dates, times and activities. It needs to be emphasised that it is most unwise to turn up at a museum with a party of children without having booked in advance, especially if you want the services of the specially trained museum teachers. After a preliminary telephone call or letter, make a visit to the schools department to plan the details of the work the children will be doing. The museum teacher will help you to translate your purpose into workable activities, making the best use of time and resources. If your visit is to form part of a particular theme or topic, take along your topic web so that the museum teacher will be able to suggest suitable loan material and other back-up work.

In discussing the timing of your class visit, do consider when a visit would be of greatest value to the topic. The Acocks Green visit was planned, for example, after the investigation of the artefacts in the suitcase, when the children's appetite for things from the past had been whetted sufficiently to stimulate them into setting up their own classroom museum.

It is important that at your meeting with the museum teacher you plan a timetable for the day, deciding if packed lunches will be taken and, if so, where they can be eaten, and checking the availability of cloakroom and toilet facilities. These basic elements, if neglected, can ruin your day! After a meeting with the museum teacher, with your intended programme for the day broadly worked out, you should then take a careful, leisurely walk round the route the children will take, with a notebook in which to record things to point out, questions to ask and potential snags (such as the uncomfortable distance of the toilets from the collection of wooden bygones!).

Transport

Back at school the question of transport will need to be addressed. A coach will probably be required if the visit is for a whole class, but don't dismiss the idea of public transport too readily. A visit by half a class with adequate adult help and a convenient bus service can be a cheap alternative, a treat for the children and a useful opportunity for learning appropriate behaviour in public!

If a coach is decided on, book well in advance and make sure the driver is aware of the correct entrances to the museum, which are often different from the normal public entrance. Timing is extremely important and should be very precisely agreed.

The question of coach funding needs to be considered (which is why public transport could be an attractive option). The alternatives are that parents are invited to pay, some kind of fund-raising is organised or the sum is provided from school funds. It goes without saying, of course, that no planning of any kind should take place without the full knowledge and approval of the headteacher.

Adult help

Planning the adult help will also be important, in terms of quality as well as quantity. Apart from yourself, there should be at least one adult to ten children. Ensure that you involve your helpers in the work being done and give them all the information they need. It may be useful if you can take your helpers to the museum beforehand.

On the day

On arrival at the museum the children left their coats on the special pegs provided and were escorted by Elvin Morris to the museum classroom. The plan for the day

(which had been explained to the children beforehand) was recapped by Elvin. The class was divided into two groups with one group remaining in the classroom, while the other group was taken round the museum.

In the classroom, the children handled, used and investigated a variety of historic objects, including an early type of vacuum cleaner, an old lamp, a Victorian button hook and a variety of laundry equipment from the turn of the century. There was a wealth of discussion between the children and the teacher and among the children themselves, revealing a degree of persistence that surprised even the class teacher herself. The children dressed up in Victorian clothing, and were told of the occasions when the various items of clothing might have been worn.

The other group, meanwhile, looked at the Pinto Collection of wooden bygones, and showed a great interest in the intriguing old toys and educational equipment. Various pictures were admired, such as Augustus Egg's *The Travelling Companions*, Ford Maddox Brown's *The Last of England* and Holman Hunt's *The Saviour in the Temple*. After a suitable interval of time the two groups changed over.

Follow-up

Once back at school, the children followed up the visit with discussion work, since it was decided that there should be no 'duty' written work. The children were asked to say what had interested them, how much they had found out and whether they felt museums were places which helped them to learn about the past. There was a range of interesting responses and considerable interest in organising a class museum. The children watched the video which had been made of their visit (which in no way inhibited them, due to Elvin's considerable skill and relaxed manner) and many of them chose to write and draw things that interested them. Everyone wrote a thank-you letter to Elvin.

The time-line

The time-line on page 36 was designed by Joan Alexander, a teacher at Acocks Green Infant School in Birmingham, where the main history topic 'Suitcase in the Attic' was tried out. One of Joan's objectives for this topic was to encourage the children's understanding of change through time. She designed this time-line as a large wall display and explained it to her class in terms of counting back in tens (which they were used to doing in maths anyway).

Joan then encouraged the children to think about the different happenings which would fit on to the chart. They started by looking at the point where they were born (the 1980s) followed by the point where their parents and then their grandparents were born. They then considered all the changes that had taken place in the life time of Mrs Smith (Joan's mother). Mrs Smith's first seaside holiday, radio, fridge, television and washing machine were recorded on the time-line and then the photographs of her mother and grandmother were looked at, in which they were wearing a particular necklace. The birth dates of these two ladies were set in the time-line and the children attempted to find out how old the necklace was. This necklace was brought into school and the children were able to examine it and try it on. After this the children attempted to place on the time-line the artefacts in the suitcase and the objects brought in by parents. Through these activities linked to the time-line the children were helped to understand the concepts of change and stability.

The time-line (see photocopiable page 36) can serve a number of purposes. It can be used as described above or it can be copied, enabling each child to record different family events with the help of parents and grandparents. The following examples show the kind of event that could be recorded:

- Great-Grandpa came to live in Birmingham when he was two years old.
- Great-Grandpa and Great-Grannie got married.
- Great-Grandpa went to fight in the Great War.
- The house we live in was built.
- My Grandpa was born.

Another way of using the time-line would be to set it out in large form and record the names and dates of kings and queens on it, to familiarise the children with the terms 'Victorian' and 'Edwardian' and the names of kings and queens since the Victorian era. You could also extend the time-line with a 'further back' section marked out in whole centuries, so that other historical knowledge the children gain can be positioned on the time-line.

It is our experience that children who are awakened to history find things out through a whole variety of sources, and are proud to share their findings with friends.

There was a time when history teaching in schools consisted only of lists of dates and kings and queens, but while we certainly want to move away from such an impoverished approach, it would be a pity to ignore the importance of such knowledge completely. John West in *Children's Awareness of the Past* (University of Keele, 1980) showed that children already had a developed sense of seriation of historical evidence by the age of seven.

The *Times Educational Supplement* of 19 December 1990 contained an article by Sylvia Collicott, Senior Lecturer in the School of Teaching Studies, Polytechnic of North London. This article, entitled 'Pulling Strings' contained details of a different kind of time-line consisting of events and dates written large and attached to a 'washing line' with pegs. This is an idea we feel is well worth trying as an addition to the kind of time-line designed by Joan. On the subject of time-lines in general, Sylvia Collicott says, 'Teachers . . . will need to prepare children for the attainment targets. Time lines can be an important medium to achieve these ends. They have multi-purpose uses: children can order events, teachers can structure task situations and all the diverse subject areas can be unified round a time line theme held together within the context of delivering a multicultural curriculum.' This is an article well worth reading.

Resources

Books

The Model Village, Nicholas Fisk, illustrated by Alan Cracknell (Walker Books).
My Class Visits a Museum, Vivienne Griffiths (Franklin Watts).

Artefacts

A range of objects like those described on page 28.

Photographs

Make a collection of old photographs to be seen as primary sources, as well as a collection of published photographs of old buildings, old cars and so on, to be seen as secondary sources.

Pictures

Try to find at least one old (ie at least 50 years old) original watercolour or oil painting, and a collection of pictures cut from magazines which portray old situations and objects.

Clothing

Make a collection of items of clothing, either borrowed from museum loans departments or collected from staff, parents and grandparents. Include items of dressing-up clothes and copies of clothing worn in former times.

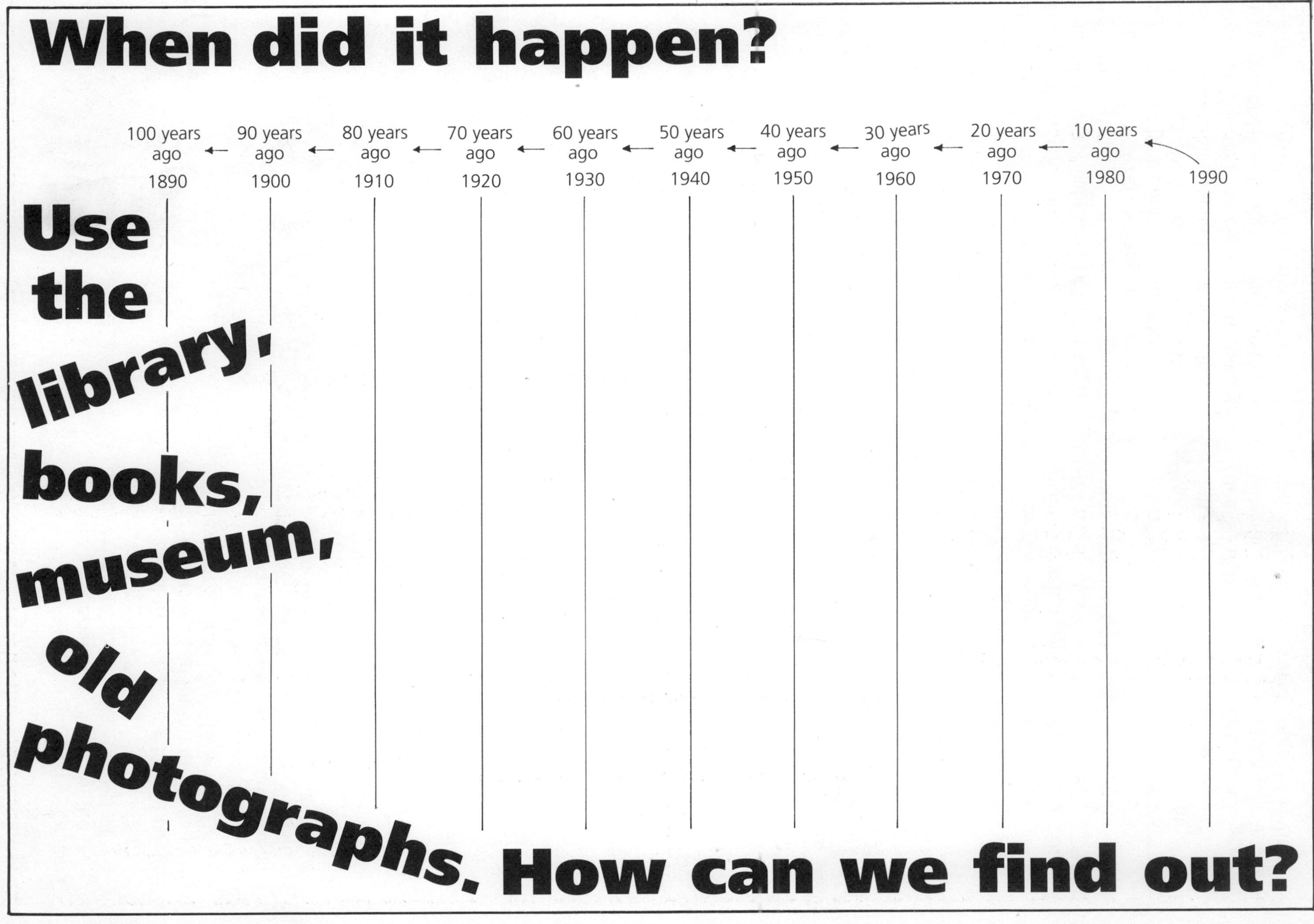
When did it happen?
100 years ago
1890
90 years ago
1900
80 years ago
1910
70 years ago
1920
60 years ago
1930
50 years ago
1940
40 years ago
1950
30 years ago
1960
20 years ago
1970
10 years ago
1980
1990
Use the library, books, museum, old photographs. How can we find out?

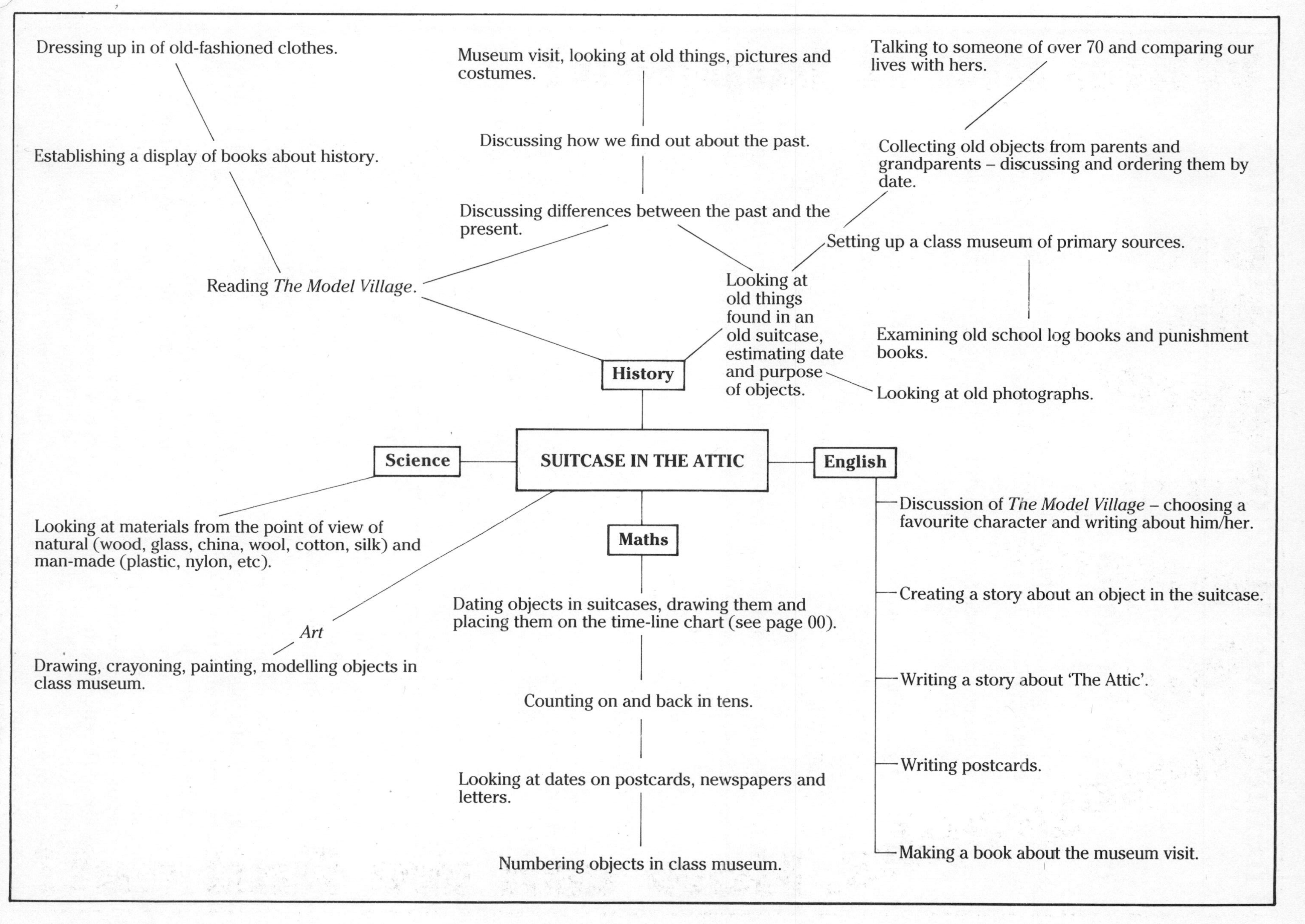

SUITCASE IN THE ATTIC
History
Dressing up in of old-fashioned clothes.
Establishing a display of books about history.
Reading The Model Village.
Museum visit, looking at old things, pictures and costumes.
Discussing how we find out about the past.
Discussing differences between the past and the present.
Looking at old things found in an old suitcase, estimating date and purpose of objects.
Talking to someone of over 70 and comparing our lives with hers.
Collecting old objects from parents and grandparents – discussing and ordering them by date.
Setting up a class museum of primary sources.
Examining old school log books and punishment books.
Looking at old photographs.
Science
Looking at materials from the point of view of natural (wood, glass, china, wool, cotton, silk) and man-made (plastic, nylon, etc).
Art
Drawing, crayoning, painting, modelling objects in class museum.
Maths
Dating objects in suitcases, drawing them and placing them on the time-line chart (see page 00).
Counting on and back in tens.
Looking at dates on postcards, newspapers and letters.
Numbering objects in class museum.
English
Discussion of The Model Village – choosing a favourite character and writing about him/her.
Creating a story about an object in the suitcase.
Writing a story about 'The Attic'.
Writing postcards.
Making a book about the museum visit.

Theme 4: Keeping ourselves healthy

Links with Attainment Targets

AT1 • use common words and phrases relating to the passing of time, *for example: old, new, before, after, long ago, days of the week, months, years;*
• observe differences between ways of life at different times in the past, *for example: the clothes worn in different periods;*

AT2 • develop an awareness of different ways of representing past events, *for example: pictures, written accounts, films, television programmes, plays, songs, reproductions of objects, museum displays;*

AT3 • find out about the past from different types of historical source, *for example: historic houses, objects in museums, paintings, photographs, coins, newspapers.*

Cross-curricular links

English: All Attainment Targets
Science: AT1, AT3
Maths: AT1, AT8

This is a health education science topic with a historical component which would lead on from the work done on food in Y1. It should probably be undertaken at Y2. The topic takes the children further back in time to the Edwardian era when standards of cleanliness and facilities for keeping clean were very different from today. Illness and the response to illness were also different, and this theme will lead to thinking and finding out about some famous people in medical history. In thinking about Florence Nightingale we move a little further back still and address the question of who is a real person and who is a fictional character.

Starting points

Approach this theme by asking the children to consider three aspects in turn:
• How do we keep ourselves clean? The discussion would give rise to talk about bathrooms, showers, washing and clean clothes.
• How do we keep our clothes and our homes clean? This would lead to talk of washing machines, dryers, vacuum cleaners and other electrical gadgets.
• How often are we ill, and what kinds of illnesses do we have? How quickly do we become well again? This would lead to talk of medicines, doctors and hospitals.

Developments

- Let the children look at pictures of bathrooms in big old houses, or visit an old house or a museum to see an old style bathroom and compare it with modern bathrooms.
- Encourage the children to consider the methods employed by ordinary people who had no bathrooms, by looking at pictures, and if possible, real examples of a wash stand, a jug, bowl and pail and an old tin bath.
- Stories could be written about bathnight in a big Edwardian household.
- Ask the children to find out from home who the first people to have baths were. This could lead to discussion about the Romans, and anecdotes about people like Queen Elizabeth I who never bathed!
- Ask the children to consider how clothes were washed in Great-Grannie's day, and arrange a visit to a museum or old house to see the laundry. A very old person (in their 80s) could be invited in to school to describe washdays of their childhood. Children could devise a drama entitled 'Great-Grannie's Washday'.
- Discuss old-fashioned ways of cleaning floors and furniture. Ask an elderly person to provide information, and try to provide living evidence using a museum/old house visit.
- Make a class collection of old laundry equipment.
- Ask the children to find out what illnesses Edwardian children suffered from (possibly by asking an old person) and what remedies were used for ailments such as toothache, colds and sore throats.
- Look at old pictures of hospitals and tell the children the story of Florence Nightingale. The school nurse might be invited in to talk about the differences between her work, training and uniform and that of Florence Nightingale.

Discussion

Ask the children questions like the following:

- What kinds of homes had bathrooms in Edwardian times?
- Where do you think people without bathrooms might have washed and bathed?
- How often do you think people bathed?
- Who do you think did the housework in those days?
- Can you think why the men didn't help much?
- What illnesses did children have then that you don't have today?
- Would a woman have become a doctor in those days?
- Would a man have become a nurse?

Resources

Books

Keeping Ourselves Healthy: An Eye Witness History Book (Wayland).
Great Lives: Florence Nightingale, Dorothy Turner (Wayland). (This could be read to the children but might need some adaptation.)
Topics in History: Alive and Well, Norman Longmate (Penguin). (This is a resource for teachers only but there are some interesting pictures.)
The Story of Medicine, Kathy and Mike Eldon (Wayland).
The Story of Medicine, Edmund Hunter (Ladybird).
Famous Names in Medicine, G Stevens (Wayland).
How They Lived – An Edwardian Household (Wayland).
Wash and Brush Up and *Home Sweet Home*, Eleanor Allen (A & C Black Junior Reference Books).
First History – Roman Times (Usborne).
Children's World: How your Body Works (Usborne).
A Very First Poetry Book, compiled by John Foster for 'The Sick Young Dragon' and 'Launderama' (Oxford University Press).
Okki-Tokki-Unga and *Harlequin* (A & C Black song books).

Pictures and artefacts

A collection of pictures and artefacts could be borrowed from libraries or museums, parents or grandparents and used as part of a school exhibition.

Film strip

The following useful film strip is available from Philip Green Educational Ltd:
F21: In Hospital.

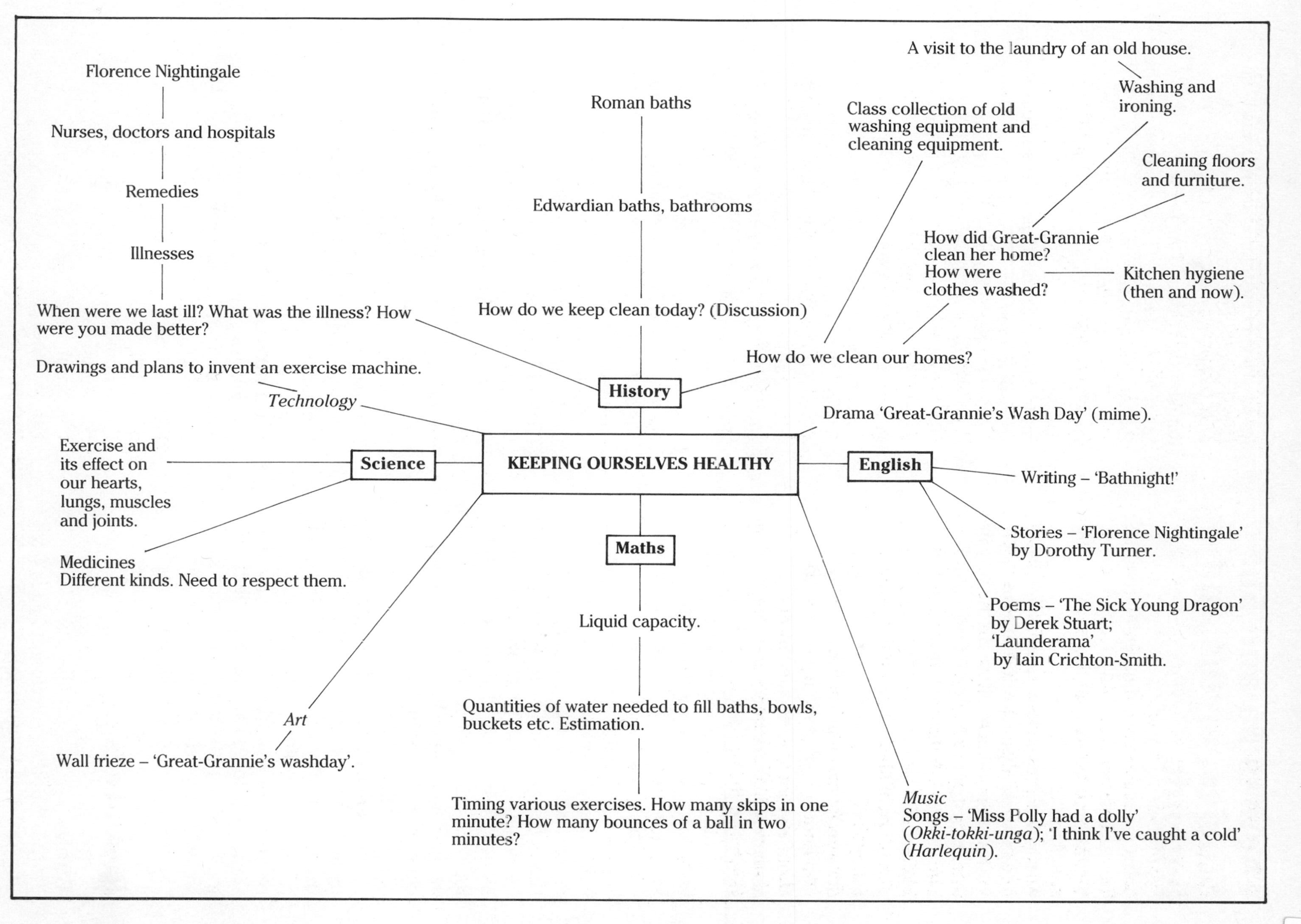

KEEPING OURSELVES HEALTHY
History
Roman baths
Edwardian baths, bathrooms
How do we keep clean today? (Discussion)
How do we clean our homes?
Class collection of old washing equipment and cleaning equipment.
How did Great-Grannie clean her home?
How were clothes washed?
Washing and ironing.
A visit to the laundry of an old house.
Cleaning floors and furniture.
Kitchen hygiene (then and now).
Florence Nightingale
Nurses, doctors and hospitals
Remedies
Illnesses
When were we last ill? What was the illness? How were you made better?
Technology
Drawings and plans to invent an exercise machine.
Science
Exercise and its effect on our hearts, lungs, muscles and joints.
Medicines
Different kinds. Need to respect them.
Art
Wall frieze – 'Great-Grannie's washday'.
Maths
Liquid capacity.
Quantities of water needed to fill baths, bowls, buckets etc. Estimation.
Timing various exercises. How many skips in one minute? How many bounces of a ball in two minutes?
Music
Songs – 'Miss Polly had a dolly' (Okki-tokki-unga); 'I think I've caught a cold' (Harlequin).
English
Drama 'Great-Grannie's Wash Day' (mime).
Writing – 'Bathnight!'
Stories – 'Florence Nightingale' by Dorothy Turner.
Poems – 'The Sick Young Dragon' by Derek Stuart; 'Launderama' by Iain Crichton-Smith.

Themes 5a and 5b: Stories, myths and legends

This theme is treated differently from the others, because:

- it is intended to span the two years of Key Stage 1;
- it is designed in two parts;
- it is primarily a literature theme.

The intention is to illustrate the way in which the history National Curriculum Programme of Study for Key Stage 1 can be applied. The relevant section says that pupils should be helped to develop an awareness of the past through stories from different periods and cultures, including well known myths and legends, stories about historical events, eye witness accounts of historical events and fictional stories set in the past.

In this particular theme we use topic webs to show how a well known myth, a legend, a story about the past, a version of a real historical event told as fiction, two stories which illustrate aspects of Victorian childhood, a story of childhood in the Second World War and a story related to a Hindu festival could all be used in a cross-curricular context. There are also two modern stories included which illustrate the way a story with sound literary value in its own right can be used to capture children's interest and lead to the learning of history in a natural way.

The stories that have been included are by no means the only ones that can be used in this way, and many teachers will see the possibilities inherent in their own repertoire of favourite stories. Suggested stories are noted and explained in the topic web, but the following resources, which are a mixture of teacher's and children's books, will also prove useful.

Resources

Books

The Story of the Post, Robert Page (A & C Black) – useful illustrations.
Roads, David Crystal and John Louis Foster (Databank Series, Edward Arnold).
Young Ideas – On the Move, Edward Ramsbottom (Macmillan).
See How it's Made – The Car, illustrated by Michael Ricketts (Macmillan).
How Things Began (Usborne).
Time Traveller – Knights and Castles (Usborne).
First History – Castle Times (Usborne).
Tales of Robin Hood (Usborne).
Ancient Greece (Usborne Pocket Guides).
Greek Myths and Legends (Usborne).
The 'Living Festivals' Series (Religious and Moral Education Press).
'Festivals' series (Wayland).
'Celebrations' series (Wayland).
'Seasonal Festivals' series (Wayland).
A Year Book of Saints, Christine Chaundler (Mowbray).
The Firefighters – An Eyewitness History Book, Anne Mountfield (Wayland).
Plague and Fire, L Cowie (Wayland).
First Guide to the Universe (Usborne).
The Know How Book of Puppets (Usborne).
The Jolly Postman, Janet and Alan Ahlberg (Heinemann).
The Little Car, Leila Berg (Magnet).
Stories from Ovid, Martin Murphy (Oxford University Press).
Saint George and the Dragon (Ladybird).
Robin Hood – His Life and Legend, Bernard Miles (Hamlyn).
Cautionary Verses, Hilaire Belloc (Puffin).
The Secret Garden, Frances Hodgson-Burnett, retold by Joyce McAleer (Carnival).
When the Siren Wailed, Noel Streatfield (Collins).

Film strips/slides

The following visual resources are available from Philip Green Educational Ltd:
F65: The 1940s.
F58: Festivals/Special Days.
F57: Winter.
F52: Summer.
F43: Autumn.
F36: Spring.
F46: Weather.
F18: Fire.

STORIES, MYTHS AND LEGENDS 1 (Yr 1)

***The Jolly Postman* by Janet and Alan Ahlberg**

History
Looking at the story of the post, and when and how it all began – early writing implements.

English
Letter-writing as a class theme. Class 'post office'.

Mathematics
Money. Buying stamps in class post office. Weighing parcels.

Science
Investigation into different kinds of writing paper and writing implements; pencils, ball point pens, felt-tipped pens (water- and spirit-based).

***The Little Car* by Leila Berg**

History
Looking at the history of the motor car through pictures, collections of toy cars and a visit to a car museum.

English
Creating, as a collaborative whole-class activity, a further 'Little Car' adventure, written from children's ideas with the teacher acting as scribe.

Mathematics
Sorting and classifying toy cars.

Science
See work on Theme 5, 'Toys' (pages 19 to 21).

The Story of Robin Hood

History
Read several versions and compare, then read *Robin Hood – His Life and Legend* by Bernard Miles, illustrated by Victor Ambrus.
Ask historical questions; was Robin Hood a 'real' person? Are *all* the stories about him true?

English
Drama – children suggesting and planning a simple play about Robin Hood for assembly.

STORIES, MYTHS AND LEGENDS 2 (Yr 2)

The Story of Persephone

English
Dramatisation planned by children.

History
Discussion of role of Greek myths. Finding out about the Greeks. Is it 'real' or made up?

Science
Focus for work on the seasons – the weather – some reference to history of science.

Mathematics
Time – seasons – months.

Saint George and the Dragon

English
Children to make 'dragons' and create stories about them. Dragon puppets – children to write plays.

History
Discussion of 'legends' – is it true?
History of special 'Saint's Days' – look at Union flag, Cf. different versions.

The Story of Sita and Rama

English
Children to dramatise story for a Diwali Assembly.

History
Discussion of when the first Asians came to Britain bringing their faith and stories with them.

***The Story of Matilda* by Hilaire Belloc**

English
Children to compose and write their own 'cautionary tales' in small groups, each contributing ideas and pictures, with one child acting as scribe.

History
Discussion of the story as a 'warning' to Victorian children. History of firefighting – old fire engines. Link with local fire-station.

***The Secret Garden* by Frances Hodgson Burnett**

English and History
Children to empathise with characters and imagine life in a big Victorian house.

***When the Siren Wailed* by Noel Streatfield**

English and History
Story read to children as an interesting, well-written story but also to give a picture of what evacuation meant to a family. Children to consider how *they* would feel.

Theme 6: Materials

Links with Attainment Targets

AT1 • use common words and phrases relating to the passing of time, *for example: old, new, before, after, long ago, days of the week, months, years;*
• observe differences between ways of life at different times in the past, *for example: the clothes worn in different periods;*

AT2 • develop an awareness of different ways of representing past events, *for example: pictures, written accounts, films, television programmes, plays, songs, reproductions of objects, museum displays;*

AT3 • find out about the past from different types of historical source, *for example: historic houses, objects in museums, paintings, photographs, coins, newspapers.*

Cross-curricular links

English: All Attainment Targets
Science: AT6
Maths: AT12, AT13

A science project on materials could include work on the history of the clothes we wear, starting by looking at our own clothing and comparing this with clothing worn by Victorians and Edwardians, building a foundation for work to follow at Key Stage 2.

This is the point at which children might find out who Queen Victoria was and who reigned after her. This knowledge could be compared with what we know of the present Queen and her family, and the children could be encouraged to ask questions such as, 'How do we know what the Queen and her family look like? Would people who were alive at the time have seen Queen Victoria and her family so often? Why not?'

Starting points

• Start a discussion about the clothes that children are currently wearing in school, drawing attention to style, fabric, colour and variety. Talk about the way in which we buy clothes (from chain stores, department stores, market stalls and through catalogues).

• Let the children draw pictures of themselves in their favourite clothes. Encourage accurate use of colours and descriptions of the materials from which the clothes are made. Each child could make a personal collection of small samples of material and mount them alongside their drawings and descriptions. This could form the first page of a book which each child could build up called 'All about clothes'.

Developments

• Look at pictures of clothes worn by Victorian or Edwardian children, both rich and poor. Make comparisons of style, colour and variety, firstly between rich and poor children and then between Victorians and children of today. Children could be shown pictures of Princes William and Harry and it could be pointed out that when they are playing at home they wear the same kinds of clothing as any other children. Some pictures of Queen Victoria's children could be shown for comparison.

- Let the children examine and try on some genuine Victorian or Edwardian clothes. Personal loans are a good source of these, as well as museum loans – it's surprising how many people possess Victorian clothing and are pleased to loan it. Examine the fabrics and ask what they are, speculating as to why the Victorians didn't use the materials we have today. Ask the children what differences there would have been in terms of washing and ironing the clothes.
- Investigate colour. Find out which colours were used most in clothes and why.
- Investigate the extent to which we wear different clothes in different seasons. Did the Victorians or Edwardians do this?
- Look at particular items of clothing and different kinds of clothing worn for particular occasions. Let the children make and draw different kinds of hats.
- Compile a dressing-up box of mock-Victorian clothing (long skirts, breeches, frilly pinafores, collars, shawls, bonnets, caps, bowlers, top hats). The children should recognise these as secondary sources and be encouraged to role-play as they wear them. This kind of clothing could well form part of a school resource bank.
- Visit a museum of costume if possible, and look at clothing of earlier times, starting with cavemen wearing the skins of animals for warmth and protection.

Discussion

Questions the children could be asked are as follows:

- Do you think there were many differences between the clothes of rich and poor children in Victorian and Edwardian times?
- What were some of those differences?
- Where did people get their clothes from in those days?
- What materials were clothes made of? How is this different today?
- Why was it not possible to use nylon or polyester in those days?
- What colours were used for clothing? Were there as many colours as there are today?
- Do you think people wore more or less clothing on their bodies than we do today? Can you think of reasons for your answer?

Resources

Books

Queen Victoria – Great Rulers in History (Ladybird).
Explainers – Living Long Ago – Clothes and Fashion (Usborne).
Simple Facts – Colours (Usborne).
The Story of Wool, Geoffrey Patterson (Andre Deutsch).
Where do things come from? Cotton, adapted from the text of Joseph Philippe (Chambers).
Finds – Fabrics, Oliver Aston (Evans).
First Ideas – Something to Wear, Edward Ramsbottom and Joan Redmayne (Macmillan).
Young Ideas – In Fashion, Edward Ramsbottom (Macmillan).
A Very First Poetry Book (Oxford University Press).

Pictures and artefacts

Pictures of Victorian or Edwardian clothes and fashions.
Pictures of the Victorian or Edwardian poor (borrowed from library collections).
Mail order catalogues of clothing and footwear.
Small pieces of different types of fabric.
A collection of Victorian style dressing up clothes.

Film strips and slides

The following visual resources are available from Philip Green Educational Ltd:
S41: Victorian Life.
F01: Clothes.

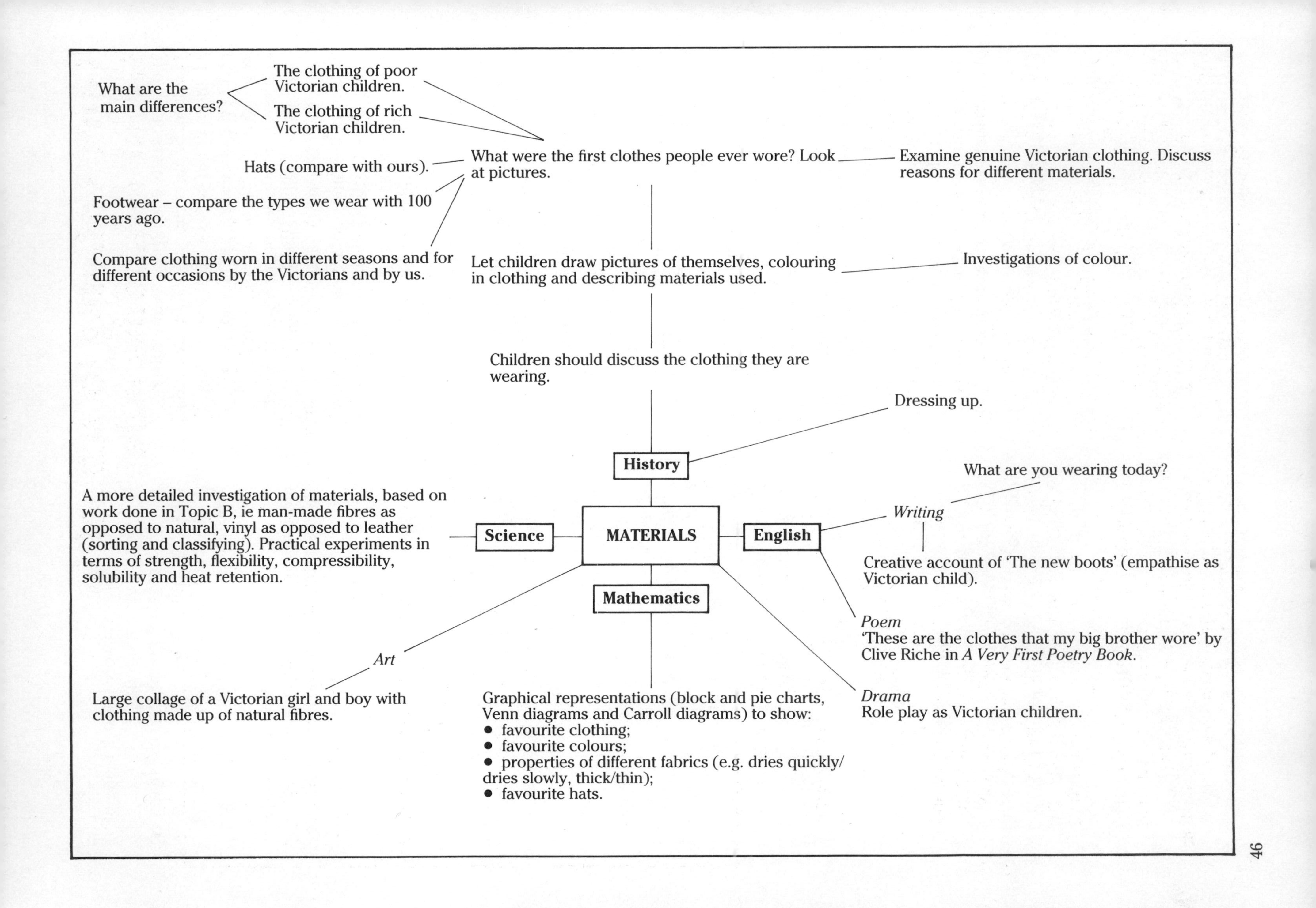
What are the main differences?
The clothing of poor Victorian children.
The clothing of rich Victorian children.
Hats (compare with ours).
What were the first clothes people ever wore? Look at pictures.
Examine genuine Victorian clothing. Discuss reasons for different materials.
Footwear – compare the types we wear with 100 years ago.
Compare clothing worn in different seasons and for different occasions by the Victorians and by us.
Let children draw pictures of themselves, colouring in clothing and describing materials used.
Investigations of colour.
Children should discuss the clothing they are wearing.
Dressing up.
History
What are you wearing today?
A more detailed investigation of materials, based on work done in Topic B, ie man-made fibres as opposed to natural, vinyl as opposed to leather (sorting and classifying). Practical experiments in terms of strength, flexibility, compressibility, solubility and heat retention.
Science
MATERIALS
English
Writing
Creative account of 'The new boots' (empathise as Victorian child).
Mathematics
Poem
'These are the clothes that my big brother wore' by Clive Riche in A Very First Poetry Book.
Art
Large collage of a Victorian girl and boy with clothing made up of natural fibres.
Graphical representations (block and pie charts, Venn diagrams and Carroll diagrams) to show:
• favourite clothing;
• favourite colours;
• properties of different fabrics (e.g. dries quickly/dries slowly, thick/thin);
• favourite hats.
Drama
Role play as Victorian children.

Topic C: Going to school in Great-Grandma's day

Links with Attainment Targets

AT1 • use common words and phrases relating to the passing of time, *for example: old, new, before, after, long ago, days of the week, months, years;*
• observe differences between ways of life at different times in the past, *for example: the clothes worn in different periods;*

AT2 • develop an awareness of different ways of representing past events, *for example: pictures, written accounts, films, television programmes, plays, songs, reproductions of objects, museum displays;*

AT3 • find out about the past from different types of historical source, *for example: historic houses, objects in museums, paintings, photographs, coins, newspapers.*

Cross-curricular links

English: All Attainment Targets
Science: AT3
Maths: AT3

This is a main history topic investigating schools about 80 years ago and earlier, giving children an opportunity to consider their own schools in some detail and then comparing them, aspect by aspect, with the schools of Great-Grandma's day. Where the present day school is actually a Victorian or Edwardian foundation there will be opportunities for looking at the school building, examining old log books and punishment books. Where the school is a modern one, an old school in the area could be looked at. One idea that can work successfully is the planning of a joint project between two schools of different ages, so that children can exchange letters, pictures, models, photographs and visits, with the two teachers joining together for the planning. This topic should build on work in Themes 1, 3, 4 and 6 and use the skills taught in Topic B.

Starting points

Spend time at this stage in recapping and revising what the children already know from previous topics and themes. They should be asked to examine school as they experience it today, considering the building, the furniture and equipment, the lessons, the teachers and aspects such as rewards and punishments.

Children should then be invited to think what it would have been like to be a child at school 80 years ago. By this stage children could plan their own work, starting with the questions 'What are we going to investigate?' and 'How shall we find out?'.

Developments

- Organise a visit to a Victorian or Edwardian schoolroom and enjoy a simulation (see Resources, page 181). Ask the children to compare all the different aspects with their own school (see topic web).
- Invite an elderly person to come to school to talk to the children about her schooldays. Encourage the children to plan in advance the questions they wish to ask. The dialogue could be taped and listened to again when the children are planning their own writing.
- Make a collection of artefacts such as pens, ink, old schoolbooks, school photographs and log books. Ask the children to devise various means to build up this collection; for example, a letter to the chair of the governors asking if any of the governing body can contribute, an advertisement in the parish magazine and in the local library, supermarket, old people's home or club. The children could also write letters to parents explaining the topic and asking for contributions to the collection. The collection may need supplementing with a museum loan. Involve the children in labelling and displaying the collection and arrange a special museum day along the lines of the one the children of Acocks Green Infant School set up and organised (see page 33). The same questions could be asked about the artefacts as for Topic B.
- Ask the children to find out what playground games used to be played and try some of them out.
- Let the children turn their own classroom into an Edwardian classroom for a day, basing some of the activities of the day on their previous visit to an old classroom.
- Bring the whole project together through a class assembly along the lines suggested in the chapter on history assemblies (see page 157).

Discussion

Questions the children could be asked include the following:

- How do you travel to school? How long does it take you?
- How did Great-Grannie travel to school? How long did it take her? What happened if she was late?
- What are your favourite lessons in school? What do you think Great-Grannie liked best? What do you think she might have hated?
- What do you do when your teacher or the headteacher come into the classroom? What did Great-Grannie do?
- Do you think teachers were very strict? What happened if children misbehaved? Do you think that was a good idea?
- What games did children play in the playground?
- What sort of things do you have to do before you set out for school each morning? What did the poorer children in Great-Grannie's day often have to do? Do you think they felt very tired in school?
- How were the classrooms heated? What happened if children came to school in wet clothes?

Resources

Books

Into the Past – At School in 1900, Sallie Purkis (Longman).
Going to School, Alistair Ross (A & C Black).
Victorian Children, Eleanor Allen (A & C Black).
Cautionary Verses, Hilaire Belloc, original pictures by TB and Nicolas Bentley (Duckworth).
School Day, Monica Stoppleman ('Turn of the Century' series, A & C Black).
Time Detectives – Great Grandmama's Schooldays, J Morgan (Macmillan Education).

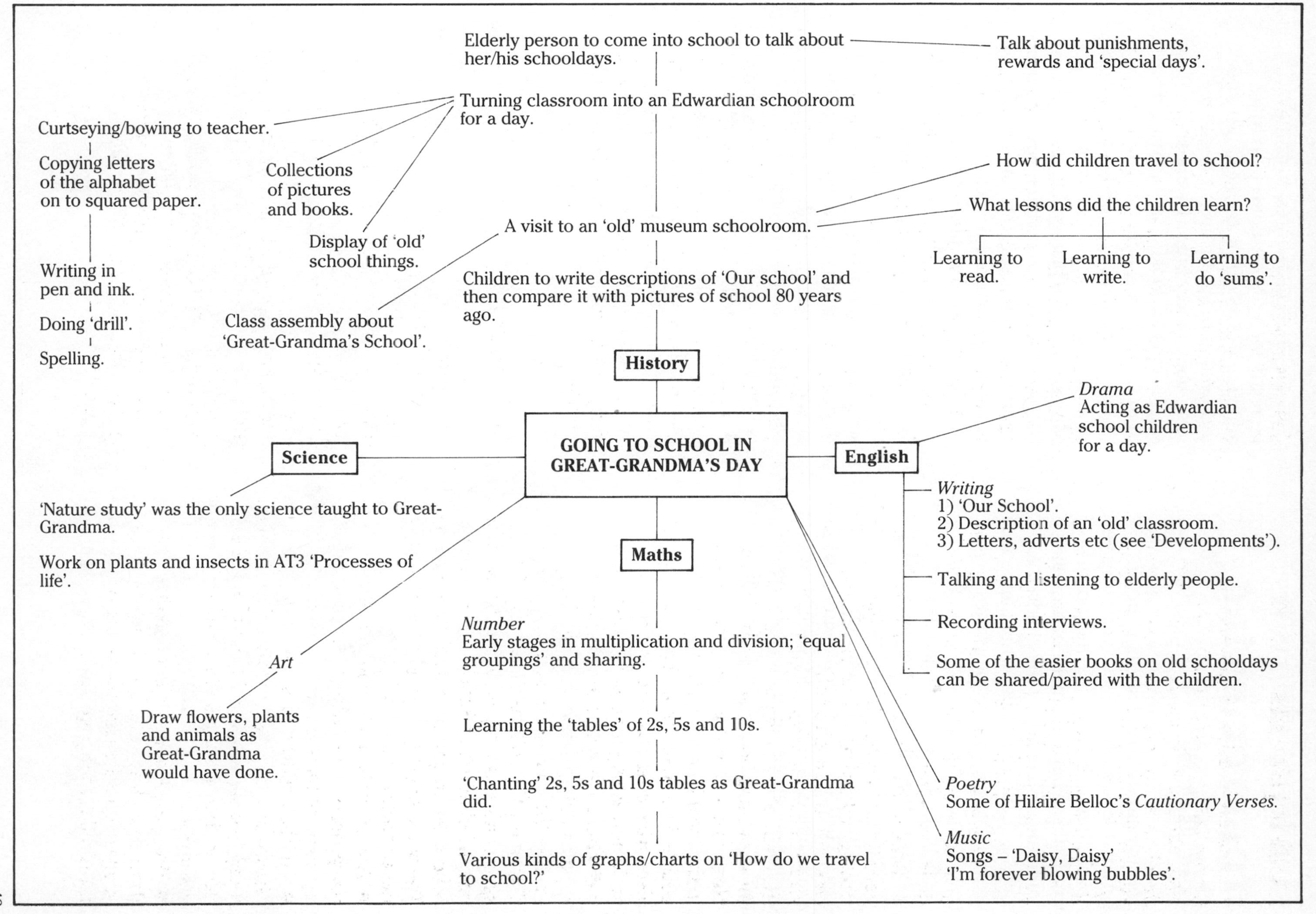
GOING TO SCHOOL IN GREAT-GRANDMA'S DAY
History
Elderly person to come into school to talk about her/his schooldays.
Talk about punishments, rewards and 'special days'.
Turning classroom into an Edwardian schoolroom for a day.
Curtseying/bowing to teacher.
Copying letters of the alphabet on to squared paper.
Writing in pen and ink.
Doing 'drill'.
Spelling.
Collections of pictures and books.
Display of 'old' school things.
A visit to an 'old' museum schoolroom.
How did children travel to school?
What lessons did the children learn?
Learning to read.
Learning to write.
Learning to do 'sums'.
Class assembly about 'Great-Grandma's School'.
Children to write descriptions of 'Our school' and then compare it with pictures of school 80 years ago.
English
Drama
Acting as Edwardian school children for a day.
Writing
1) 'Our School'.
2) Description of an 'old' classroom.
3) Letters, adverts etc (see 'Developments').
Talking and listening to elderly people.
Recording interviews.
Some of the easier books on old schooldays can be shared/paired with the children.
Poetry
Some of Hilaire Belloc's Cautionary Verses.
Music
Songs – 'Daisy, Daisy'
'I'm forever blowing bubbles'.
Science
'Nature study' was the only science taught to Great-Grandma.
Work on plants and insects in AT3 'Processes of life'.
Art
Draw flowers, plants and animals as Great-Grandma would have done.
Maths
Number
Early stages in multiplication and division; 'equal groupings' and sharing.
Learning the 'tables' of 2s, 5s and 10s.
'Chanting' 2s, 5s and 10s tables as Great-Grandma did.
Various kinds of graphs/charts on 'How do we travel to school?'

History drawn from recurring themes

Throughout the infant stage, there are certain themes which recur year after year. Apart from their intrinsic educational worth, these have the merit of providing continuity and enabling the children to look back and remember what happened in previous school years. Sometimes a class news book is kept in which important happenings are recorded and described, often with the teacher acting as scribe. If these books are kept from previous years they can be read to, by and with the next class. They are an excellent primary source and can illustrate one very valuable way of finding out about and understanding the past, even if, as in this case, it is the recent past.

By the time children reach Y2 they will be ready for a further dimension to be added to the recurring themes and, with this need in mind, we are adding to the main body of Key Stage 1 work some suggestions for looking at recurring themes from the historical point of view. Some teachers may wish to develop this aspect as an alternative to, or in combination with, some of the history themes. The National Curriculum certainly justifies this approach when it suggests 'an introduction to historical personalities and events through stories from pre-history to the present day; poetry, pictures, TV and radio, local, national and topical festivals'. In the Programme of Study for Key Stage 1 it is suggested that learning can take place through taking advantage of ceremonies, anniversaries etc, when they arise, to contribute to an understanding of local, national and world history. It is suggested that the repertoire of stories should be drawn from a variety of cultures and periods. This suggestion has been borne firmly in mind in the inclusion of a theme entitled 'Stories, myths and legends' and is also considered as we look at the potential

for valuable learning in history through recurring curriculum themes.

Harvest

A central part of celebrating harvest is the focus on food and farming (see theme on Food, page 22) which can lead to work on old-fashioned methods of farming.

- Try to organise a farm visit, followed by a visit to a farm museum. A good example of such a museum is Cogges Manor Farm in Oxfordshire where the farm is actually run as it would have been 100 years ago. The cows are milked by hand, the plough is pulled by a horse and crops are grown without the aid of chemical fertilisers. The farmhouse parlour itself is a perfect example of how an Edwardian farming family worked, lending itself to stories about the daily life of people in the countryside 100 years ago.
- Explore changes in the way food is transported; compare canals, roads and railways. A canal trip could be arranged.
- At harvest time we think of the gold colour of the corn, which could lead to the story of King Midas. The story of Persephone (see 'Stories, myths and legends') relates to the explanations the ancient Greeks gave for the changing of the seasons, which could allow for some study of Greek myths and how they can be interpreted. It is important for children to appreciate that myths can tell us a great deal about the people who evolved them.

Resources

Books

Stories for Seven-year-olds, edited by Sara and Stephen Corrin (Puffin):
'Persephone' by Freda Saxey and 'The Golden Touch' by Nathaniel Hawthorne. (Young Puffin).

Museum

Willenhall Lock Museum, Walsall Street, Willenhall, Walsall.

Bonfire night

- Teach the children the rhyme:

'Remember, remember, the fifth of
November,
Gunpowder, treason and plot.
I see no reason why gunpowder treason
Should ever be forgot!'

This could lead to the story of Guy Fawkes (celebrated in drama, drawing and writing) and some investigation into life in the days of King James I.

- Ask the children to find out all they can about the Houses of Parliament.

Resources

Stories of Special Days and Customs (Ladybird).
James I and the Gunpowder Plot (Ladybird).

Christmas

- Explain to the children about the winter solstice when, even before the birth of Jesus, people celebrated the shortest day and decked their homes with evergreen branches.

• On 13 December tell the children the story of St Lucy and how it is celebrated in Sweden today. When the Christians were being persecuted in Rome about 1,800 years ago they hid down in the catacombs. Lucy brought them food and blankets and on her head she wore a garland on to which were fixed candles so that she could be seen as she was approaching and could see her way in the dark catacombs.

Nowadays, in Sweden, the eldest girl in the household gets up early on December 13, dresses in a white dress with a red sash and takes coffee and saffron buns to the rest of her family in bed, to remind everyone of St Lucy (or St Lucia). The girl also sings a special song. The children could act this story, make Christingle crowns and make coffee and saffron buns.

• Describe a Victorian Christmas using pictures of all kinds. Explain the origin of the Christmas tree, with some account of Prince Albert, comparing him with the Duke of Edinburgh. Read a version of *A Christmas Carol* to the children and make comparisons between Tiny Tim's Christmas and our kind of Christmas. A Christmas frieze could be based on episodes of this story.

Resources

The Stories of Our Christmas Customs (Ladybird).
A Christmas Carol retold from Charles Dickens (Ladybird).

Pancake Day

The children could be told of the origin of the word 'shrove' and the explanation of why people once had to eat up all the eggs and fat before Lent. Connect this with the Roman custom of making and eating cakes in worship of the goddess of ovens, Fornax. The link with the word 'Carnival' (farewell to flesh or meat) could be explained along with the meaning of 'Mardi Gras'.

Resources

Stories of Special Days and Customs (Ladybird).

Summer holidays

• This could start with a celebration of May Day, with stories of how the Romans honoured the goddess Flora, goddess of flowering plants. A traditional May Queen could be chosen, with children dressing up to dance round the maypole and stories of how from the Middle Ages onwards people did this to celebrate the coming of spring.
• Children's own holidays at the seaside could lead to finding out about the Victorian seaside holiday. The ways in which people made journeys could be explored, looking at the start and development of railway travel.
• Grandparents could talk about holidays at home during World War Two, with discussions about entertainments in the park.

Resources

Books

Entertainment in 1900, Stephen Attmore ('Into the Past' series, Longman).
A Family in World War Two, Stewart Ross ('How They Lived' series, Wayland).

Visits
Visit to a steam railway, for example the Severn Valley Railway.

Diwali

Many teachers will want to give opportunities to think about community festivals, mainly because they are celebrated by many families as part of their religion, but also because it is important for all children to be aware of the diversity of culture in our society and the need to understand faiths other than their own. Diwali provides a good opportunity to look at the story of Rama and Sita and to consider what kinds of things it tells us. The children could look at all aspects of the festival, finding out when it started and why. Asian children could ask grandparents about life in the sub-continent when they were young. (See 'Stories, myths and legends', page 42).

Resources

Rama and Sita – Folk Tales of the World, Govinder Ram (Blackie).
Diwali, Howard Marsh (Living Festivals series, Religious and Moral Education Press).

Road safety

Most schools take an annual look at road safety, and involve the local police. This gives an ideal opportunity to learn about how the police force first began and what existed before then. An excellent wall frieze could be built up around this theme, and local police could be asked to help.

Resources

Law and Order, Frank Huggett (A & C Black).

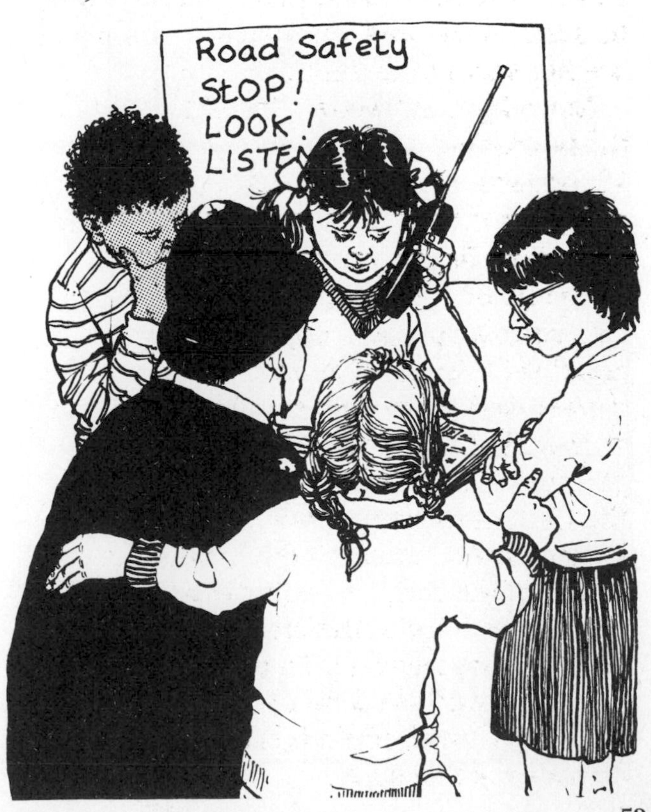

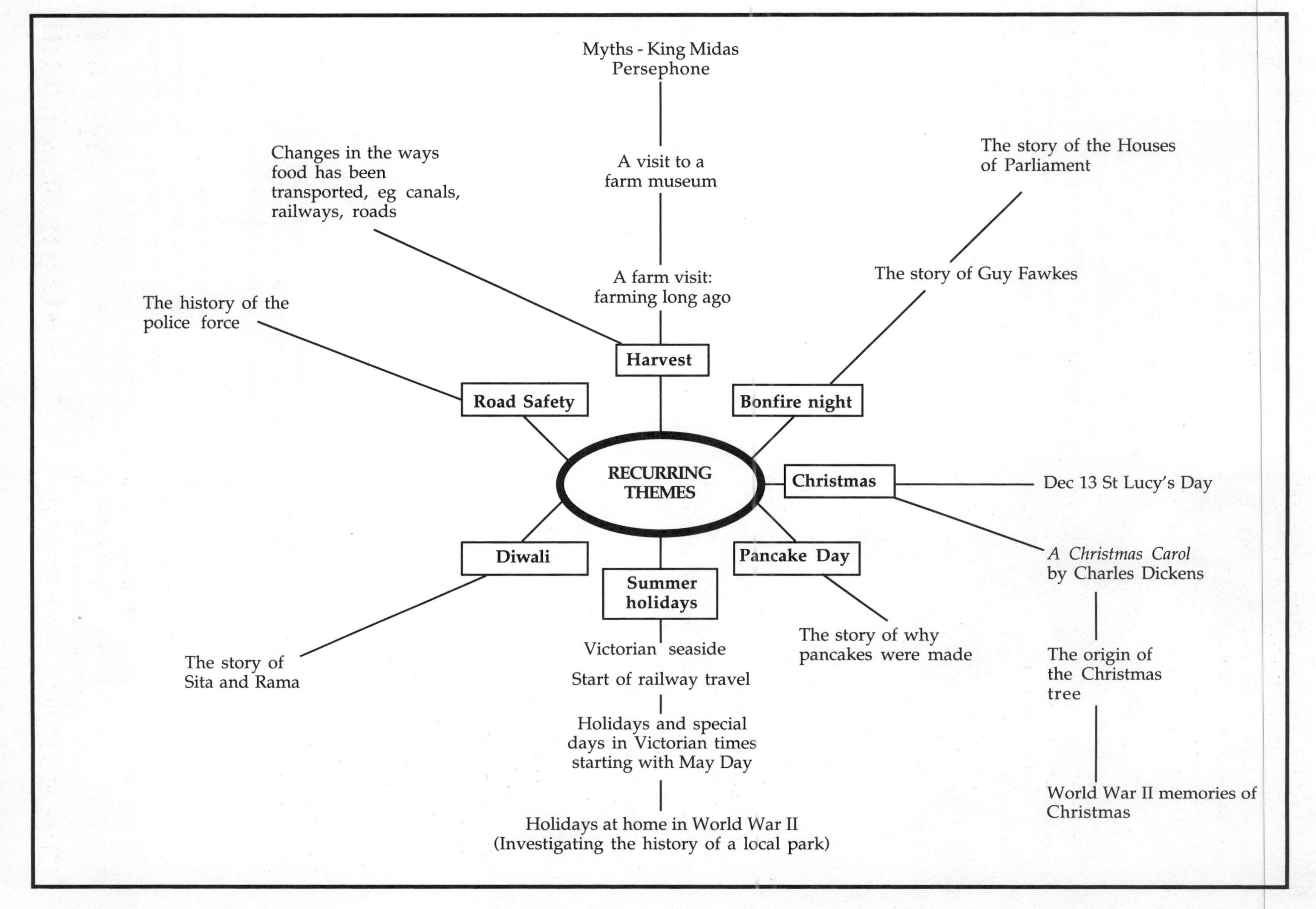
RECURRING THEMES
Harvest
A farm visit: farming long ago
A visit to a farm museum
Myths - King Midas Persephone
Changes in the ways food has been transported, eg canals, railways, roads
Road Safety
The history of the police force
Diwali
The story of Sita and Rama
Summer holidays
Victorian seaside
Start of railway travel
Holidays and special days in Victorian times starting with May Day
Holidays at home in World War II (Investigating the history of a local park)
Pancake Day
The story of why pancakes were made
Christmas
Dec 13 St Lucy's Day
A Christmas Carol by Charles Dickens
The origin of the Christmas tree
World War II memories of Christmas
Bonfire night
The story of Guy Fawkes
The story of the Houses of Parliament

Using the parish church

As an alternative, and where appropriate, we suggest that children in the middle of Y2 be invited to study the parish church. This could provide links with RE and geography or environmental studies, and could lead to a genuine interest in places of worship as a whole, Christian and non-Christian. Such a topic will set the scene for a consideration of the historic traditions that have led to the foundation of various places of worship, and an understanding of the diversity of culture in the local environment. The Final Report of the History Working Group said:

'The vicinity of the school is an important source of historical evidence, whether it is an old village or a new estate. Teachers should use the local environment to enable pupils to develop their powers of observation and to ask historical questions'. (5.5)

'Teachers should help pupils to begin to focus on selected aspects of the environment, *for example one particular building*, and then encourage more extended explorations of their environment, *for example comparing buildings of different periods*.' (5.6)

The parish church is likely (but by no means certain) to be one of the oldest buildings in the area. If the church is fairly modern, it is appropriate to ask the children why the church came to be built when it was and where people who lived in the area (if there were any!) went to church before. The church's foundation date could be fitted on to a time-line (see page 36) either in the section for the past 100 years or on an extension designed to cover the centuries before. The appropriate person to help with the study of the church would be the vicar, who will probably be delighted to give access to old records, and may be willing to show children around in the interests of historic awareness rather than religious observation.

The study of the church could be divided into the following areas:

- the people;
- the building;
- inside the church;
- the churchyard.

The people

Introduce the children to the vicar, and ask him to explain his role. The children could ask him how long he has been vicar of the parish, and how many past vicars there have been and when they held office (this could, of course, involve going back several centuries on the time-line). The vicar could also explain the role of offices such as bishop. (In one school where such a study was undertaken the children were actually able to visit the bishop's palace.)

Ask the children to discuss the people who built the church (such as medieval craftsmen, Victorian stonemasons or twentieth century architects). They might like to ask some questions about all the people who use the church today. This could yield some interesting information about different social groups ranging from the babies who come to Mother and Toddler groups and are brought for baptism to the elderly who come to lunch clubs.

The building

Children could look at the shape of the windows and doors, and examine the building materials used. Ask them to look for bricks, stone (of different kinds depending on the geological composition of the area), wood (used in different ways) and glass (particularly stained glass).

Reference could again be made to the period of the church and the changes in style through the ages. The tower or steeple could be examined and questions asked about its purpose. Stories might be told of people taking shelter in church towers during wars. For example, the detached belfry of Pembridge church in

Herefordshire provided shelter during the Civil War, and Tredington church in Warwickshire was damaged by bullet holes at around the same time. The church bells could be investigated and their functions, past and present, considered.

Inside the church

The overall shape of the church could be looked at and its significance discussed. Different areas such as the chancel, nave, altar, font, pulpit and choir could be explained. Children could look at wall tablets with names and dates and examine war memorials and monuments.

The seating in the church could be considered, and the children could find out whether pews or chairs are the earliest form of seating. Box pews might be explained, along with the social distinctions that people once observed. The floor could provide an interesting source of study, with children looking for brasses and inlaid memorial tablets. (Some brass rubbing could be undertaken with permission). There may be some interesting old hymn and prayer books.

The churchyard

The most interesting features of a churchyard will probably be the tombstones, and the children can look for dates, trying to link them with other aspects of history they have been studying during the Key Stage 1 years. Family relationships could also be explored, and children could look at surnames and discuss whether any local people, particularly children in the school, still have those surnames. It might be interesting to link this aspect of the work with a study of the school's history. Ask the children to find out whether any famous or well-known people are buried or commemorated in the churchyard. In one class studying one of Birmingham's older suburbs, the children were enchanted to find a famous artist commemorated, and the tomb of the family of the wife of a former prime minister. The children then asked questions of a number of local people and found the houses where these people had lived. They were pleased to find a print of a painting by the artist showing their area as it was over 150 years ago.

Follow-up work

The children can record their findings about the parish church through writing, drawing, junk modelling and painting. It might also be good experience for the children to take photographs and write captions for them.

An important follow-up to the study of the parish church would be for children to study other places of worship in the area, starting perhaps with a Methodist or United Reformed church or a Quaker meeting house. Similar approaches to those used in the parish church study could be adopted, and some of the differences could be noted. A visit to a mosque and a Hindu temple could be made with the help of Hindu or Muslim leaders and of Muslim and Hindu parents where possible. A synagogue could also be visited and children could discuss some of the customs relating to different faiths. Children could try to find out how long the various places of worship have been where they are, why they were founded at that particular time and either what the building was previously used for or what was on the site before it was built.

Using a botanical garden

The Final Report of the History Working Group states 'Pupils should begin to make simple comparisons between the past and the present, and so gain an increasingly systematic sense of the relative positions of different events within a time span.'

We have used our local botanical gardens with children at both Key Stages 1 and 2, and although the objectives we originally identified were not primarily concerned with the teaching of history, we were not surprised to find that a considerable amount of good historical learning actually did take place. When one reflects firstly that gardens do, in themselves, relate fundamentally to the concepts of growth and change, and secondly that many fine botanic gardens were laid out as leisure facilities in the Victorian era, it becomes obvious that children will gather historical knowledge from a project based in such a garden. If the project is carefully planned as a history experience, that knowledge will be richer and will lead to fuller understanding. We are indebted to Bill Graham of the Birmingham Botanical Gardens for the information he has given us and for the intellectual discipline that he, as a geographer and scientist, has applied to the use of the gardens for teaching history.

Children can appreciate change and growth as they observe the long-term changes in plants which, in the process of evolution, have left behind more primitive forms, sometimes known as living fossils. Comparisons can be made between these and the modern plants to which they are related. Examples of these ancient plants are the cycads (dinosaur plants) and the ginkgo (maidenhair tree).

Growth of plants takes time, especially in

the case of some trees, which may have a life span well in excess of ours. The age of a tree can be determined by counting its rings, and this can be related to historical events. The age of a living tree can be roughly determined by measuring its girth. Young children can use a piece of string marked off in years to make calculations. Trees could be placed in chronological order.

Timber from trees was an important resource for the construction of houses and ships. Ask the children to find out which type was used for various items of furniture, for constructing houses and for building ships. A group of children working on a project connected with the Mary Rose worked out the sizes of beams required and surveyed the trees to see if they were suitable for use for that purpose. They then calculated the present day cost of the work.

Since we know that the Victorians used botanical gardens for a day out, we were able to reconstruct such a day with children dressed up in Victorian costume, playing with hoops and other Victorian toys as well as listening to the band! Children could also study old photographs and posters of such events (there is a very attractive *Child Education* poster showing a day out in public gardens in the Victorian era; see References and resources, page 185).

Many of the plants in botanical gardens were introduced into this country by Victorian travellers, who collected plants from different parts of the world. Some botanical gardens have gardens which represent particular periods in history, such as the cottage garden being constructed at Birmingham Botanical Gardens. Other sources of garden history can be found in many National Trust gardens and at the Museum of Garden History founded by the Tradescant Trust in London.

Many botanical gardens have good examples of Victorian and Edwardian architecture, such as bandstands, fine iron-framed hot-houses and decorative railings.

Chapter 3
Key Stage 2

The Core History Study Units

The work undertaken at Key Stage 1 will have provided a sound platform from which historical work can be developed at Key Stage 2.

This work must be covered by pupils from ages seven to eleven during the twelve terms of Y3, Y4, Y5 and Y6. Schools must undertake five or six of the Core Study Units. Either 'Victorian Britain' or 'Life in Britain since 1930' may be left out in favour of a further Supplementary Study Unit.

A school plan for history could look like this:
Y1 Term 1 Britain since 1930 (Core Study Unit 4)
Y1 Term 3 The Benin (Supplementary Study Unit C)
Y2 Term 1 Victorian Britain (Core Study Unit 3)
Y2 Term 2 Tudor and Stuart times (Core Study Unit 2)
Y2 Term 3 Ships and seafarers (Supplementary Study Unit A)
Y3 Term 1 Explorations and encounters (Core Study Unit 6)
Y3 Term 3 Invaders and settlers (Core Study Unit 1)
Y4 Term 1 Local history (Supplementary Study Unit B)
Y4 Term 4 Ancient Greece (Core Study Unit 5).

This chapter takes each core study unit and attempts to develop the historical information as well as giving some practical ideas. We aim to point the teacher in the right direction rather than do all the work. Further reading will be required, and we give a selection of appropriate books at the end of each section, as well as the resources listed on page 181.

Teaching aids for history

Books

Several schools will probably be attempting to borrow bulk loans from local libraries at once, now that nationally prescribed topics will be undertaken by many schools at about the same time. Schools will probably find that a range of books will have to be bought once the school policy for history has been decided.

Using museums at Key Stage 2

As pupils will be following a four-year plan at Key Stage 2, the history co-ordinator for the school will be able to incorporate visits to museums and sites of interest when drawing up the school history policy.

Throughout this book we encourage teachers to talk to museum staff and make use of their knowledge when planning visits or borrowing artefacts. Museum education officers will be able to advise on the kinds of activities on offer and suggest ideas for using the museum's resources, as well as keeping you aware of forthcoming special activities. If headteachers can be persuaded to release a member of staff for the purpose, the time spent planning a visit with the help of museum staff will probably prove invaluable.

The Avoncroft Museum of Buildings in Bromsgrove is an example of a museum that brings history alive for pupils. We spoke to Dr Simon Penn, the director, who explained that the museum was interested in the social use of houses as well as the technology involved in their construction. For example, children can be shown how the use of domestic energy has changed, and how this is reflected in the buildings. The appropriate artefacts and rooms can be used to give pupils a hands-on

experience of how Great-Grandma organised her washday. As with most museum sessions, teachers would need to pre-book this type of activity.

We happened to visit the museum when an English Civil War activity was in progress. We saw actors in role living in the smoky conditions of a wattle and daub town house, and Cavalier soldiers surprised us as they drew swords to duel in the street! Dr Penn explained that 2,000 children had taken part in 100 one-hour sessions during the Civil War Week, undertaking such activities as skinning rabbits, making wattle and daub panels, dyeing fabric, baking bread and learning some of the military skills of the period. It is well worth finding out if a local museum could offer your school such an educationally sound approach to history.

Many museums have craftsmen and women who will demonstrate such traditional skills as nail-making, flour-milling, weaving, paper-making and candle-making. Some museums offer children the chance to join in with bread-making, milking, canal boat legging, riding in a horse-drawn cart or even taking part in a Victorian lesson in a genuine classroom of the period.

Visits could be made to the local municipal museum, where there is likely to be a selection of interesting artefacts. If there is a chance of using a local bus service to get to the museum, this can help to reduce the cost of the trip.

Follow-up work

You could ask the children to form groups to undertake mini-projects on the aspects of life they see reflected in the museum, from agriculture to transport or domestic life. They could then report back to the class as a whole. The ability to sum up and present their findings is an important skill for the children to learn.

If you wish, the whole class could make a presentation to the rest of the school based on their museum visit. A slide show or a video would probably enhance this, and if parents are invited to attend, it might also reinforce the notion of the value of museum visits.

Many museums are willing to loan artefacts to schools, although some of the rarer items will be replicas, of course. A collection of kitchen gadgets could be used to stimulate work relevant to technology in the National Curriculum, if the pupils are set the task of designing another system or tool to cope with the task for which a particular implement was designed.

CSU1: Invaders and settlers

	Pupils should be taught about:
invasions and settlements from 55 BC to the early eleventh century	• the Roman conquest and settlement of Britain; resistance to Roman rule, including Boudicca; Britain as part of the Roman Empire; the departure of the Legions Anglo-Saxon invasions and settlements, including the rule of Alfred, King of Wessex; the conversion of England by Roman and Celtic Christians Viking raids and settlement; Britain as part of a wider Viking world
reasons for invasion	• the search for land, trade and raw materials
way of life of the settlers	• everyday life in town and country houses and home life religious life
the legacy of settlement	• place-names and language myths and legends styles of art and architecture

Starting points

We recommend that the three main invasions are studied in chronological order before one invasion is studied in depth. We suggest that a large, stout map is made showing the United Kingdom and Ireland, and Western Europe from Brittany up to the North of Norway. This could be done by tracing a map on to acetate and projecting it on to a piece of card pinned to a wall (the size can easily be adjusted to suit). Pupils could then draw over the outline, first in pencil, then in thick felt-tipped pen.

If the map is mounted on a table or set of flat desks, it can be the base for simulations of each invasion. A coat of varnish or a layer of clear adhesive plastic would protect the map in use. Balsa models or cardboard cut-outs of boats can be used to represent the invading forces, although changes in detail would, of course, need to be made for each set of invaders. Coloured pins, counters or tiny blocks can represent the invaders' original settlements, the places they raided, the places they colonised and the location of the invaded inhabitants. The movement of the invaded inhabitants to other parts of the country can be simulated.

As each invasion is studied, mini-features such as a Plasticine Hadrian's Wall or Offa's Dyke can be added. A video camera could be fixed over the map and the single frame facility used to make a cartoon-like representation of each invasion. This could be shown to other classes and parents, along with models, costumes, pictures and readings.

The Roman conquest

The Celts

The lifestyle of the Celts in Britain needs to be studied so that the subsequent impact of the Roman invasion can be understood. Some major features of Celtic life included hill settlements, hill-top forts with massive earthworks, iron tools, elected chiefs, Druid priests, skilled use of chariots, love of jewellery, lack of a written language, farms, equal rights of property ownership for women and men, advanced medical and surgical skill and a lack of class distinction.

The Roman expeditions

The expeditions of 55 and 54 BC did not result in a Roman settlement in Britain. The expedition of AD 43 did, however, as the Romans had learnt the lessons of 55 and 54 BC. A safe landing port was chosen at Richborough, and over 40,000 soldiers from the second, ninth, fourteenth and twentieth legions with auxiliaries crossed from Boulogne to Richborough, and landed unopposed.

The Romans fought their way towards London, and met fierce resistance at Medway, but after a two-day battle, they continued, meeting little serious opposition. Emperor Claudius arrived at Colchester to accept the surrender of the eastern Belgae tribe. Soon the Romanisation of Britain was in full swing.

The Roman army

It may seem odd to say that a major strength of the Roman army was that its soldiers would follow orders. However, the same was not always true of the opponents. The Romans were well armed and trained; they were paid regularly; they had good chances of promotion, and at the end of 25 years of service each soldier could expect a pension and a plot of land. To sum up, they were in the position of professional soldiers fighting part-time soldiers.

The legionary soldier had high status, and was considered the backbone of the striking force. He had to be able to build as well as fight. The roads, which were built soon after the conquest, were an essential part of Roman strategy as they ensured that troops could be moved quickly to trouble spots.

Make a Roman road

What you need

Pea gravel and sand from a builders' supplier, fine gravel from an aquatic supplier, crushed white chalk, a baseboard, clay, sand, kiln (optional).

What to do

Place a shallow strip of clay about 10cm wide on the board. Then put a layer of coarse gravel about 1cm deep over the clay. The edge of this strip should then be walled up with clay. Cover the gravel with a layer of crushed white chalk about 0.5cm deep, then wall this up in the same way. Repeat the process with a further 1cm layer of fine gravel, a 0.5cm layer of crushed chalk and 1cm of fine gravel, each walled up with clay. The wall should slope inwards (Figure 1). Make some tiles to represent the stone slabs which cover the top layer. Roll some modelling clay out to a depth of about 4mm and cut it into small squares when firm. The squares can be fired in the kiln or allowed to dry in the air. Lay them on the top of the fine gravel, using a little sand to bed them in. The end

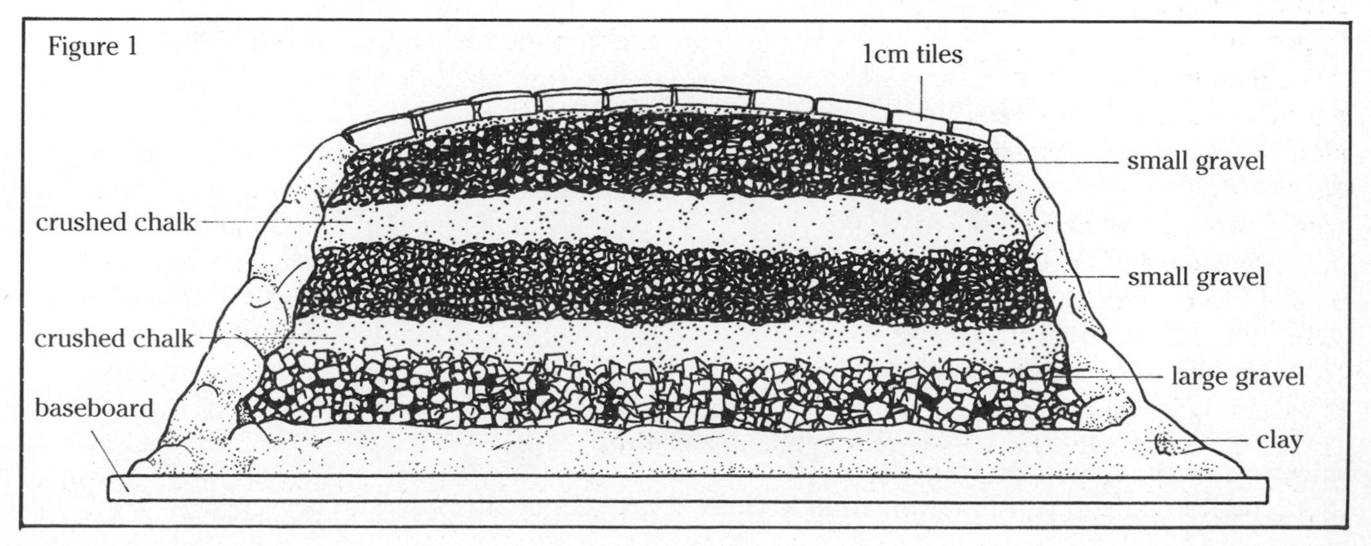

of the model should show the construction in cross-section.

Roman shields

What you need

Large cardboard boxes, scissors, paint, string.

What to do

Using Figure 1 for reference, cut out shield shapes from card for each child. Allow the children to paint them and fit string for handles.

Ask the children to practise the famous 'tortoise' formation, as in Figure 1.

Sponges could be hurled at the formation to test how effective it is!

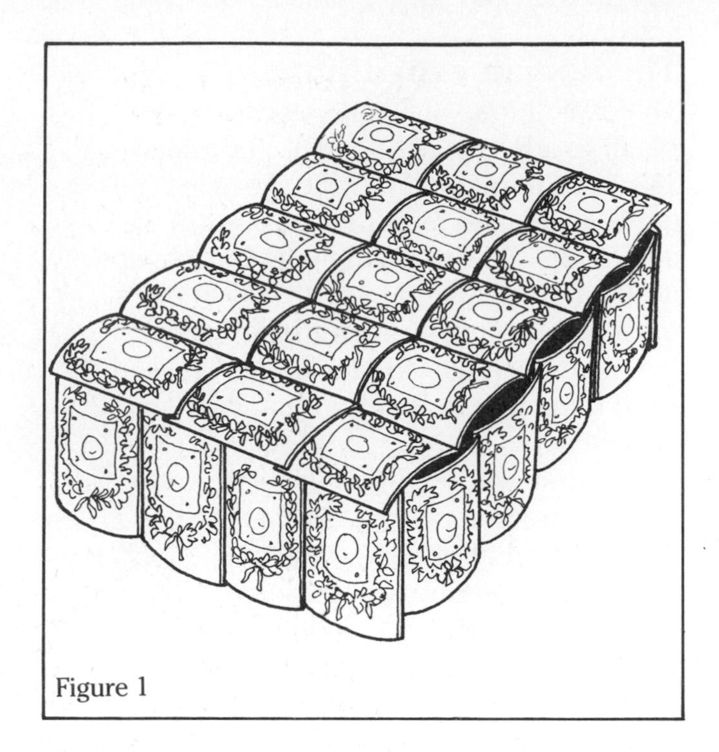

Figure 1

Resistance

In AD 60 King Prasutagas died. He was the ruler of an East Anglian tribe called the Iceni. In an attempt to protect his family, Prasutagas had willed half of his riches to the Roman Emperor. However, this plan backfired when Roman agents came to demand the property, and treated the Iceni badly. When the Iceni protested, the king's widow Boudicca (Boadicea) was whipped and her daughters assaulted. This incensed the Britons, and a rebellion soon spread throughout south-east Britain. London, Colchester and St Albans were destroyed and the inhabitants killed. The Romans considered leaving the country, but a victory by Paulinus' troops ended any resistance to Roman rule.

Roman domestic life

Pupils will need to understand that large Roman households depended upon slaves to do the work. Out of town, Romans lived in villas with rooms opening on to a courtyard or corridor. Some rooms would have been heated by hypocausts, and most villas had baths. The best rooms would have had mosaics and painted plaster walls.

Pupils should compare the housing and lifestyles of the native Britons who did not become Romanised with the Roman lifestyle.

Mosaics

What you need

Graph paper, felt-tipped pens, self-hardening clay, paint, plaster, baseboard.

What to do

Ask the children to make their own mosaic designs using graph paper and felt-tipped pens.

Make the mosaic tiles by rolling out self-hardening clay and cutting it into small squares. Paint the tiles when dry.

Mix some plaster of Paris and spread it flat on a baseboard, then allow the children to embed their tiles in it in their chosen design.

To make some 'Roman murals' to accompany their mosaics, allow the children to paint designs on damp plaster of Paris spread over a baseboard.

Hypocaust

What you need

Cardboard box, toy bricks or cotton reels, kitchen tiles, craft knife, hair drier.

What to do

Cut two holes 5cm wide in the corners of the bottom of a cardboard box so that they are diagonally opposite each other. Ask the children to arrange a minimum number of bricks or cotton reels on the bottom of the box so that they will support a floor of tiles.

When they have completed this task and the tiles are in place, allow the children to try out their hypocaust by blowing hot air through the system using a hair drier.

Towns and town life

Maps exist which show Roman London, and these can be compared with modern-day London by tracing the Roman map on to an OHP transparency and projecting it on to a map of modern London.

From the middle of the second century town construction reflected Roman confidence and optimism. Large towns were a new feature of Britain and there was plenty of room within the walls for growth. After the Romans had left and the towns were deserted, it became apparent that Roman towns were carefully planned rather than left to evolve. Towns were fortified, centred on a basilica and forum, and covered from 40 to 140 acres. The local senate met at the basilica, where local business was carried out and justice dispensed. Craftsmen would work in shops around the forum. The baths were used as a social centre as well as for bathing. Water would be brought into towns through covered conduits.

The Britons soon adapted to Roman town life, and even native workmen used Latin and produced Roman-styled goods. The country area as a whole had to bear the cost of town upkeep.

Town planning

What you need

Pencils and paper, copies of Roman town plans, large map (see page 62), art straws, water.

What to do

Ask pupils to plan their own Roman town, bearing in mind the need for a forum, a basilica, baths, an amphitheatre (probably outside the walls) and fortified town walls with four gates. The streets should be straight. These plans could then be compared to plans of known towns such as Calleva (Silchester). Drawings could be made based upon known Roman architectural styles.

Let the children use art straws to form a model conduit, pushing the end of one straw into the next. Carry out tests to see how far gravity-fed water will run.

Christianity in Britain

Worship of the Roman gods and the Britons' nature gods continued for more than three centuries after the invasion. Very few people had become Christians by the third century, and many of these were cruelly persecuted. From AD 313, however, after the conversion of Emperor Constantine to Christianity, Christians were able to worship openly. Britons worshipping their old gods were now sometimes persecuted.

A Christian chapel dating from about 365 was discovered in Lullingstone, Kent.

Hadrian's Wall

When Emperor Hadrian visited the north in AD 121-122, he decided to build a wall from east to west. The wall took five years to build, and much of the work was done by legionaries. It was laid on stone foundations and was over six metres high and three metres wide. The side facing the enemy was built on stone and mortar, the inside from rubble and wet clay.

Some soldiers were stationed on the wall itself, living in the mile castles, while others were camped several kilometres behind. At intervals between the mile castles there were turrets, possibly used for signalling. A ditch behind the wall, known as the *vallum*, is all that remains of the ditch and mounds that marked the limit of the Roman Empire.

Exploring Hadrian's Wall

What you need

Large map (see page 62), drawing and writing equipment, stout card, self-hardening clay.

What to do

First of all, ask the pupils to mark the course of the wall on the large map of the United Kingdom, Ireland and western Europe from Brittany to the north of Norway. Then you can ask them to use the details of the construction of the wall for mathematical investigations. The wall was 120km long, and it is thought that each kilometre would have used 25,000 tons of building stone. Groups of eighty soldiers would have tackled forty metre lengths at a time.

If they wish, the children could make a cross-sectional drawing of Hadrian's Wall to scale, as well as scale models constructed from card and clay. You could also encourage the children to explore in written work the reaction of tribes who were involved in cross-border raiding.

The legions leave

The end of Roman rule in Britain was a gradual process and there were a number of contributory factors.

- Britons and Saxons had been allowed into the army, which gradually became weak and undisciplined. A force was sent by the Emperor Theodosius to restore order in Britain.
- At the start of the fifth century part of the Roman army was sent to fight in Europe, which reduced their presence in Britain.
- The Saxons had been attacking Britain from about AD 250, starting with pirate raids. In AD 446, pleas to Rome for help in fighting them off were ignored.

The Roman way of life lingered on for a while, but eventually the fine villas were abandoned by their wealthy Romano-British owners. Roads were no longer used and the worship of nature gods returned.

Saxon piracy and settlement

As the power and influence of Rome diminished, so the audacity of Saxon attacks on the British shores increased. By AD 300, Saxon raiders from north Germany and Holland were looting villages inland as well as coastal hamlets. Forts were built from the Wash to the Isle of Wight as defences.

From about 340, tribes from Scotland and Ireland invaded from the north and reached the Thames. Saxons and Franks attacked from the south. The once proud and disciplined Roman army had become weak and disillusioned.

Many people buried their tools and treasure during this time of unrest. The Mildenhall Silver treasure is dated from this period.

The invaders who settled in Britain after the Romans left came from Holland, North Germany and Denmark. The Angles, Saxons and Jutes are usually referred to as the Anglo-Saxons or the Saxons. Large numbers of warriors made forays to Britain, and returned for their families, cattle and possessions when they decided it was safe to settle down.

Vortigern, king of a large part of Britain, offered the new settlers land in exchange for helping to fight off fresh invaders. In about 450 these new allies turned on their host, led by the brothers Hengist and Horsa, and took over much of south-east England. The Saxons expanded further into Britain until they controlled much of the country. Those Britons who did not live under Saxon dominance moved to north-west England, Scotland, Wales and south-west England.

Cornwall and Wales were occupied by Britons, and Scotland mostly by Picts, Scots, the British tribes and the Angles. Celtic language, music and art were common to the areas not occupied by the Anglo-Saxons. The islands of Shetland and Orkney were settled by Norwegians escaping the poverty of their homeland. Other Norwegians settled in the Hebrides, Galloway and the Isle of Man.

The boats used by Saxon invaders were open, like a large rowing boat with pointed prow and stern. 14 or so benches would support the oarsmen. The boats were up to 70 feet in length, 14 feet wide and could carry 40 people. They must have been far more manoeuvrable than the clumsy Roman galleys. One such boat was found preserved in a peat bog.

The body of a warrior has also been found preserved in peat. He wore a finely woven tunic, trousers with short stockings, a large, square woollen cloak and leather sandals.

Mapping the invasion

What you need

Large map (see page 62), pins, string, coloured counters.

What to do

Use the large map to show the lands in Germany, Holland and Denmark that the Anglo-Saxons left, the routes that they took to move to Britain and the land that they occupied in Britain. Pins could hold string in place to show the borders, and coloured counters could show which tribes lived where.

Celtic resistance to the Saxons

Some historians place King Arthur in the fifth or sixth century. The legend may well be based upon the exploits of Artorius, the leader of a band of Romanised soldiers. He is said to have used cavalry expertly and assisted Britons who were being harassed by the Anglo-Saxons. Many people believe his headquarters were located in Cornwall.

Pupils today may have a more accurate picture of Celtic warriors in the fifth century than previous generations, because a recent television series about Arthur was set in this period, rather than the twelfth or thirteenth centuries usually associated with the Knights of the Round Table.

Celtic adventures

What you need

Writing equipment, reference books about the period.

What to do

Ask pupils to write about the adventures of a Celtic warrior from this period, who could be either female or male. They should describe the types of weapons and method of travel used, and the location of enemies. A serial, written a chapter a week, and planned to coincide with the aspect of history studied for that week, could be used as a focus for investigating the dress, travel, trade, weapons and population spread of the Anglo-Saxons and Celts, as well as the religion and domestic life of the time.

Saxon and Celtic kings

When the Anglo-Saxons began to settle in England, Wales was inhabited by many tribes, each with their tribal king. Some had very small kingdoms indeed. From the early part of the seventh century these tribes raided across the border with England. This raiding was encouraged by the kings, as under traditional Welsh law they were entitled to a third of all goods captured. By the beginning of the ninth century there were a number of kingdoms, including Gwynedd, Powys, Deheubarth and Morgannwg. In the early part of the tenth century Hywel Dda ruled over Deheubarth, Gwynedd and Powys. His laws, which were based upon traditional Welsh custom, were considered good.

The first king to regard himself as ruler of England was King Offa (757 to 796). He ruled East Anglia, central and south-east England, as far north as the Humber, and south-west up to a curving border from modern day Bristol, through Windsor, to Portsmouth. To show the raiding Welsh where his kingdom ended so that they might expect harsh punishment if caught across the border, he had a dyke constructed. Between 787 and 796, Offa's Dyke was dug between Flint and the upper Wye. It was not a defensive barrier, but served as a powerful symbol of Offa's strength. King Offa is also remembered for the silver pennies he had minted and for the fact that in 789, towards the end of his reign, a small band of Viking raiders invaded the coast of Wessex and killed the King of Wessex's representative who greeted them as traders.

Saxon and Celtic art

What you need

Pictures of illuminated manuscripts and Saxon and Celtic jewellery, felt-tipped pens, paper, self-hardening clay, paint, varnish.

What to do

Let the children practise Saxon and Celtic lettering, drawing their own initials in the style of illuminated manuscripts, perhaps with dragon head endings to lines. The children may also like to make replicas of Saxon brooches from self-hardening clay, which can then be painted and varnished.

Christianity returns to England

The Anglo-Saxons worshipped nature gods such as Erce the earth mother and Woden the father god. The Christianity of the Roman period survived in Wales, Scotland, Cornwall and Ireland. The Celtic Church was based on remote monasteries which sent out roaming missionaries to spread the Christian message, rather than establishing churches in towns. It could not, therefore, use the Church of Rome's method of basing a ruling bishop in a town. The Celtic Church developed independently of Rome, its missionaries wandering where the spirit moved them.

Celtic Christians came to Scotland in 563. Twelve monks led by Columba made the remote island of Iona their base. A Northumbrian king, Oswald, eventually invited the Celtic missionaries to preach in England.

Pope Gregory had long wanted to re-convert England to Christianity. In 597 he ordered a band of monks led by Augustine to England. King Ethelbert of Kent, although a pagan, was married to a Christian princess. He gave Augustine a small church in Canterbury. In 601, Pope Gregory proclaimed Augustine Archbishop of England.

A Celtic monk called Aidan was prominent in preaching to the Northumbrians, and he based himself on the island of Lindisfarne in 634.

There were major differences between Roman Christianity and Celtic Christianity. King Oswald's successor Oswy called a great council to debate these differences at the monastery of Whitby in 663. The King sided with the Roman Church, but aspects of the Celtic Church were retained.

Anglo-Saxon cross

What you need
Cardboard, Plasticine, plaster of Paris, pencil, broad and fine lino-cutting tools, dowel, wooden base, drill.

What to do
Ask the children to make a mould for the cross as in Figure 1, using strips of cardboard held in place with Plasticine. Then they can mix some plaster of Paris, pour it into the mould and allow it to set.

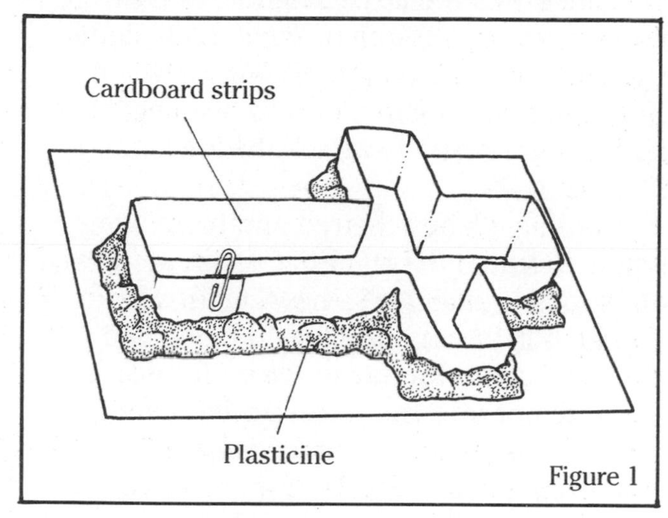

Figure 1

When the plaster cross is dry, the children can remove it from the mould and draw a simple pattern on one face of the cross using a pencil (Figure 2). Carve away the background with a broad lino-cutting tool, and add the fine detail with a narrow one.

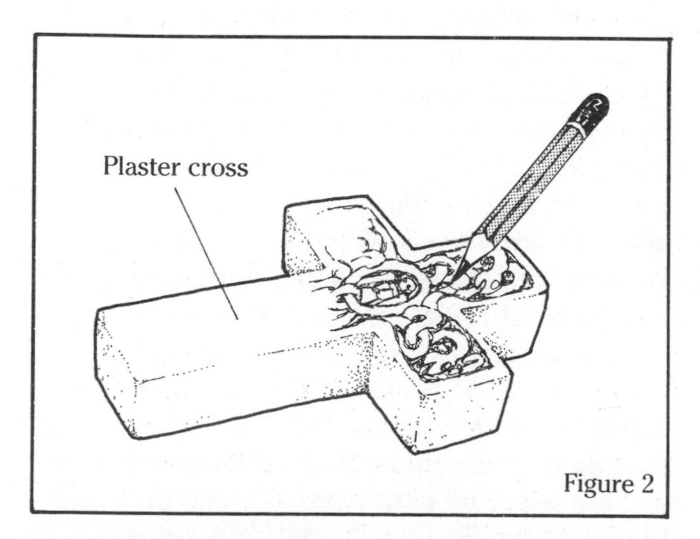

Figure 2

To make the cross stand upright, insert a piece of dowel through the base of the mould before filling it with plaster. Drill a hole in a piece of wood to act as a stand for the cross and push the dowel into the hole as in Figure 3.

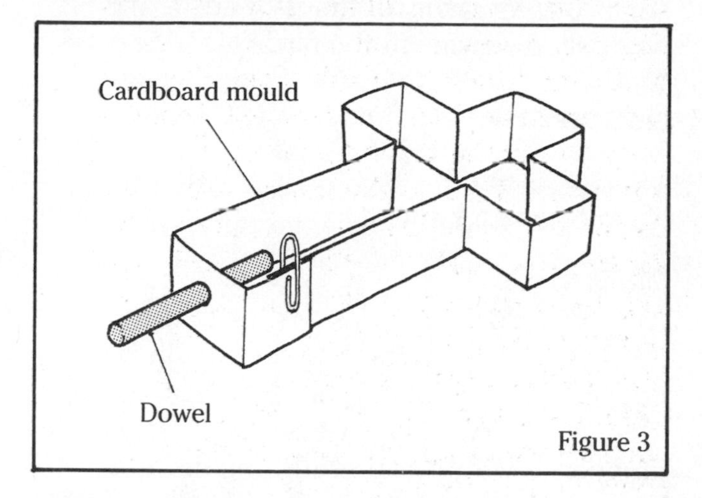

Figure 3

Crime and punishment

The Saxons had their own legal system which included the following laws:

- Trial by ordeal. This involved the accused having to hold a red hot bar in order to prove his innocence.
- Those accused could swear innocence before a public jury, using an elaborate series of oaths. They had to be backed up by others swearing oaths in their defence. A falter in the oath swearing was deemed to be a sign of guilt.
- Runaway slaves and suspected witches were killed, and wrongdoers could be punished by branding and cutting off hands, ears or tongues.
- Some crimes could be compensated for by paying a fixed fine. Every man had his allotted wergild, which was the amount to be paid if he was killed or unlawfully injured. Relatives could forgo wergild and start a blood feud.
- In the absence of a police force, criminals would be chased by hue and cry, a Saxon equivalent of the wild west posse.
- Women were given equal status in divorce cases. They took half of the property if they kept any children.

The rule of kings

Saxons accepted the rule of kings and the bloodline of royalty. The Witan was an assembly which gathered to advise the king. It was probably made up of thegns (nobles) and included bishops after the coming of Christianity.

Every freeman owed his lord the duty of serving in the army in times of need. This was called service in the fyrd.

Saxon law

What you need
No special equipment.

What to do
Ask the children to consider the fairness of Saxon law and discuss whether the laws depended upon luck rather than justice. They could try to swear elaborate oaths of innocence without faltering, and discuss whether, in fact, there was some rough and ready justice in the laws. Would a guilty man be more nervous and therefore more likely to falter in the oath swearing, for example?

Let the class role-play a crime, the hue and cry and the summoning of the criminal before the people. They could then choose an appropriate punishment.

The coming of the Vikings

After the small Viking raid of 789, attacks on coastal settlements became increasingly common. Just as the Romans had defended themselves against the Saxon raiders, so the Saxons had to defend themselves against the new invaders.

Although these raiders are known collectively as Vikings, they came from Norway, Denmark and Sweden, each an independent country, and did not refer to themselves as Vikings. Reasons for their raids and eventual colonisation of other countries included the shortage of arable land in their home countries, a love of exploration and adventure, and their new freedom after the death of Charlemagne, king of the Franks. Charlemagne died in 814 and, as no heir was agreed, there was no longer a strong king to oppose the Vikings, and they were able to raid along the great rivers of Europe.

In 793 the holy island of Lindisfarne was attacked. The raiders stole treasure, and killed some monks, taking others as slaves. In 795 Iona, the base of St Columba, was attacked and looted. The raiding and looting continued throughout the ninth century, and by 865 not a church less than a day's ride from the coast was left standing.

In the same year a large army of Danes landed on the east coast. The Saxons were not able to beat off such a large force, particularly as the large kingdom of Offa had broken up into many smaller kingdoms by 865. The Danes captured large parts of England, from Northumbria to Reading, and by 870 were ready to attack the kingdom of Wessex.

The Saxon king Ethelred and his brother Alfred defeated the Danes at Ashdown. In 871 Ethelred died and a new Danish army landed. Alfred negotiated with them, and gave the Danes money in return for a promise not to attack Wessex. They kept largely to that agreement for five years. After that, the Danish army split into two factions. One faction, led by King Guthrum, attacked Wessex and overcame parts of what are now Wiltshire and Hampshire. Alfred fled with his lords to Athelney in Somerset, then gathered an army around him and marched northwards to Guthrum's headquarters at Chippenham. Alfred beat the Danes in a pitched battle and besieged them for 14 days.

After Guthrum and some of his chiefs agreed to be baptised as Christians, the treaty of Wedmore was drawn up. The Danes ruled England north of Watling Street, Mercia remained a separate kingdom and Alfred remained as ruler of Wessex. The treaty of Wedmore in 878 resulted in the Danelaw, the partitioning of England.

King Alfred

Alfred was the youngest of five brothers, and so he would not have expected to become king. He was born in 849, the son of King Ethelwulf of Essex. He became king in 871 at the age of 22.

After the treaty of Wedmore, Alfred ordered warships to be built to defend the coastline. These ships were twice as long as other English ships, with 60 oars or more. They were faster and steadier in the water than the Viking ships. Alfred is sometimes regarded as the founder of the British navy.

As well as being recognised as a great warrior, Alfred was interested in learning and invited scholars to settle in Wessex. He learned Latin himself and translated many books. He devised a set of laws, known as Alfred's dooms, to protect the poor and weak. In 886 he rebuilt London. He died in 901.

Boats

The Viking longship was strong, fast and seaworthy, and it is in such vessels that Lief and Thorvald sailed to America. The way they were constructed enabled the boats to flex in stormy seas. Much is known about the type of boats the Vikings built and sailed, because boats were used for the burial of chieftains and royalty, and some have been sufficiently well preserved to reveal details of their construction. In 1880 such a funeral craft was excavated at Gokstad in Norway. A replica of the ship was built and sailed to America in 1893.

The study of the Viking longboat and journeys could be undertaken elsewhere if the supplementary study unit on ships and seafarers through history is chosen as an option.

Viking voyages

What you need

The large map (see page 62), card, stapler, sticky tape, paint, scissors, long pole, shorter pole to act as crosspole, old sheet dyed in a bright colour, large cardboard boxes, thin strips of softwood, drill, string.

What to do

Ask the children to mark the Vikings' voyages of migration and exploration on the large map. Once again, countries of origin and places of colonisation should be marked. Journeys of trade and exploration from Gurgan on the eastern extreme of the Caspian Sea, to Iceland, Greenland and Vinland (Newfoundland) could be plotted on a smaller scale map, with settlements included.

Encourage the children to make a simple model of a longboat from two strips of card drawn and decorated to represent the ship's timbers and carvings. Staple these together at each end and bow them out to give a free-standing model. Larger models can be made from thicker card, curved and stuck in place around a long cardboard box in the middle to give it strength. Let each pupil make a personal shield to fasten on the sides.

A dramatic classroom display could be made using a pole the height of the classroom as a mast, with a crosspole fastened at the top. The bottom could be placed on the floor against the wall and the top allowed to hang forward at an angle of 15 degrees. An old sheet which has been painted or dyed could be hung from the boom to make the sail. The bow of a longboat could be made out of card from packing boxes, stuck together at the figurehead. This could be free-standing on the floor, sticking out from the wall a metre or so. A rough sea scene could be added as a background, on the wall behind the sail. For extra effect, pupils could tape-record sea sound effects.

To understand how Viking boatbuilders made flexible joints, pupils could use two strips of thin softwood, overlap them by about 3cm and clamp them in position while they drill holes through the overlapping section about 2cm apart. When the clamps have been released, let them try to join the pieces of wood using string.

Funerals

Ships were central to the burial or cremation of important Vikings, as they symbolised the long voyage which the deceased was about to undertake in the afterlife. Excavated burial ships have been found to contain artefacts which were deemed essential for the voyage to Valhalla. Slaves were killed and placed in the ship to serve the master on the voyage.

Let the pupils study funeral customs as part of an investigation into Viking beliefs. Ask the class to work in groups to investigate Viking gods and Viking funerals, and then report back to the whole class.

Viking craftsmen

The Vikings produced magnificent wooden carvings on everyday objects, including elaborate chess sets. Their boats were often covered with intricate carvings, and weapons were often inlaid with bronze, brass or silver.

The Viking jewellers were skilled in working gold and silver, and detailed coins were minted. Much jewellery has survived, some excavated from archaeological digs at the sites of graves, other pieces rediscovered in the twentieth century after being buried for safety in times of crisis. Jewellery was buried with important chiefs or royalty, such as the Viking queen whose grave was discovered at Oseberg.

Chess sets

What you need

Card, scissors, felt-tipped pens, plaster of Paris, varnish, petroleum jelly, Plasticine, knife, paint, clay, kiln.

What to do

Try to obtain a replica of a Viking chess set as a museum loan for the children to use as reference. Let them draw the chessmen on card, cut them out and decorate them, and make card stands for the pieces so that real chess games can be played with them.

A plaster chess set can be made by carving a piece from plaster, then coating it with varnish. When the varnish is dry, cover the entire surface with petroleum jelly and then cover the piece with Plasticine. Carefully cut through the Plasticine so that it comes away in two pieces, as in Figure 1. Join the two pieces of Plasticine together again so that they form a hollow mould. Fill the mould with plaster of Paris and leave it to harden. When the plaster has set, peel away the Plasticine and varnish the chess piece. Let the children make an entire chess set in this way, making different moulds for the various pieces.

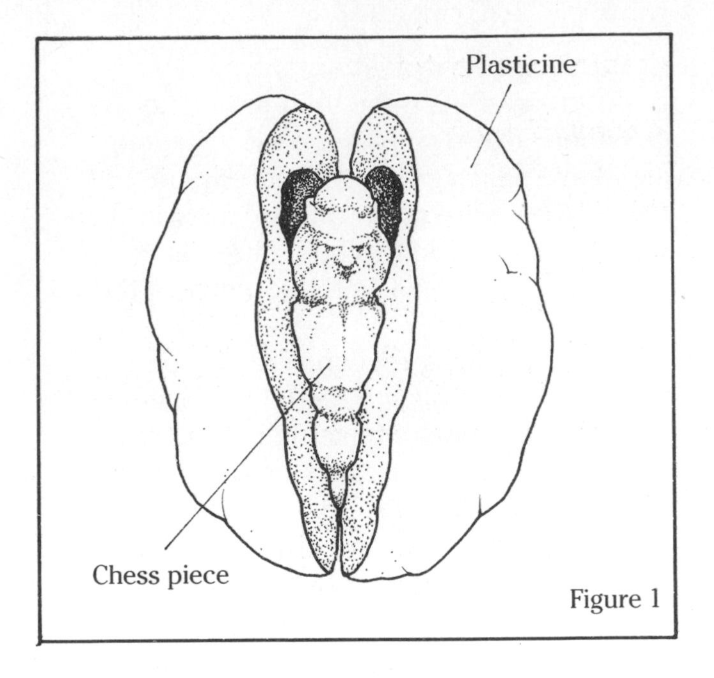

Figure 1

Larger chess pieces could be made from clay and fired in a kiln.

Inlay

What you need

Clay, carving knife, yellow Plasticine, pictures of the great axe of Mammen.

What to do

Show the children pictures of the great axe of Mammen and discuss the inlay work.

Ask them to make clay replicas of the axe, or to invent their own designs. They can carve patterns on the axes when the clay has hardened. If they wish, they can roll yellow Plasticine into long thin strings and press it into the grooves to represent gold, cutting away the excess with a knife.

Runes

Memorial tablets and grave goods have been found which bear runic inscriptions. Some reference books give the original 24 letter runic alphabet, while others give the 16 letter version believed to have been in use in the tenth century.

Runic inscriptions

What you need

Soft wood or plaster blocks, carving knives, writing materials.

What to do

Let the children carve an approximation of their own names in runes on soft wood or plaster blocks using Figure 1 for reference.

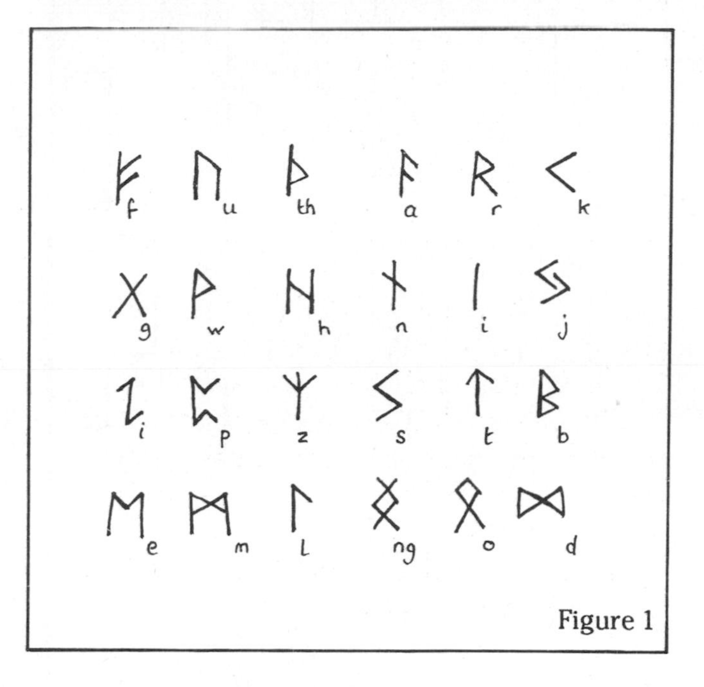

Figure 1

Ask them to try to transcribe photocopies of runic inscriptions into modern day letters. Ask them why the transcription is not in English.

Viking women

Although Viking women were expected to carry out the household chores, rear children and weave cloth, some wealthy women were farmers and traders in their own right, which was not the custom in all parts of Europe. While Vikings warriors were away from home, their wives managed the farms and often defended them by fighting off raiders.

The women were also responsible for teaching children the traditional stories about famous Viking adventures and achievements. These stories were known as sagas and were passed on from generation to generation. They usually contained lengthy genealogies giving the entire family histories of the characters.

Viking sagas

What you need

The large map (see page 62), translations of Viking sagas, tape-recorder.

What to do

Let the children read modern translations of the sagas, and plot out the locations and journeys on the large map.

Ask the children to make their own sagas, perhaps containing their own family genealogies, and tell them to the rest of the class. You could ask one pupil to tell a story in the style of a saga, and tape-record it. The story should then be retold several times and the final telling recorded as well. Pupils could listen to the two versions and discuss the differences between them, and the reasons for these differences.

The battle of Stamford Bridge

The defeat of King Harald Hadrada at Stamford Bridge in 1066 is usually told as a minor aspect of the battle of Hastings. Pupils will need to know that it also marked the end of the Viking age.

Resources

Everyday Life in Roman and Anglo-Saxon Times, M Quennell and C H Quennell (Batsford & Putnams).
Everyday Life in Roman Britain, M Quennell and C H Quennell (Batsford).
Great Adventures of the Vikings, J Geipel (Bell & Hyman).
Headline History 55 BC to 1485, J Ray (Evans).
Roman Britain, R R Sellman (Methuen).
Roman Soldiers, 'Starters' series (Macdonald).
Saxon Britain, J Hamilton and A Sorrell (Lutterworth Press).
The Celts, R Place (Macdonald).
The Romans, J Forman (Macdonald).
The Saxons, T D Triggs (Oliver & Boyd).
The Vikings, J Anderson (Puffin).
The Vikings, M Gibson (Macdonald).
The Vikings, S Nickels (Jackdaw Pack).

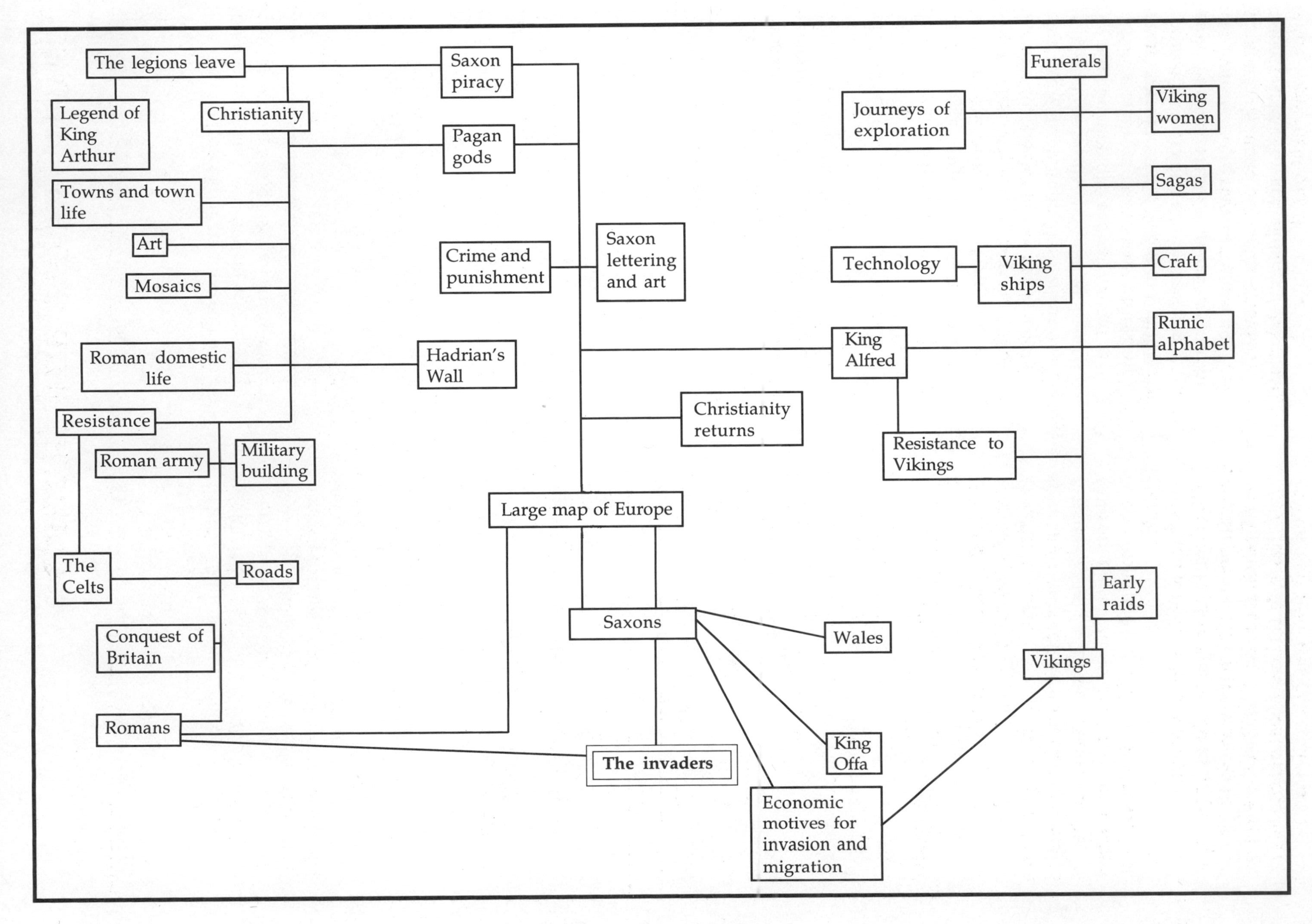

The legions leave
Saxon piracy
Funerals
Legend of King Arthur
Christianity
Journeys of exploration
Viking women
Pagan gods
Towns and town life
Sagas
Art
Crime and punishment
Saxon lettering and art
Technology
Viking ships
Craft
Mosaics
Runic alphabet
King Alfred
Roman domestic life
Hadrian's Wall
Christianity returns
Resistance
Resistance to Vikings
Roman army
Military building
Large map of Europe
The Celts
Roads
Early raids
Saxons
Wales
Conquest of Britain
Vikings
Romans
King Offa
The invaders
Economic motives for invasion and migration

CSU2: Tudors and Stuarts

	Pupils should be taught about:
rulers and court life	• Tudor and Stuart rulers major events, including the break with Rome, the Armada, Gunpowder Plot, Civil War and Restoration the courts of the Tudor and Stuart monarchs
people in town and country	• the way of life of different groups in town and country trade and transport the Great Plague (1665) and the Great Fire of London (1666)
scientific and cultural achievements	• scientists, including Newton, and their discoveries architects and their buildings music and drama, including Shakespeare
exploration and empire	• explorers, including Drake and Raleigh, and their voyages the beginnings of the British Empire
religious issues	• religious changes religion in everyday life King James's Bible

Starting points

Monarchy

This long period was heavily influenced by the monarchy and the struggle against its power. A family tree from Henry VII to Queen Anne, the last of the Stuarts, would provide a useful point of reference for the wide range of this unit.

The class could be divided into four or more groups to make the family tree. Possible divisions could be made from Henry VII to Edward VI, from Mary Tudor to James I, from Charles I to Charles II (including the Protectors), and from James II to Anne.

If large sheets of card are used, the family tree could be displayed lengthways around the room. Each group should aim to finish at a point half-way up the card with the line continuing to the monarch with which the next group is starting (see Figure 1). Pictures can be mounted in appropriate places, to illustrate the events and people mentioned.

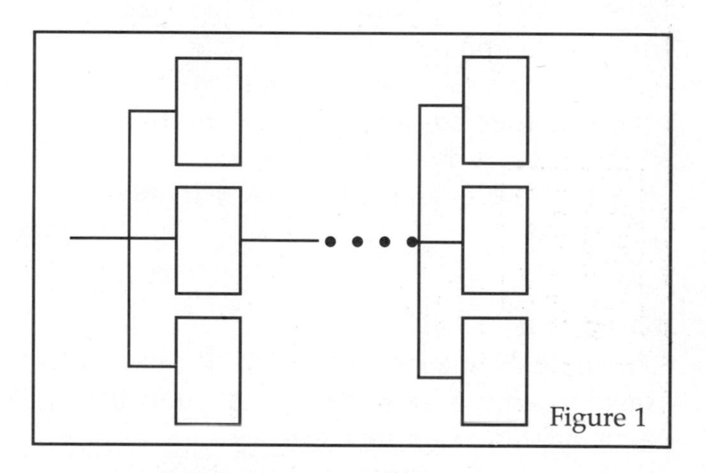

Figure 1

Cultural and scientific developments

The Elizabethan era is often thought of as a glorious age, and writers such as William Shakespeare, Christopher Marlowe, Ben Jonson, Philip Sidney and Edmund Spenser were renowned for their poems, plays and stories.

Watching plays was a favourite Elizabethan pastime, and strolling players would perform in the courtyards of inns. The first theatres were built in the form of such courtyards. The Globe and the Swan at Bankside and the Fortune theatre at

Cripplegate were amongst the first purpose-built theatres.

The theatres were closed by the Puritans, but opened again in Charles II's reign. The Globe and the Fortune had by this time been destroyed, and the King's Theatre and the Duke of York had become the most important.

Tudor musicians would have played upon the lute, viol, flute and virginals. The period of the Tudors and Stuarts saw many changes in popular fashion, and pupils could document these and present their findings in chronological order.

An important technological development was that of guns. During this period they became more reliable and more powerful, and subsequently armour and castles became less important.

It was a period in which the world was proved to be a sphere, and it was discovered that the earth was not the centre of the universe. Elizabethan writers like Bacon were able to challenge the acceptance of classical knowledge. Galileo and Kepler changed men's thinking.

Newton's theory of gravity, Boyle's chemical theories and Harvey's discovery of the circulation of blood were each important seventeenth century scientific achievements.

Religion

The topic of religion can be tackled from the viewpoint of religious persecution and recrimination. Children will need a background knowledge of how the State from the time of Henry VIII onwards treated those who held different religious views.

Henry VIII

If, as is suggested in the National Curriculum, well-documented events are studied, then the break by Henry VIII with the Roman Catholic church should be taught, as should his six marriages. His desire to leave a male heir partly explains both facts.

The reign of Henry VIII

What you need

Reference books about the period.

What to do

Ask the children to devise a dramatic presentation based on the turbulent events during the reign of Henry VIII. Divide the class into groups to research and make notes on the following people:

- each of Henry's six wives;
- Cardinal Wolsey;
- Sir Thomas More;
- Thomas Cranmer;
- a displaced monk and nun;
- Henry himself.

Ask the groups to arrange their notes into a dramatic presentation narrated by their central character. For example, Sir Thomas More could say, 'At first I wanted to be a monk, but then I trained at Oxford to be a lawyer. One of my friends there was Erasmus, from the Netherlands. I came to London to practise, and became a member of parliament. I was surprised and a little worried when the King asked me to be Lord Chancellor . . .'.

When all the groups have devised their presentations, they can be linked in chronological order by a narrator who will give the background information. Encourage the children to develop their presentation as far as you think appropriate, perhaps using it as an assembly, or adding costumes and music to create a play to be shown to the parents.

Elizabeth I

By the time Henry's daughter, Elizabeth I, was on the throne, Roman Catholics in England felt a strong conflict of loyalty between Church and State. Missionaries began to work secretly to convert people in England and Wales back to the Roman Catholic Church. They relied on Catholics to hide them, and wealthy families often had 'priest holes' specially constructed for this purpose in their houses. Harvington Hall, to the south-west of Birmingham on the A450, has some excellent examples of priest holes.

During Elizabeth's reign there were several plots to overthrow her and replace her with a Roman Catholic queen, namely Mary, Queen of Scots. Such plotting resulted in Mary's execution in 1587. Her son, James I of England, eventually succeeded Elizabeth.

Priest holes

What you need

Cardboard boxes, scraps of wood and fabric, paint, sticky tape, staples, adhesive, scissors.

What to do

Use the idea of priest holes as a basis for work involving role-play, imaginative writing and technology. Ask a small group of pupils to act as priests trying to find hiding places, while other pupils take on the roles of the family hiding them. Let the rest of the class be the soldiers searching for the priests.

If the layout of the room allows for it, the children playing priests could really try to hide. They will need to find or construct a hiding place which cannot be spotted from the outside, but which is easily accessible and has good ventilation, warmth and access to water and food.

Let the children plan their designs and construct them in a suitable part of the school. They could use cardboard from old boxes and scraps of wood and material, and the finished model can be painted. To assess the design, ask a relative stranger to the school to walk around and try to spot the hiding places.

The Armada

Elizabeth imposed fines for refusing to attend Church of England services, and punished known Catholics. During her reign, up to 300 Roman Catholics were executed, which led the Spanish to believe that Britain was an enemy of God. The religious aspect is an important part of the background to the Spanish Armada. King Philip II of Spain saw himself as the champion of the Catholic faith, and wanted to send his ships to defeat the Protestant queen.

The Armada was sighted off Plymouth on 14 July 1588, and beacons were lit from Cornwall to York. The Armada was engaged off the Isle of Wight on 19 July. The large Spanish ships were somewhat top-heavy, and carried many troops, which meant that although the English ships were not much smaller, they were much more manoeuvrable. They also had superior fire-power, and could come up to a Spanish ship, fire and be off before the Spanish could reply.

On 22 July, the Spanish anchored off Calais and eight English fireships were sent in. Fighting continued all that day. On 23 July, the wind drove the Spanish out into the North Sea, and the English chased them up to Scotland where they ran out of ammunition and gave up the chase. Many Spanish ships were lost in storms as they headed north of Scotland and west of Ireland. Depending on your sources, either 53 Spanish ships were lost or only 55 reached Spain.

The battle at sea

What you need
Thin card, paper, matchsticks, balsa wood, adhesive, paint or felt-tipped pens.

What to do
Ask the children to make a large table-top map of the UK and Ireland, so that they can simulate the defeat of the Spanish Armada. They will need to make 132 models of Spanish ships and about 100 English ships, as well as eight English fireships. They could also make models of the warning beacons. Figure 1 shows a design which could be used for the model ships, which should be about two or three centimetres in length.

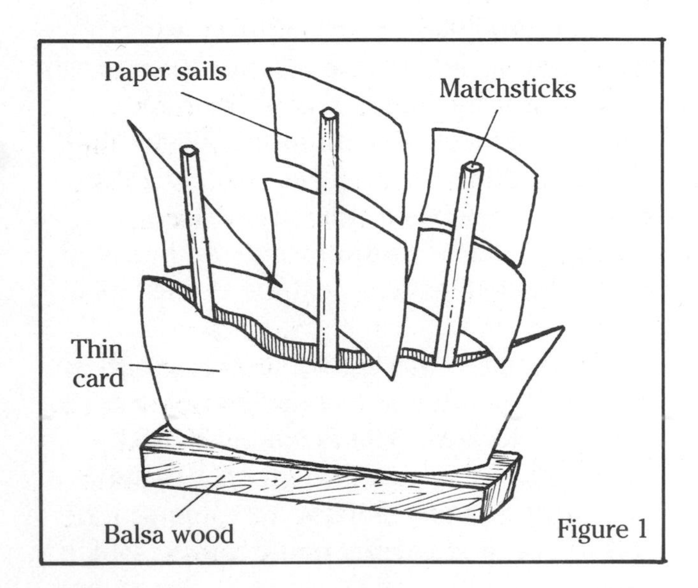

Figure 1

James I and the Gunpowder Plot

King James believed that he ruled by divine right. He was very much concerned with religion, and arranged for the Bible to be translated from Latin into English. The result of this was the Authorised Version or King James Bible.

In 1605 a conspiracy led by Guy Fawkes, Robert Catesby and other Catholic nobles plotted to kill the King by blowing up Parliament. This was a consequence of years of religious suppression by the State. James had lived in fear of just such an assassination attempt, as his own father had been killed by assassins at the Scottish court. When news leaked out about the plot, the conspirators were rounded up, tortured and executed. We feel that it is especially important that children know this story to explain why guys are burnt in effigy on Guy Fawkes Night.

Encourage the children to examine the story of James I from a security viewpoint, imagining the problems that he felt he had. They could list his enemies, and draw up proposals to keep him safe from them. For example, he wore a padded doublet to protect himself and slept surrounded by thick mattresses.

The Pilgrim Fathers

The sailing of the Pilgrim Fathers to America in 1620 could also be studied as an example of religious persecution.

Charles I, who was king at the time, governed with a small group of ministers. One of these, William Laud, Archbishop of Canterbury, was strongly opposed to the Puritans having any influence in the Church of England. The Puritans disliked the use of colourful images, statues and elaborate music in churches and church services.

Archbishop Laud wanted to drive them out of England, and in 1620 the *Mayflower* sailed for America from Plymouth with a small band of Puritans, determined to start a new way of life based on their ideas of simple worship. Thousands more followed them to settlements such as New England, but those who stayed behind harboured a resentment that was to lead to civil war.

The pilgrims arrive

What you need
Writing equipment.

What to do
Pupils could role play the arrival of the Pilgrim Fathers in the *Mayflower*. They could debate the options available for finding food, building shelter, obtaining drinking water and growing food. This

could be presented as a set of optimum criteria for deciding where to settle; for example, by a stream with arable land, with woodland to provide nuts for food and timber for houses. A river could double as a source of fresh water and fishing.

Ask the children to devise a list of rules for settlers to follow for the common good, bearing in mind the Puritans' simple way of life.

The Civil Wars – 1642-45 and 1648

The Scottish occupation of Newcastle in 1640 highlighted the fact that Charles had no strong standing army. The majority of Scots also had a simple puritan way of life and resented Charles I's attempts to impose the English prayer book on them.

In 1641 Parliament passed an Act stating that it must meet at least once every three years. Led by John Pym, Parliament demanded the right to control the army, and to appoint the King's Council of Ministers. Charles decided that he had given up enough power. On January 3 1642 he entered Parliament with an armed guard and demanded that five MPs accused of treason be handed over.

On January 10, with anti-Royalist feeling growing in London, Charles moved to Hampton Court. The Queen fled abroad with the royal children.

On 22 August 1642 Charles raised his standard at Nottingham, and went on to rally support from Wales and Cheshire. When he began to advance on London, the Parliamentarian forces moved to intercept him, and the two armies met at Edgehill in Warwickshire. This was the first major battle of the Civil War.

In 1644 the Scottish army entered the war on the side of Parliament. In the winter of 1644-1645 the Parliamentarian New Model Army was formed, based upon strict discipline. After the battle of Naseby was won by the Parliamentarians in 1645 the first phase of the Civil War was as good as over.

In 1648 Charles escaped from Hampton Court. The Scottish army changed allegiance, and were beaten by the Model Army at Preston. After this, Parliament wanted Charles I to rule again with restricted powers. Cromwell was bitterly opposed to this, and the Army took over London, including the House of Commons. Charles I was tried, and executed on January 30, 1649.

Royalists and Parliamentarians

What you need
Reference books about the period.

What to do
Pupils need to study the basic facts. They should realise that the armies were comparatively small and that the whole nation did not take up arms. Ask them to debate or write about which side they would have supported, using evidence they have researched rather than feelings. They need to understand the irony of a king being beheaded in the cause of parliamentary reform.

Ask the children to examine the differences in uniform and protective wear between the two armies, and compare their tactics. For example, the failure of Prince Rupert's cavalry to regroup after breaking through at Edgehill can be compared to the tight discipline of Cromwell's troops at Naseby.

The Commonwealth and the Restoration

The period following Charles I's execution was very unstable. Holland, France, Spain and Scotland declared war on the Commonwealth, the Irish rebelled, Prince Rupert attacked Commonwealth ships in the Atlantic and factions within Parliament looked to settle old scores. Cromwell personally suppressed the Irish revolt in 1649, leaving a legacy of hatred that has remained to this day.

Prince Charles, the son of Charles I, twice attempted to win back the throne, supported by a Scottish army, but Cromwell twice defeated him and he escaped and fled to France. In 1653 Cromwell expelled Parliament. For five years Cromwell ruled as Lord Protector, during which time Roman Catholics were allowed a degree of religious freedom and Jews were allowed to enter the country. Cromwell died in 1658, and his son ruled after him until 1659, when Prince Charles was invited to return to become king. He landed at Dover during May 1660.

Summaries of events

What you need
A large frieze board or expanse of wall, three large sheets of paper in different colours, writing equipment.

What to do
Encourage the children to consider the main significant events of Cromwell's rule and of Charles II's Restoration. Divide a large frieze board or wall into three sections, each backed with a different colour and labelled respectively 'Advantages', 'Disadvantages' and 'Undecided'.

Ask the children to write short summaries of the main events of the period, such as the execution of Charles I, the increased power of Parliament, Cromwell's suppression of Ireland, the rise of puritanism, the reform of the church and legal systems, the tolerance of Catholics and Jews, the godly laws of Cromwell the Protector, the Restoration of Charles II, the revenge of Parliament on the Regicides, the laws that forced all councillors to take Holy Communion, the persecution of the Quakers and the continued persecution of Catholics after the Restoration.

Ask the children to stick their summaries on to the frieze according to their views of events. The finished frieze might well have the same events stuck on under three different headings.

A class discussion could be based upon the finished frieze, and the differences of opinion debated.

The Plague

The main circumstances leading to the Plague of 1665 need to be studied by the pupils. Dirty streets, a limited and polluted water supply, an increase in fleas carried by black rats (themselves more common as the port of London became increasingly busy), crowded living conditions and a lack of any effective treatment all contributed to more than 70,000 deaths in 1665 in England. Samuel Pepys' diary provides an eye witness account from June 7 to December 31.

Difficult decisions

What you need
Reference books about the period.

What to do
The subject of the Plague can be quite morbid, dealing as it does with death and mass burial, but one way of tackling it might be to ask the class to role-play a scene where a group of villagers want to prevent the Plague from reaching their village. A second group of children could be people fleeing from London looking for refuge. The villagers would have to take decisions based on real facts. They would need to know how people thought the Plague was transmitted, as well as actions that prevented it, such as isolation. Perhaps the party fleeing London pay so well that they are allowed in. A death from plague could be introduced by the teacher in role as a messenger, and further decisions would need to be made. A follow-up activity could involve a comparison of the children's decisions with actual stories of decisions taken by villages in 1665, such as that taken by the villagers of Eyam.

Ask the pupils to suggest measures that could have been taken at the time to prevent the rapid spread of disease. They will need to investigate the levels of hygiene, human habits which attracted rats and the medical notions then current that the human body had four humours that needed to be kept in balance.

The Great Fire of London

The Great Fire of 1666 can be connected to the Plague in London in the sense that after the fire, streets became wider and cleaner, and therefore less disease-ridden. Narrow streets contributed to the spread of the fire much as they did to the spread of the Plague. Pupils will need to understand the way in which buildings were constructed at the time. It may have been planned for pupils to study Tudor buildings in detail in the supplementary study unit on houses and places of worship. If not, we suggest that pupils look at wattle and daub and timber-frame construction. They will also need to look at how close the buildings were to each other, particularly the top storeys.

Important events during the fire include the use of the Thames as a safe escape route, the acrid smoke from burning warehouses, the use of trained bands to fight the fire, the unsuccessful attempt to clear a fire break at the River Fleet, the change of overall control from the Lord Mayor to The Duke of York, the energetic examples of Charles II, the use of gunpowder to blow a wide fire break, and the resulting homelessness of more than 100,000 Londoners.

Understanding the Great Fire

What you need

A variety of materials including wood, rope, straw, metal, bricks and fabrics, matches, thin paper, scissors, Plasticine, metal trays, stopwatch, map of London in 1666, washing-up liquid bottle, waxed cotton, dowel, black paper, paint, tissue paper.

What to do

- Demonstrate the comparative flammability of materials. Wood, rope, straw, metal and bricks could be tested in controlled conditions. A second adult must be present to supervise the pupils while you conduct the demonstrations.
- A second experiment, again conducted by yourself with the help of a second adult,

would be to cut out some thin paper silhouettes of timber houses. Use Plasticine to stand them upright in a grid pattern on a metal tray, with the ends almost touching. A match should be applied to the middle point and a note made of the time taken for the flames to spread to the whole set of houses.

A second tray with the same number, shape and size of houses could be set out, but with a much bigger gap between them. The match should be applied to the same middle point, and the time taken for the flames to spread or die out should be noted again.

This experiment should be done outside, on tarmac or concrete, on a still day. It would be best to try it out in advance to judge the gaps needed for the first set to catch fire quickly, and the second set more slowly.

Ask the children to draw conclusions as to why the flames spread more quickly in one set of houses, and to make comparisons with the layout of London prior to the fire.

- Photocopy a map of London as it was in 1666 on to an OHP acetate sheet and project it on to a large sheet of paper. Ask the children to trace the details, which will give a useful enlargement. Four copies should be made, one for each day of the fire. The progress of the fire can then be shown from 2am on 2 September to Wednesday 5 September, when the fire was brought under control.

- Study fire-fighting methods and ask the children to make a working model of a 'squirt' from a washing-up liquid bottle with the bottom cut off. The cut off bottom should be trimmed so that it fits inside the body of the bottle. Then the children can cover it with waxed cloth and fasten it to the end of some thick dowel, as in Figure 1.

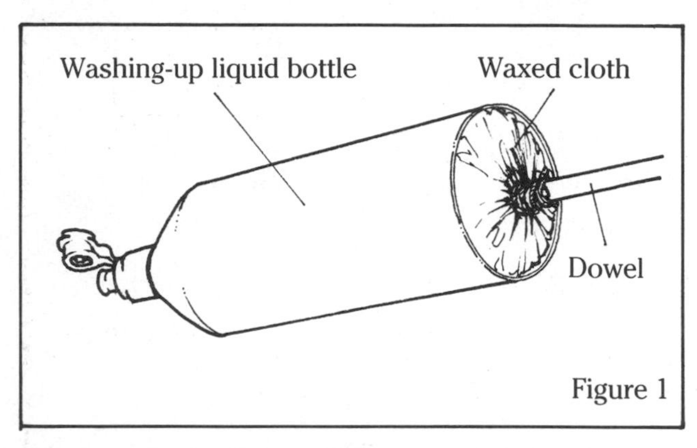

Figure 1

- Let the children work either in groups or individually to produce a dramatic picture by painting flames over a sheet, or by sticking on tissue flames. Silhouettes of houses and pre-fire buildings such as St Paul's and London Bridge could be cut from black paper and stuck on to the flames. Pupils could compare this pre-fire silhouette with today's skyline.
- Schools in or near London could follow the course of the fire along existing streets, which have not changed course a great deal since the fire of 1666. The Museum of London has a special display about the fire, complete with sound and light effects.

Further work

We suggest that the class is divided into small groups to research and report on the lives of ordinary people in Tudor and Stuart times. For example, they could look at a monk during the Reformation, a sailor in the English fleet fighting the Armada, a musician or actor at Elizabeth's court, an English Roman Catholic in 1575, a farm labourer in the Fens in 1650, a London apprentice in 1666, an architect of 1670, a lady of fashion and a Puritan lady of 1684, a Yorkshire wool spinner of 1662, tin miners in Cornwall, copper miners in the Lake District in 1670, a tobacco merchant in Bristol in 1670 and a beggar in 1601. Shakespeare, Drake, Raleigh, Isaac Newton, Sir Christopher Wren and William Harvey should be studied, perhaps by larger groups reporting back to the whole class, with opportunities for questions, so that all pupils learn about these specific characters.

Resources

Elizabeth I, J Hope Simpson (Hamish Hamilton).
Elizabeth I, G Regan (Cambridge University Press).
Henry VIII, W Norman Pittenger (Franklin Watts).
How They Lived 1485–1700, M Harrisom and O M Royston (Basil Blackwell).
Life in Stuart London, P Miller (Methuen).
Plots, Traitors and Spies 1653-1685, J Wroughton (Macmillan).
Puritan Times, A Clarke (Batsford).
Queen Elizabeth I, B Zamoyska (Longman).
Living in Samuel Pepys' London, R J Unstead (A & C Black).
Struggle for Power 1485–1689, R J Unstead (Macdonald).
Living in The Elizabethan Court, R J Unstead (A & C Black).
The Fire of London, R Matthews (Wayland).
The Pilgrim Fathers, F W Nolan (Macdonald).
The Queen, Nobles and Gentry, P Speed and M Speed (Oxford University Press).
The Reign of James I, C Russell (Methuen).
The Story of Britain in Tudor and Stuart Times, R J Unstead (Transworld).
The Stuarts, A Steel (Wayland).
The Tudors, C Morris (Batsford).
The Spanish Armada, C Walter Hodges (Oxford University Press).
Tudor Country Life, P Fincham (Longman).

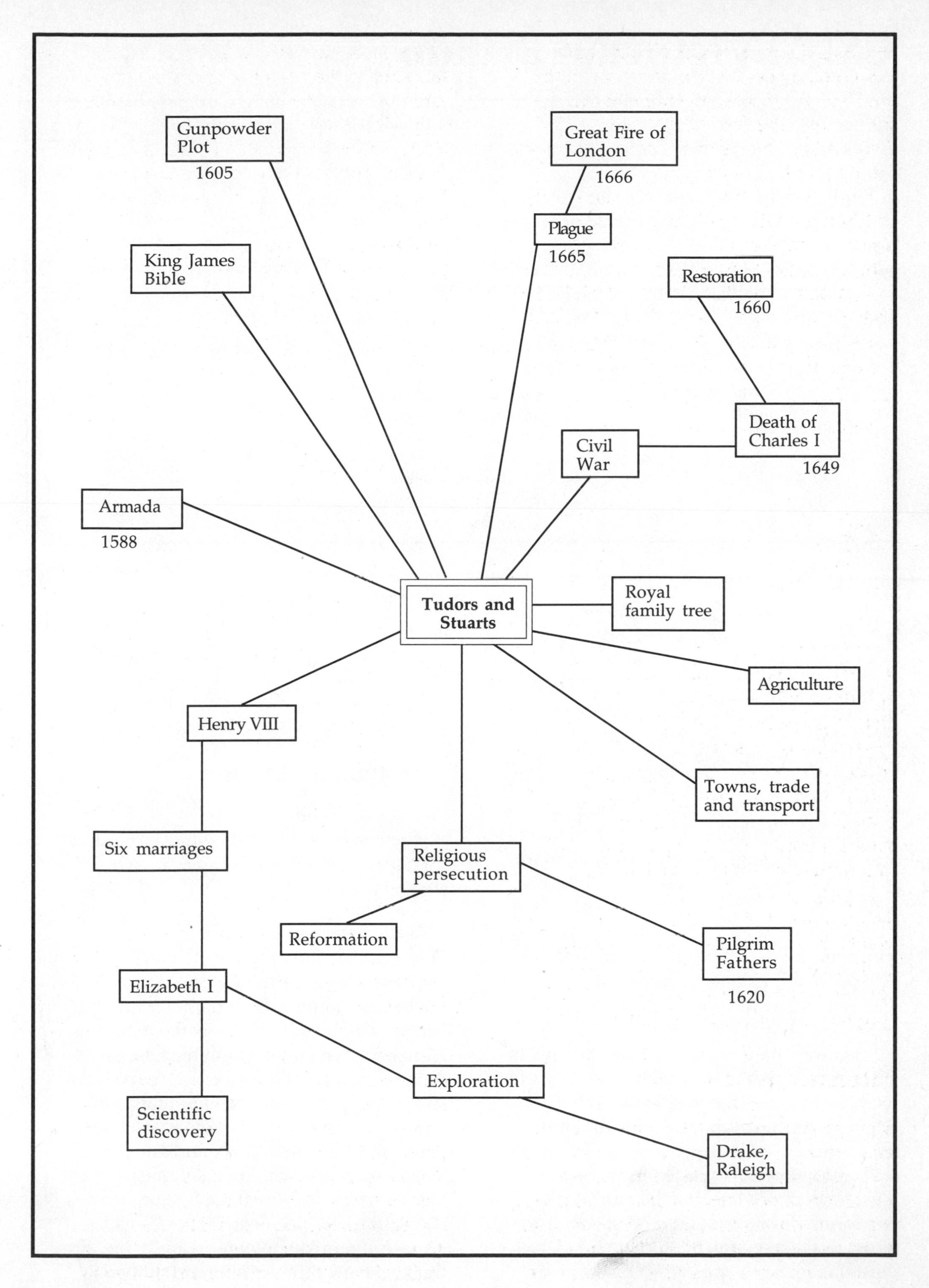

Gunpowder Plot
1605
Great Fire of London
1666
Plague
1665
King James Bible
Restoration
1660
Death of Charles I
1649
Civil War
Armada
1588
Tudors and Stuarts
Royal family tree
Agriculture
Henry VIII
Towns, trade and transport
Six marriages
Religious persecution
Reformation
Pilgrim Fathers
1620
Elizabeth I
Exploration
Scientific discovery
Drake, Raleigh

CSU3: Victorian Britain

economic developments	Pupils should be taught about:
	• steam power, industry and mass production child labour new forms of transport, including railways the growth of towns trade and growth of the British Empire
public welfare	• public health education
religion	• the importance of religion in the lives of the Victorians
scientific and cultural achievements	• inventions and scientific discoveries buildings and public works art, photography and literature
domestic life	• Victorian families houses and home life leisure and pastimes

The study of the Victorian era, 1837-1901, is rewarding because of the multitude of relevant artefacts that surround us, the vast amount of literature and photographs that are available, the quality and quantity of museum exhibits and the legacy that our ancestors have handed down in terms of systems and attitudes that have survived to this day.

This project could be undertaken as a year-long programme of study, and there is enough work suggested in this section to take up two lessons a week for 36 weeks. This takes into account the weeks needed to settle pupils into a routine after the summer holidays, to put on Christmas or Eid productions and to carry out assessment at the end of the academic year.

Teachers may decide to take the unit as a term-long theme, in which case they will be able to select the suggestions that complement work planned for the other two terms.

The topic web on page 90 shows how each aspect of Victorian life can be explored and developed, and shows how most of the avenues of study are interlinked.

Starting points

Choose starting points which generate enthusiasm for the project, set the project within a historical time reference and give a general overview of the era.

The generation game

What you need
Set of cards as detailed below, large sheet of paper, self-adhesive paper, scissors, felt-tipped pens.

What to do
Make up a set of cards, each card representing a particular person, and giving the name of the character and the age at which he or she became a parent. Teachers can either compile these cards themselves or let the children make them. We suggest that 30 cards are made with women's names and the age at which they gave birth, from 18 to 40, and another 30 cards are made with men's names and the age at which they became fathers, also from 18 to 40 (see Figure 1).

To build up a simulated family tree, first make a card representing a child of a

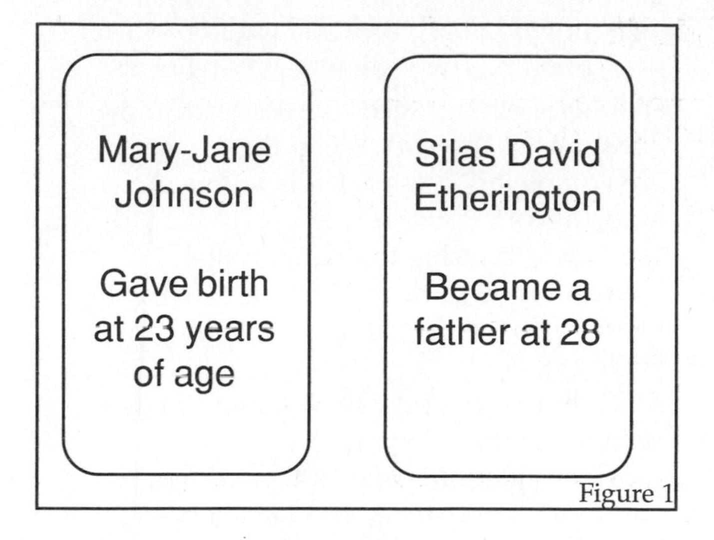

Figure 1

similar age to the pupils carrying out the task. Then the children can pick 'parents' for the child, selecting one card from the 'mother' pile, and one from the 'father' pile. Ask the children to use the information on the cards to work out when the parents were born (the current year minus the pupil's age minus the age the fictional parents on the cards became parents).

Next, let the children take a second card from the 'mother' pile and a second card from the 'father' pile. These characters represent the mother's parents. Again, the dates of the grandparents' births can be worked out. Let the children continue the sequence with the grandparents' parents, their parents, and so on, back to 1830 or so. Then they can repeat this for the father's line.

Let the children make some sticky paper figures and stick them to a large sheet of paper to represent the family tree, adding the dates of birth and lines from parents to children. The idea is to enable pupils to conceptualise in human terms the time span between the present day and the Victorian era.

A time-line made up from strips of paper one metre long, using alternating colours, can be pinned up around the classroom wall. This will also help pupils make the mental transition from the present to the Victorian era. Important dates should be marked on the time-line.

Teachers may wish to elaborate the generation game as pupils gain in experience, by adding a pack of sibling cards. Perhaps the pupils could work out a set of rules so that the number shown on a thrown dice gives the number of siblings.

When the children have studied the Victorian age in some detail, allow them to return to the game. Pupils could then use their research to add more detail to the Victorian families in their family tree.

Some parents might be willing to share their known family tree back to the Victorian era.

Victorian detectives

What you need

Copies of a local street map, Ordnance Survey maps, reference books on Victorian architecture, large sheets of paper, overhead projector, thick card, scissors, sticky tape, adhesive.

What to do

Take the children out to look for evidence of Victorian architecture. Unless your school is on a new estate or in a new town, there will certainly be examples of Victorian buildings, street furniture, canals or railways. Your school might be one of the thousands of schools built during that period.

Encourage the children to look for clues. Some will be very obvious, such as dates on houses, terraces, bridges and post boxes. The dates when canals and railways were built are well documented. Less obvious clues will include street names such as Victoria Road, Albert Road, Queensway and Jubilee Terrace. Like all good detectives, pupils will need to look for supporting evidence to prove that it was Queen Victoria, not Elizabeth, that Queensway was named after. Children will need to be shown that there are stylistic differences between late Georgian, Victorian and Edwardian buildings.

Provide the children with photocopies of a street map on which to mark any evidence of Victorian buildings. Afterwards, make a study of Ordnance Survey maps of the district to cross-check the children's detective work, and to extend their research.

If you are not surrounded by Victorian buildings, a walk or bus ride will usually bring you near to some. Pupils will need more than one look, as they will need to use reference books to confirm or deny their first judgements.

The work can be presented in a number of ways.

- The pupils' small maps and notes can be kept in their project files and used for later reference and as a basis for compiling large wall displays.
- A large map showing the location of Victorian features can be made by photocopying a small street map on to an acetate, projecting this on to a large sheet of paper and copying the map with thick felt-tipped pens. Features can be added using drawings or adhesive paper shapes to represent buildings or street furniture.
- Large cardboard cut-outs of Victorian buildings can be made using thick cardboard. Encourage the children to draw a set of buildings to scale, about 1.5m high, paint them and fix them to a corridor wall to make a striking street scene. You could also mount a display of photographs taken by the pupils on their detective visits.

Research projects

Once the pupils have an understanding of the position of the Victorian era in time, they need to have some basic knowledge about it. This knowledge could include the methods of transport and how these developed over almost seven decades, the variety of housing conditions, the changes in pastimes, the effect upon society of developing industry, the growth of towns and the influence of religion on people's lives.

We recommend that the class is organised into groups, each of which tackles one area as a mini-research project. Each group should then make a presentation to the rest of the class. This might include both a verbal and a pictorial presentation. The remainder of the class should be encouraged to ask constructive questions at the end. When the projects are completed, a mini-display of each group's work could be set up.

It is worth trying to gain parental interest in the project. Many homes have Victorian artefacts, such as washing dollies, bed-warmers, stone jars, books and so forth. Parents may be willing to loan such items for a display.

When the pupils are motivated by the work they have done, and have a basic knowledge and understanding of the era, it is time to consider a school visit (see pages 60 to 61).

The remainder of this section sets out some further areas of study. For each subject there is information about important events, as well as examples of diverging points of view to be considered, ideas for activities and details of cross-curricular links.

Queen Victoria

During her reign, Victoria became a national symbol, not least because hers was the longest reign in the nation's history.

She was often viewed as an ideal wife and mother, especially following her retreat into mourning after Prince Albert's death in 1861. She was an opponent of women's rights, and her moral attitudes had a lasting effect on the nation.

It is also important to think of Queen Victoria in her capacity as head of the British Empire.

Victoria and her Empire

What you need
Reference books on the period, world maps of 1890 and of the present day.

What to do
- Let the children research and illustrate the family tree of the Queen and her consort, showing how many of her children

and grandchildren became European royalty.

• Ask the children to compare world maps of 1890 and the present day to see the extent of the British Empire and find out how modern nations have replaced the old colonies. Follow this up with an investigation into countries which retain close links with Britain. Ask the children to think about the movement of population from countries once united under the British Empire, and to what extent this has led to our present multicultural society. At a simple level this could lead to an understanding that some colonies became members of the Commonwealth, which entitled their nationals to British citizenship.

Social reform

During Victoria's reign a number of social reforms came into being, and the following points should be considered:

• The London Police Force was established in 1829.

• Employment of women and children in the coal mines was stopped in 1842.

• Child employment was limited to the over-eights, and women and children's work was limited to ten hours a day by the Factory Act of 1847. This, in effect, limited most men to a ten-hour day because they were dependent on the women and children to assist them.

• Most working class men were able to vote by 1867.

• The vote was extended to farm labourers in 1884.

• The degradation of prison life was attacked by reformers such as Elizabeth Fry (1780-1845).

Industry

The Victorian age was a time of great industrial expansion. Children should be aware of the following factors:

• Britain became the wealthiest nation on earth because of industry.

• People crowded into industrialised slums, drawn from the poverty of the land.

By 1850 the country population and the town population were equal, but by 1900 there were more people living in towns than in the country.

• Children were employed because they were easily bullied and did not have to be paid a great deal. Wagonloads of orphans were brought from the country to work in the cities, and parishes were glad to be rid of their responsibility.

• The Irish famine led to migration of workers to England (1845-1857).

• Late Victorian industry was threatened by foreign competition.

• Industrialisation led to new professions becoming respectable. The mechanical engineer, the civil engineer and the accountant were accorded much higher social status than before.

Inventions

Pupils could research the range of domestic inventions that eased the burden of those who worked in the home. They could also study the inventions that made communications and transport far more efficient. The system of canals was at its height during the Victorian period. The Suez Canal was cut in 1869, which made sea voyages to the East easier.

At the start of Victoria's reign slow coaches, eight-horsed wagons with wide wheels to prevent them sinking in the mud, transported goods at less than walking speed. By the end of her reign, fast trains carried goods all over the country and motor cars were being driven.

Telephones were in general use, electricity became available for domestic and industrial use, and telegrams could be sent across the Atlantic. Photography was invented and refined during this period. Improvements were also made in medicine, nursing, antiseptics and anaesthetics.

Pupils could learn about these inventions through a study of the personalities involved.

Housing

The movement of people from the country to the town to work in the factories led to a high demand for housing. Large houses were partitioned so that many families could rent one room each. New buildings were quickly thrown up near to the factories, without adequate sanitation. Slum conditions were commonplace. Towards the end of the nineteenth century, philanthropic organisations set about clearing some of the slums and building model housing estates. Not all factory owners were uncaring about their workers; some built substantial houses for them.

Pupils could compare the information they find in textbooks about slums with the pictures of large Victorian houses, many of which still exist today.

Leisure

The children could explore the rise in popularity of cycling, day trips, phonographs and gramophones, the music hall, football, tennis and other pastimes.

Religion

Church-going was a regular feature of life in the country. As the population shifted towards the towns, the habit of church-going lost some of its hold. The Methodist Church seemed to have more influence than the Church of England upon the working people. The Salvation Army carried out the kind of work they still do today, such as looking after those sleeping rough.

Culture

Some pupils might wish to read books by Victorian authors such as Stevenson, Kipling, Hardy, H G Wells, Conrad, Conan Doyle and Dickens. The children might be surprised at how many of the stories they are familiar with without having read the books.

Pupils could look at reproductions or, better still, original works by the Pre-Raphaelite artists. They could compare the subject matters chosen by these artists with the everyday life they have researched.

Pupils could make a diagrammatic representation of the changes in fashion over the period.

Explorers and innovators

Study the journeys of explorers such as Mary Kingsley, Speke, Burton, Livingstone, Burke, Wills and King in Africa and Australia, with an emphasis on the technology available to the explorers. Journeys could be charted on large wall maps.

Pupils could study the ideas, discoveries and inventions of the Victorian era by looking at the lives of personalities such as Elizabeth Fry, Florence Nightingale, Isambard Kingdom Brunel, Charles Dickens, Sir Robert Peel, Charles Darwin, Joseph Lister, Louis Pasteur, Fox Talbot and Dr Barnardo.

Resources

A Day in the Life of a Victorian Domestic Servant, L Davidoff and R Hawthorn (George Allen & Unwin).
Age of Machines: 1815-1901, R J Unstead (Macdonald).
A History of Everyday Things in England 1851-1914, M Quennell and C H Quennell (Batsford).
A Victorian Factory Worker, S Ross (Wayland).
Changing Society in Victorian England, I Doncaster (Longman).
George IV to Victoria, G Wills (Wheaton).
Growing Up in Victorian England, S Ferguson (Batsford).
Life in Victorian London, L Seaman (Batsford).
People of the Past: The 19th Century (Oxford University Press).
The Age of Dickens, P Rooke (Wayland).
The Hartlebury Children's Tutor, (Hereford and Worcester County Museum).
Victoria's Reign, A Cammiade (Methuen).
Victoria, Queen of a Changing Land, R Poulton (World's Work).

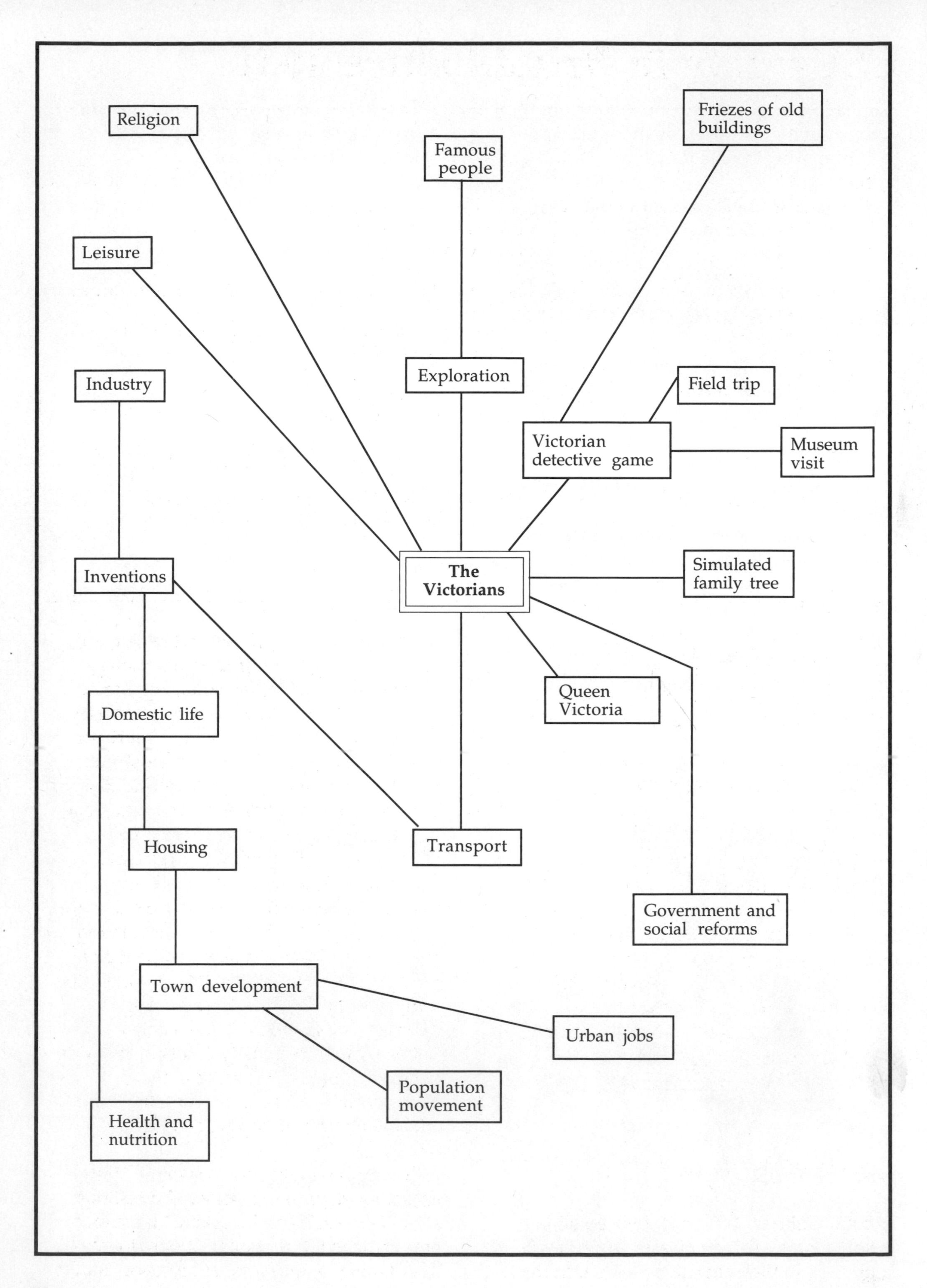
Religion
Famous people
Friezes of old buildings
Leisure
Industry
Exploration
Field trip
Victorian detective game
Museum visit
Inventions
The Victorians
Simulated family tree
Domestic life
Queen Victoria
Housing
Transport
Government and social reforms
Town development
Urban jobs
Population movement
Health and nutrition

CSU4: Life in Britain since 1930

	Pupils should be taught about:
economic developments	• the decline of heavy industries the growth of new industries changes in transport
the Second World War	• the impact of the Second World War (1939 to 1945) on Britain
social changes	• changes in the role of men and women and in family life immigration and emigration
scientific developments	• inventions and discoveries concerns about the environment
religion	• religious changes and their effect on everyday life
cultural changes	• popular culture, including fashion, music and sport the impact of radio, the cinema and television

All the units in Key Stage 2 build upon work done at Key Stage 1, but this unit in particular uses the skills and knowledge gained by pupils in the previous Key Stage. They will have looked at their own histories and at events in the lives of people around them. They will have used artefacts and pictures to study the past. They should have been given the opportunity to explore the recent history of their parents' and grandparents' generations through talking to them about the events of the past, as well as the physical environment and society.

We recommend that pupils start this unit by looking at events in their own lives and move backwards in time to 1930, learning about and recording changes from the present and comparing the present with the recent past.

Starting points

Ask the children to record their personal school history. Which classes have they been in? Did they change schools from Key Stage 1 to Key Stage 2? Have they joined any out-of-school organisations such as brownies, cubs, Sunday school or Koran school, and how old were they when they joined? Have they taken up any sports or other hobbies? Have they had pets? Can they remember what their favourite toys and television programmes were one year, two years, three years ago? Have their tastes in food changed over the years?

The results could be set down as a personal time band of seven or eight years for each pupil. Each piece of information recorded could be represented by a 2cm-wide strip along the band. School would be fairly continuous from the age of four onwards, while other facets such as hobbies might be mostly empty strips with occasional blocks coloured in to correspond with the time when the pupil was following that hobby (see Figure 1 on page 92).

Teachers should consider carefully the extent to which more personal questions about home life can be asked. I have met parents who felt that a questionnaire about their family history was an intrusion, and it may be more sensitive to pursue the school, hobby or pets type of history.

The compiling of these personal histories could be followed up by inviting an adult who remembers the 60s, 70s and 80s to sit in on a lesson and answer questions. Somebody in their forties would be ideal. It would be important to have a sympathetic adult who understood children.

The pupils would need to prepare their questions in advance, and record the answers in some way. Typical questions would be about fashion, domestic appliances, inventions, music, work and schooling. It would be possible to set an exercise based on the organisation of the visit. A system could be planned for inviting the speaker, arranging a time, meeting the speaker, gleaning information, recording that information and thanking the speaker.

Pupils could follow up the speaker's visit with research into the 60s, 70s and 80s from books, magazines, videos and newspapers. Groups could tackle areas such as fashion, inventions, space travel, music, cars, home interiors, sport, television and other media changes.

Introduce the issue of the right of Commonwealth citizens to live in Britain, and consider the way in which such citizens were encouraged to immigrate, often to take poorly-paid unskilled work. A speaker who immigrated to Britain in the 60s could be invited to explain why she or he made that decision, what were the problems encountered and whether the adopted country lived up to expectations.

Changes in domestic and working life could be charted alongside important events in Great Britain during this period. Pupils could look at the miners' strike of 1984-85 from the point of view of the miners and then from the point of view of the coal board. The abolition of the death penalty, the lowering of the voting age to 18, joining the EEC in 1973, equal opportunities legislation during the 1970s and the rise of unemployment to three million in the 1980s are all major changes which affected society. These issues are complex, and may have to be taught as a discrete input rather than researched by individual pupils or groups.

To gain direct experience of 60s culture, children might enjoy dressing up in 60s fashions and dancing to music from that period (which often seems to feature high in the charts). This could be followed up by art work such as clothes designs based on flower power and op art.

Artefacts should be readily available for a class display, such as early digital

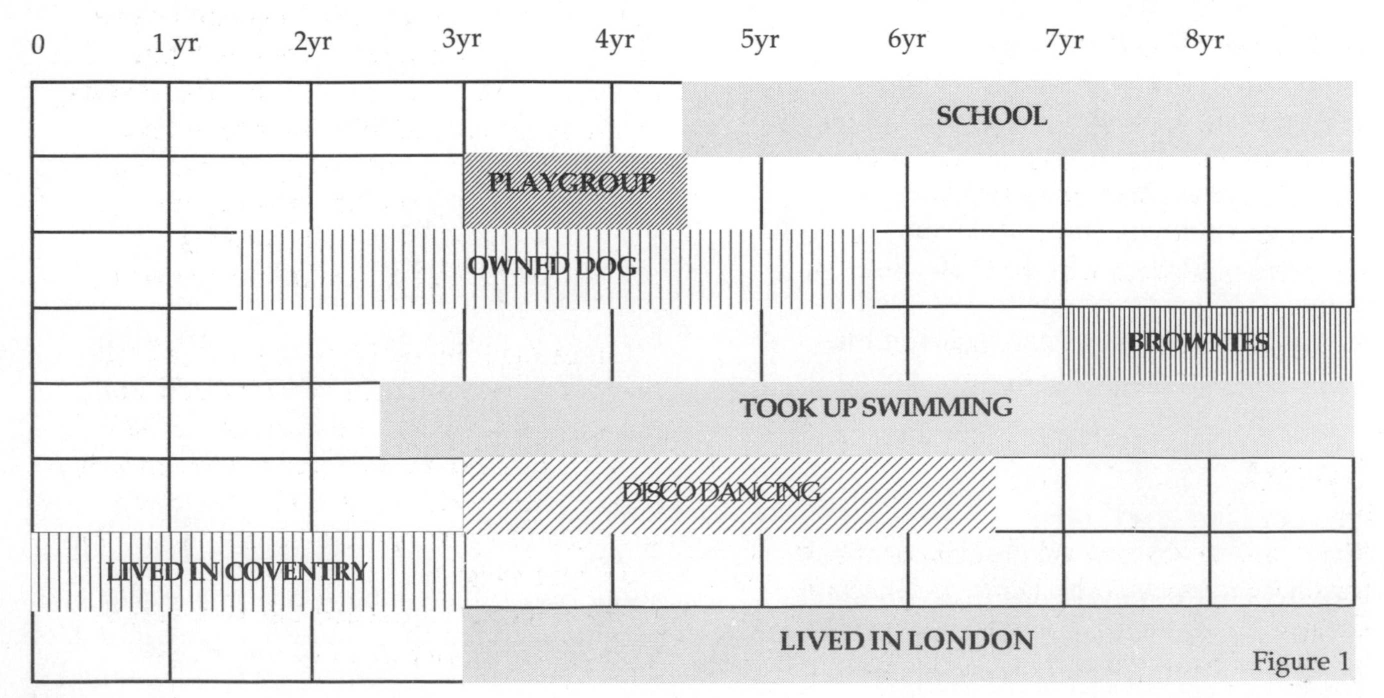

Figure 1

watches and calculators, transistor radios, toys, records, photographs, domestic utensils etc.

Media

Differences and similarities between current newspapers, magazines and films and those of 10, 20, 30 and 40 years ago can be studied using library copies of old newspapers, often kept on microfiches, old and current films on video, and current and so-called classic programmes, also on video. The videos of older films and television programmes can also be used to look at clothes, cars, fashions and housing.

The radio

The popularity of the radio during the thirties could be taken as a starting point for work presented as radio news bulletins. Pupils could tape-record reports of key events of the thirties, based upon factual research, and these could be played to the class. A card mock-up of a period radio, or even better, a real period radio, could be used in front of the tape-recorder speaker. It would be fairly easy to connect the output from a tape-recorder to the speaker of an old radio, for extra authenticity.

National Grid

The National Grid was completed in the early thirties, and a subsequent boom in the sales of electric irons, cookers, fires, washing machines and refrigerators eased the domestic burden of middle-class families.

Designs of 1930s appliances could be compared with those of today.

Sport

Many sports have world records or world bests. Graphs could be made to compare these over 40 years. The mile record could be plotted for each record since 1954.

1930 to 1939

Children should know in general terms why there was a trade depression in the western world following the Wall Street Crash of 1929. This helps to explain why three million people were unemployed in 1933, why wages were cut in many jobs and why whole communities depending on one industry found that unemployment became a way of life.

This gives the background to the Jarrow Hunger March of 1936 in which about 200 men marched the 300 miles from Jarrow to London to draw attention to the closure of the Jarrow shipyard.

The Jarrow March

What you need

Writing equipment, map of England, large sheets of paper.

What to do

The Jarrow March could give rise to a mini-project within the unit. Base some maths work on calculating how far the men could march in a day. Pupils could measure how far they can walk in fifteen minutes, and base their calculations upon that. They would need to take into account the hunger of the men, decide whether a large group walks more or less quickly than one person, for how long each day a group could march and how much time would be spent stopping to eat. The results could be compared with the actual time the march took, which was just over one month. Discuss with the children the reasons for any wide discrepancies between their estimates and the actual time.

Encourage the children to make a large map showing the route of the march and the stopping points, and organise a role-playing session on the theme of the march. Some of the children could be marchers who want to give up, and others those who are eager to go on.

The children could use this role-play to keep an imaginary diary of the march.

The war years and post-war Britain

We suggest that the concept of Britain at war is introduced to the class by the teacher. Pupils will need to know why hostilities were entered, and will need to know about the so-called Phoney War period, when many people were as yet unaffected by war. This unit concentrates on the Home Front, and will consider the war as it affected civilians. However, the evacuation at Dunkirk, the Battle of Britain and the assembly of troops prior to D Day will also be considered as they took place on, above or around Britain. It must also be remembered that major social changes such as planning for a welfare state also took place in wartime.

Mothers and children under five years of age were evacuated from London and other big cities straight away. Primary school children soon followed with their teachers.

There are opportunities for children to read true accounts of how evacuated children felt. Again, adults with real experience of evacuation could tell them about it. Pupils could empathise with their counterparts of 1939, and write imaginary accounts or letters home to parents. Pupils could role-play the conflict between parents wanting their children to be safe, but not wanting them to go away to strangers. Many country people were shocked by the poverty of children that they took in.

Battle of Britain

The Battle of Britain, fought during the summer of 1940, was a battle in which the aircraft are often remembered as vividly as the pilots. The front line aircraft were fairly evenly matched, each having advantages and disadvantages. The system that the RAF used to bring their aircraft into action made up for the fact that there were fewer RAF fighters overall. Air Chief Marshall Dowding had instigated a system which used radar and observers to warn of incoming enemy aircraft. Controllers ordered squadrons of aircraft to intercept. Although this system was criticised by those who felt that the aircraft should be brought into action in a large wing, the enemy did not gain the air superiority they needed to invade, which vindicated Dowding's system.

Operations room

What you need
Intercoms if available, cardboard aircraft silhouettes, map of the playground, coloured markers, jackets, gloves and back-packs for the 'pilots', large cardboard boxes.

What to do
Pupils could study the sequence of events which followed the spotting of enemy aircraft by sight or by radar.

An 'operations room' could be set up in part of the school. If it is possible to use intercoms from one room to another, observers in the playground could phone in observations to the control room. The children could represent enemy aircraft by moving around the playground with aircraft silhouettes of the appropriate scale, and markers could be moved around a large map of the playground to plot their movements.

Meanwhile, other pupils could be waiting in a third area to represent pilots at readiness. The 'controller' could use another phone line to order them to scramble, or send a written mesage via a runner. The 'pilots' could pull on jackets, gloves, 'parachutes' (back-packs) and run to their cockpits (mock-ups made from large cardboard boxes with a seat inside).

The time between the sighting of enemy aircraft and readiness of the pilots for take-off could be recorded. The children could form groups and rotate the jobs, and ways of being more efficient could be discussed and tried out.

Parachutes

What you need
A range of junk materials, different types of fabric, needles and thread, sticky tape, adhesive, scissors, string.

What to do
Many airmen's lives were saved by using parachutes. As a technology task, pupils could identify the qualities needed for an emergency parachute, construct scale models and test them out against their criteria.

Encourage them to consider the following points:
- reliability and efficiency;
- ease of opening;
- ease of manufacture;
- the system used for folding.

High-visibility clothing

What you need
A variety of floating materials, fluorescent paint, fabric scraps of different colours, inks and food dyes.

What to do
For airmen ditched in the sea, it was vital to be spotted and rescued as soon as possible. Ask the children to:
- experiment with floating markers that could be seen from a boat;
- compare the visibility of colours for clothing;
- experiment with liquids that stain and colour the sea, thus drawing attention to the ditched pilots.

Bombing
As the Battle of Britain waned, so the bombing of cities intensified. Homes were provided with shelters. The Anderson shelter was made from six sheets of curved steel bolted together. It was buried four feet into the ground and had earth piled over it. The floor area measured six feet by four feet. It usually contained four bunks, but six could be squeezed in. The Morrison shelter was built like a large table, but made from steel with wire mesh at the sides.

Pupils could discuss the pros and cons of using one or the other type of shelter. The Anderson was cold and damp because it was located outside. On the other hand, the Morrison was used inside the house but involved a risk of the user being trapped inside it.

Shelters

What you need
Cardboard boxes, corrugated card, aluminium foil, fine netting, weights, soil.

What to do
Let the children build replicas of Anderson and Morrison shelters for a static display, or make a cut-away large scale model to show the cramped conditions.

Models of the Anderson shelter, built to scale from corrugated card, could be tested for strength. Ask the children to devise a fair test, such as dropping a gradually increased set of weights from a set height, to see at what point the shelter collapses. Earth could be laid over a second model to test the improved protection this gives.

Rationing

What you need
Old recipe books and ingredients, stove, vegetable seeds, plant pots and compost (or access to a plot of land).

What to do
Pupils could find out what sorts of foods were available and plan a wartime menu for a day. If facilities allow, they could try cooking a meal based on the food available during wartime. Perhaps visitors who lived through this period could be invited in to sample the meal, and of course to provide the pupils with first-hand information.

Let children read about the 'dig for victory' campaign, and then plant some vegetables in a plot or in pots in the classroom. These vegetables could eventually form part of the wartime meal.

Dad's Army
Within a few weeks of the appeal for Local Defence Volunteers on May 14 1940, more than a million men had enlisted. By August the LDV was renamed the Home Guard, and eventually it was given the nickname of Dad's Army.

If the pupils study a map of Europe showing the displacement of the enemy, they will appreciate the serious concern about invasion. They can find out more about the measures taken to make invasion difficult, such as wiring the beaches, removing road signs, putting stakes into open spaces to frustrate glider landings, putting tank traps along roads, placing pill boxes at key points and banning the use of church bells except as a warning of invasion. The need for a body of troops at home to keep a vigil against invaders should be discussed.

Once pupils have found out these facts, which can be shared via groups reporting back, watch some videos of the BBC series *Dad's Army*. Ask the children to look out for the anti-invasion features, and other facts of domestic wartime life. Characters carry gas masks, food is rationed, black market goods are illegally offered for sale, petrol is rationed and the ARP warden is often heard to bellow, 'Put that light out!'

Women at war
Consider the social changes that war brought to many women. As in the First World War, women took over many of the jobs traditionally done by men. An act of parliament enabling women to be called up was passed in 1941, and women not in employment were directed to certain jobs, such as working in munitions factories. The pupils could debate the rights and wrongs of people being ordered to do certain jobs.

New clothing was rationed, not so much because of shortage but rather because factory capacity was needed for war work. People therefore became adept at recycling old garments, mending worn clothes and making new clothes out of unrationed material. This was known as 'make do and mend'.

Wartime clothing

What you need
Old clothes, dye, scraps of net and bright fabric, braid, buttons, feathers, dried flowers, paint, cardboard boxes, sticky tape, needles and thread, scissors.

What to do

Encourage the children to try to turn old clothes into a special party dress or suit. Pieces of dyed net curtain could be added to old dresses, dull jackets could have bright buttons sewn on and braid put round cuffs and pocket edges. Old hats could be adorned with feathers, painted leaves and dried flowers.

These items of clothing could then form part of a display, with life-sized figures cut from old cardboard boxes, painted and dressed in the clothes.

Decisions that changed society

The following events proved highly significant in the changes that occurred in post-war Britain.

- 1942: the Beveridge Report on social security in Britain was published.
- 1944: the Education Act became law.
- 1946: the Bank of England was nationalised; the Royal Commission recommended equal pay for women; the National Insurance Act was passed.
- 1947: the coal mining industry was nationalised; the school leaving age was raised to 15.
- 1948: British Rail was nationalised; the National Health Service was introduced.
- 1949: the iron and steel industries were nationalised.

The pupils would need to be aware, in broad terms, of the reasons for passing such acts, but would need a great deal of teacher support if asked to deal with the political and social implications.

The entitlement to free health care and to free education up to the age of 15 can be studied in terms of what life was like for those who could not afford health care and education before the war, and in terms of the legacy that these acts have left us today.

Important issues of the 50s would include the urgent need to build homes, the end of rationing, the development of supermarkets, the increase in popularity of both television and dance halls as forms of entertainment, and the rise in wages.

Other significant events

Other issues that could be studied include:

- the abdication of Edward VIII;
- the emergence of paid holidays;
- the existence of a partial health service for those paying National Insurance contributions;
- the return to fuller employment as the nation rearmed.

Resources

Between the Wars, F Wilkins (Batsford).
Between the Wars: Britain in Photographs, J Symons (Batsford).
Children in the Second World War, S Purkis (Longman).
At Home in the 1950s, S Purkis (Longman).
At School in the 1950s, S Purkis (Longman).
Family in the Fifties, A Hurst (A & C Black).
Family in the Sixties, A Hurst (A & C Black).
Growing Up in the Fifties, J Pascall (Wayland).
Growing up in the Swinging Sixties, S Cleeve (Wayland).
At Home in the 1930s, S Purkis (Longman).
In the Town in the 1930s, G Middleton (Longman).
Work in the 1930s, E Merson (Longman).
Jubilee Terrace, C Shenk (A & C Black).
The Battle of Britain, A Hobbs (Wayland).
The General Strike, A Mountfield (Wayland).
The Home Front, M Yass (Wayland).
The Modern Age, P Speed and M Speed (Oxford University Press).
We Were There, G Cawte (Blackwell).

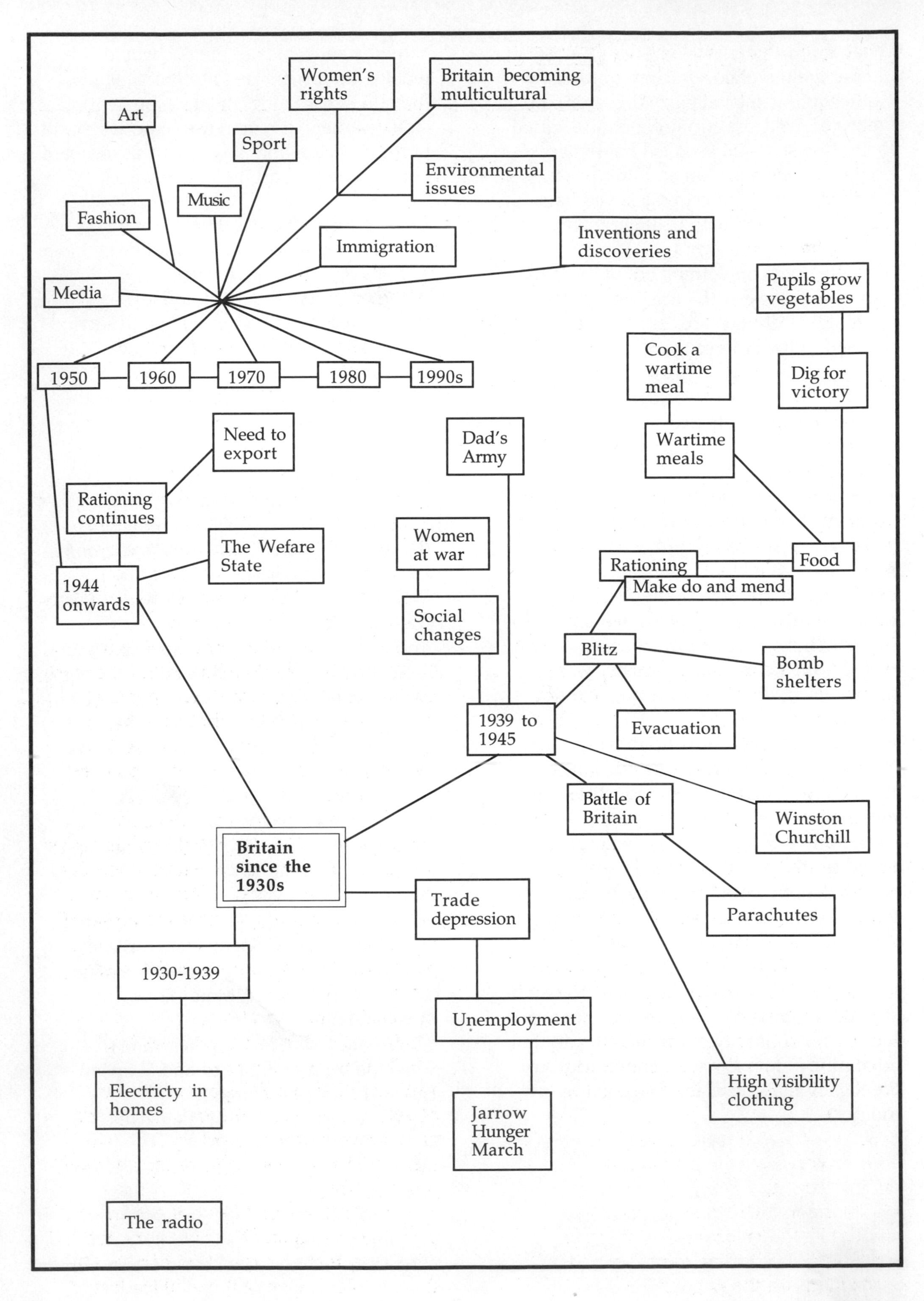
Women's rights
Britain becoming multicultural
Art
Sport
Environmental issues
Music
Fashion
Immigration
Inventions and discoveries
Media
Pupils grow vegetables
Cook a wartime meal
Dig for victory
1950
1960
1970
1980
1990s
Need to export
Dad's Army
Wartime meals
Rationing continues
Women at war
The Wefare State
Food
Rationing
Make do and mend
1944 onwards
Social changes
Blitz
Bomb shelters
1939 to 1945
Evacuation
Battle of Britain
Winston Churchill
Britain since the 1930s
Trade depression
Parachutes
1930-1939
Unemployment
High visibility clothing
Electricty in homes
Jarrow Hunger March
The radio

CSU5: Ancient Greece

	Pupils should be taught about:
the city state	• Athens and Sparta citizens and slaves
the economy	• agriculture and trade sea transport
everyday life	• the lives of men, women and children sport
Greek religion and thought	• Greek gods and religious practices myths and legends scientists and philosphers
the arts	• architecture, art, drama and literature, and how they reflected Greek society
relations with other people	• the Persian Wars Greece and Rome
the legacy of Greece	• language, politics, sport and the arts

Starting points

Pupils will need to know the geographic location of Greece. The unit does not require a study of the rise and fall of Greek civilisation as essential information, but pupils would benefit from a summary of the history of Greece from 1500 to 200 BC. Teachers will know how detailed or simple to make their presentations of the essential information for the pupils. The following information is included for the benefit of teachers:

- Up to 1400 BC: Crete ruled Greece.
- 1400: the power of Crete declined.
- 1200: the power shifted to mainland Mycenae and Tiryns in the Peloponnese.
- 1180: possible date of the Trojan war.
- 1100 to 800: a time of migration. The Achaeans were overcome by the Dorians.
- 1000 to 800: the Aegean islands and the coast of Asia Minor were occupied by Greeks. The *Iliad* and the *Odyssey* were composed.
- 800 to 600: there was an expansion of Greek colonialism all around the Mediterranean.
- 776: the first Olympic games.
- 572-497: Pythagoras.
- 549-546: the Persian king Cyrus took Greek lands on the Aegean.
- 490: the Persians were defeated by a small army of Athenians at Marathon. Pheidippides had run 140 miles in two days to ask the Spartans to help, but they refused because they were celebrating a moon festival. His 26 mile run to Athens to give news of the victory may be more legend than fact. The Athenian army marched back to Athens in time to face the Persians, who had sailed there expecting an undefended city.
- 480: Athens, Sparta and other smaller states combined to fight the Persians under Xerxes. A small force of Spartans defended the pass at Thermopylae. Athenian ships defeat the Persian navy near the island of Salamis.
- 479: the Persian army was defeated in central Greece.
- 469: Socrates was born.
- 447 to 438: the Parthenon was built.
- 428: Plato was born.
- 431 to 421: first Peloponnesian war. Athens and Sparta continued to raid and plunder each other's territory. The two exhausted sides agreed to peace after ten years' fighting.
- 413 to 404: second Peloponnesian war. In a move to expand their territory, the Athenians sent an expedition of over 140 ships to Sicily. One of the dual leaders of

the expedition, Alcibiades, was recalled to be tried. He deserted to the Spartans, and advised them to send an army to Syracuse in Sicily. The whole Athenian army was killed or taken prisoner. In 413 the Spartans built a fortified base at Decelea, on the border of Athenian territory, from which they mounted raids. In 405 Lysander, the Spartan admiral, captured the entire Athenian fleet. Athens was blockaded, and accepted the terms of surrender.

- 399: Socrates was condemned to death.
- 359 to 336: Philip of Macedon conquered Greece.
- 336: Alexander the Great became king.
- 323: Alexander died.
- 323 to 283: Euclid.
- 146 BC: Greece was conquered by Rome.

Well known stories and facts can be put into their historical context. The story of Helen of Troy, Pheidippides' run from Marathon, the Spartans defending the pass at Thermopylae and the conquests of Alexander the Great could be enjoyed as exciting adventure stories, and could be marked on a time-line.

Cities in Greece

The study of the emergence of the city state in Greece could focus mainly on Athens and Sparta. The children should be aware of the move from monarchy to rule by the aristocracy. In Athens this happened at about the time of the Olympiad in 776 BC. They should also know that tyrants seized power from time to time.

In 508 Athens was transformed into a democracy. This meant that free-born men had the right to vote in the Assembly and were eligible for jury service; women, slaves and foreigners who lived locally had none of these rights. A council of 500 was elected to discuss laws, which were then passed or rejected by the Assembly.

Once a year the Assembly met to decide if anyone deserved to be banished. The word ostracism stems from the fact that the names of those put forward for banishment were written on a piece of broken pottery (ostrakon in Greek). If enough members of the Assembly agreed that someone should be banished (for whatever reason), he would be driven from the city.

By 428 BC the Athenian democracy had reached a point where the politicians were artisans rather than wealthy landowners. Leaders such as Cleon the tanner responded to popular feeling rather than providing strong leadership.

The defeat of the Athenians by the Spartans in Sicily resulted in a short period of oligarchy (rule by the few) in 411 BC. This lasted for a few months only.

Children and home life

The different ways of bringing up children in the two cities could be contrasted. Spartan babies were examined at birth and only healthy ones allowed to live. Spartan boys had to leave home at seven years of age to learn how to be soldiers. The training was harsh, and total obedience was expected. Spartan men continued to live as soldiers in barracks up to the age of thirty or more. Spartan girls were also given athletic training.

The Spartans depended on a subject race of slaves, the Helots, to do the work which released male Spartans for military duty. A special force of secret police kept the Helots in order.

Athenian boys started school at seven and would learn to read, recite poems and stories by heart and play the lyre or the double flute. Physical education was also highly valued. Boys (or their parents) would often choose to learn advanced mathematics, astronomy or rhetoric from one of the many teachers in Athens, if they could afford to continue with their studies.

Athenian men started their military training at eighteen years old and finished it at the age of twenty. The Athenians were famous for having lively, inquiring minds, and flocked to hear new teachers.

Athenian girls were educated at home and taught what was considered necessary to enable them to become good mothers and household managers. Occasionally girls were admitted to the classes of philosophers and teachers such as Plato, though this was unusual.

The Athenians depended upon slaves to do a lot of their work, which in turn released them to take part in the democratic assemblies.

Cities and slavery

What you need
Reference books about the period.

What to do
Pupils need to understand that slavery was used by Greek city states. Some slaves were treated very harshly, and some quite kindly. Explore through role play the concept of being enslaved. Encourage the children to develop the scenario of imported slaves being sold to the Spartans and Athenians, and the slaves contemplating their fates.

Discuss how present day society compares to Athenian and Spartan society. What city would the children choose to be brought up in?

Trade

Pupils could mark the shores and islands colonised by the Greeks on a map of the Mediterranean. They could use information books to try to find out what the Greeks might have traded with other countries. Greece exported wine, oil, pottery, woollen goods and metal goods. Corn, salt, fish, leather, timber and slaves were imported.

The harbour of Piraeus was connected to Athens by two roads and a river. These roads and river were protected along their five mile length by two walls, called the Long Walls.

Pupils would need to know that the city states traded independently rather than as one unified Greece, and that iron rods were used as currency at first, and then coins. These coins are worth further study by pupils. The Greeks adopted the use of coinage from the Lydians. The Athenian drachma was the standard wage for a day's work. Six obols were worth one drachma, one hundred drachma were worth one mina and sixty mina worth one talent. It is thought that the Spartans continued to use iron bars as currency instead of coins in order to limit the accumulation of large personal fortunes.

The coins of Philip of Macedon, father of Alexander the Great, were copied (very badly) and used in iron age Britain.

Science

The Greeks made many important contributions to science, starting with the early philosophers who created theories about why the universe is as it appears to be. Aristotle was also influential, as apart from his philosophical works he was also very interested in natural history, and categorised and described a great many animal species.

Hippocrates, who taught between 440 and 390 BC, is remembered today mainly because of the oath doctors take, which is named after him. Hippocrates studied the patient's symptoms and prescribed careful diets and exercise, using a scientific approach rather than a mystical one. The idea of the profession being more important than the reward is credited to Hippocrates.

The mathematician Pythagoras discovered relationships between sets of numbers. Pupils could try out some of the simple relationships that he found, for example, that the first four integers make ten (1+2+3+4=10). This equation can be laid out using counters to make a triangle, with four counters on each side and one central counter (Figure 1). Pythagoras also found that the first three odd numbers came to nine, which became a square when laid out using counters (Figure 2). Pupils could try to copy and possibly extend these patterns.

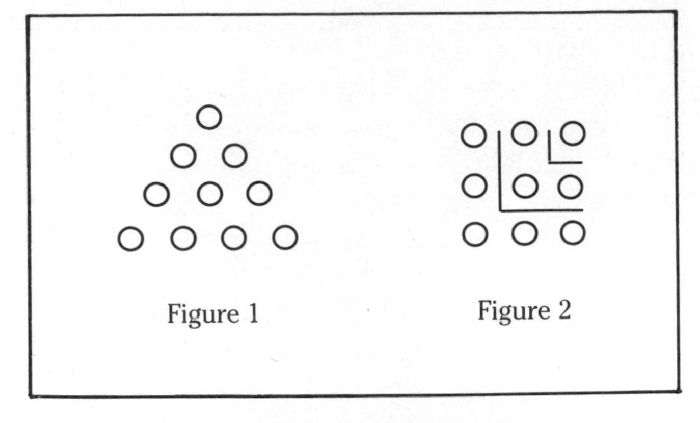
Figure 1 Figure 2

A water-powered clock was built in Athens, and housed in the Tower of the Winds beneath the Acropolis. As water dripped into a tank, a float rose. The float was connected to a counterweight by ropes and chains. The rope passed over a drum which turned the clock face. The tank had to be emptied every twenty four hours.

A water-powered clock

What you need
Wood, nails, hammer, five-litre plastic drinks container, water tank, piece of wood or tennis ball, light counterweight, cotton reels, card, string, dowel, adhesive, sticky tape, scissors, water.

What to do
Ask the children to make a simple version of the Athenian water-powered clock.

You may find it is best to make a wooden frame for the apparatus like the one shown in the diagram. Insert thin pieces of dowel through three cotton reels, and set them up in the frame as illustrated (Figure 1). Attach a card disc to the central cotton reel to act as a clock face, and fix a pointer to the end of the dowel supporting the central reel, so that it will move round the clock face.

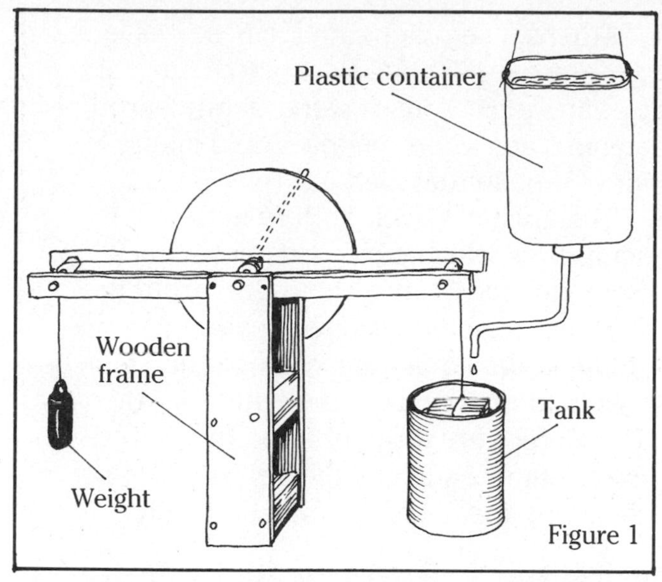

Figure 1

Take a piece of wood or a tennis ball to act as the float, and attach it to one end of a piece of string, with a counterweight at the other end. The counterweight will need to be lighter than the float; it may be necessary to experiment in order to get the weight ratio right.

Pass the string over the cotton reels, winding it three or four times around the central reel. Fix a five-litre container above

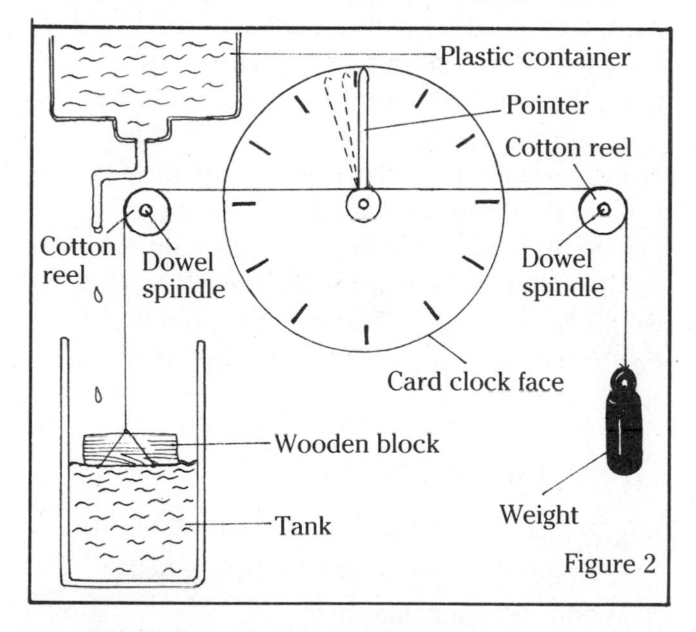

Figure 2

the apparatus as shown in Figure 2, and punch a small hole in it so that the water will drip through slowly. Place a tank underneath to catch the drips, and put the float in the tank. As the level of the water in the tank rises, the float will rise too, and the string will turn the central cotton reel, which will make the pointer rotate slowly round the clock face.

The gods

The ancient Greeks firmly believed in the existence of gods and goddesses who took human form, and lived on Mount Olympus. As we recall from Greek legends, these gods could be kind, cruel or fickle; sometimes they set tasks to test humans, while at other times they would come to their aid. There were special deities for each city, for occupations, for feelings, for women, a god of the underworld and gods for aspects of nature. In fact, there were gods allocated to most things.

You could allocate a god to each of the children and ask them to find out about them. They could look at Zeus the supreme god; Poseidon his brother, lord of the sea; Hades, also Zeus' brother, lord of the underworld; Apollo, god of the sun, prophecy, poetry and music; Hermes, messenger of the gods; Aphrodite, goddess of love; Athena the warrior goddess, goddess of wisdom; Artemis, goddess of hunting, the moon, the night and protector of women. Ask the children to make a verbal report back to the rest of the class when they have found out about their gods.

Sport

Participation in sport fulfilled the Greek ideal of a healthy body and a healthy mind. It kept men prepared for war, but at the same time also helped to keep the peace between the city states to some extent.

Every four years at Olympia the Greeks engaged in a five-day competition in honour of the gods. All competitors had to be able to prove that they were Greek, and swore an oath to the gods that they would take part without cheating. Events included horse racing, chariot racing and running races of one, seven, twelve, twenty and twenty-four lengths of the stadium. Long jumpers were allowed hand-held weights to assist them, the discus and javelin were thrown, wrestling and boxing took place, and there was a free-for-all version of one to one fighting called the pankration.

Olympic games

What you need

A large space such as the school playground, chalk, plastic plates, dowels, 500g weights.

What to do

Pupils might enjoy making their own version of the original Olympic games. Chalk out a scaled-down version of the stadium on the playground, or mark it on the playing field. The stadium at Olympia measured 606 feet by 30 feet, but this could be reduced to 60m by 3m.

Plastic dinner plates could be used for the discus and metre-long dowels for the javelins. The children could try long jumping, using 500g weights in each hand to assist them. They could also set up running events based on the original number of stadium lengths.

Architecture and art

The earliest Greek temples were made out of oak, with heavy pillars supporting thick beams. The proportions were determined to a large extent by the strength of the wood.

Later stone temples used the same proportions. As architects became more used to working with stone and understood its properties, pillars became more slender and ornate. The natural colour of the marble would have been painted over with bright colours.

The Doric style of architecture is thought to have culminated in the building of the Parthenon. This temple, set high above Athens in the Acropolis, was started in 447 BC, designed by Ictinus and built of pentelic marble. The stones in many Greek buildings, including the Parthenon, were fastened together not with cement but by iron rods inside the columns and iron clamps tying the blocks together. The builders went to a lot of trouble to ensure a perfect fit. The heavy stones were lifted into place using only simple cranes and pulleys.

Athens, like other Greek cities, was laid out in a careful plan. Because of the warm climate, most houses were planned around a courtyard where people could spend a lot of time in the open air.

The ancient Greek pottery and sculptures which survive depict scenes from life at the time. The friezes from the Parthenon include scenes of young men riding in the Panathenaic procession which was held in honour of the goddess Athene. The Greeks are thought to be the first to carve statues such as the Venus of Milo, depicting the naked body realistically.

Temples

What you need

Cardboard tubes and boxes, polystyrene tiles, paints, adhesive, scissors.

What to do

It may not be appropriate for pupils to learn in detail about the Cretan, Doric, Ionic and Corinthian styles of Greek architecture, but they could make some simple three-dimensional model facades of temples. They could use cardboard tubes from the middle of kitchen paper rolls for the columns, long narrow boxes for the stone beam across the top and a shaped polystyrene tile for the triangular section above the beam. These could be painted in bright colours to give an idea of how they might have looked. The model facades could be used as part of a display about the Greek gods.

Greek vases

What you need

Black sugar paper, white or orange wax crayons, scraper, stapler.

What to do

Many scenes from ancient Greek life and legends were depicted on their pottery. Pupils could imitate the stylised figures found on Greek vases by covering a piece of black sugar paper with a thick layer of white or orange wax crayon. It helps to build up the thickness if the crayon is

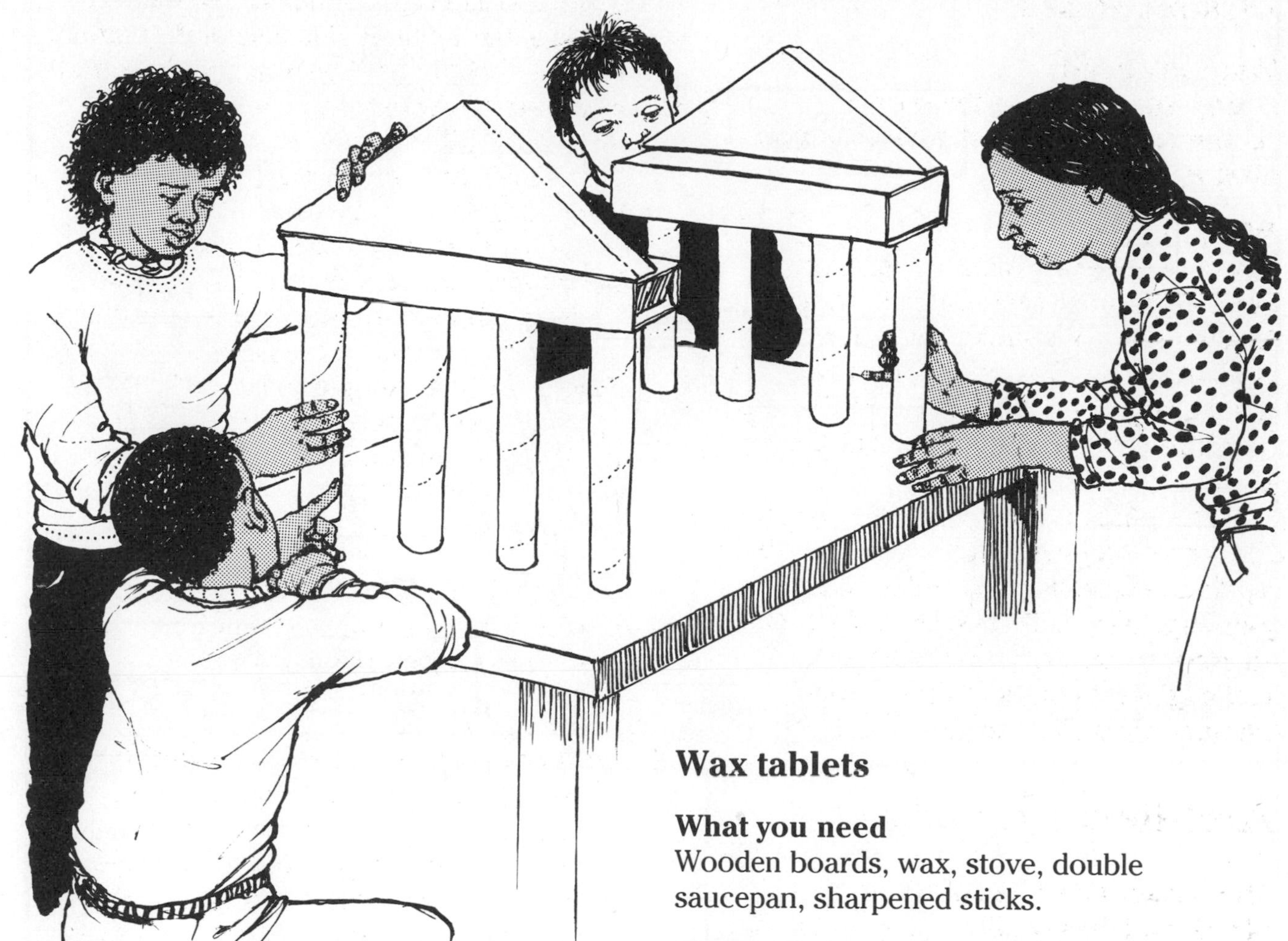

applied horizontally and then vertically. When a thick layer has been built up, figures and designs taken from pictures of Greek pottery can be scraped through the wax. The paper could then be rolled into a cylinder and stapled, to show the design on a curved surface.

Literature

Pupils would need to know that the ancient Greeks produced many great playwrights, poets and authors such as Homer, Sophocles and Euripides, and great historians such as Herodotus. Pupils might enjoy stories from Homer's *Odyssey* or *Iliad* in a simplified form.

The Greeks wrote on wooden boards coated with wax. The words were scratched into the wax using a sharp stylus.

Wax tablets

What you need
Wooden boards, wax, stove, double saucepan, sharpened sticks.

What to do
- Prepare tablets for the children by melting wax in a double saucepan and pouring it over a wooden board. Pupils could write on these in the Greek alphabet using sharpened sticks.
- Demonstrate to the children the connection between the Greek and Roman alphabets, and the way in which our alphabet evolved.

Books

Ancient Athens, E J Sheppard (Longman).
Ancient Greece, C Burland (Hulton).
Ancient Greece, D Taylor (Methuen).
Ancient Greece, M and C Quennell (Batsford).
Ancient Greeks (Macdonald).
Ancient Greeks, C Horton (Hamish Hamilton).
The Buildings of Ancient Greece, H and R Leacroft (Brockhampton).

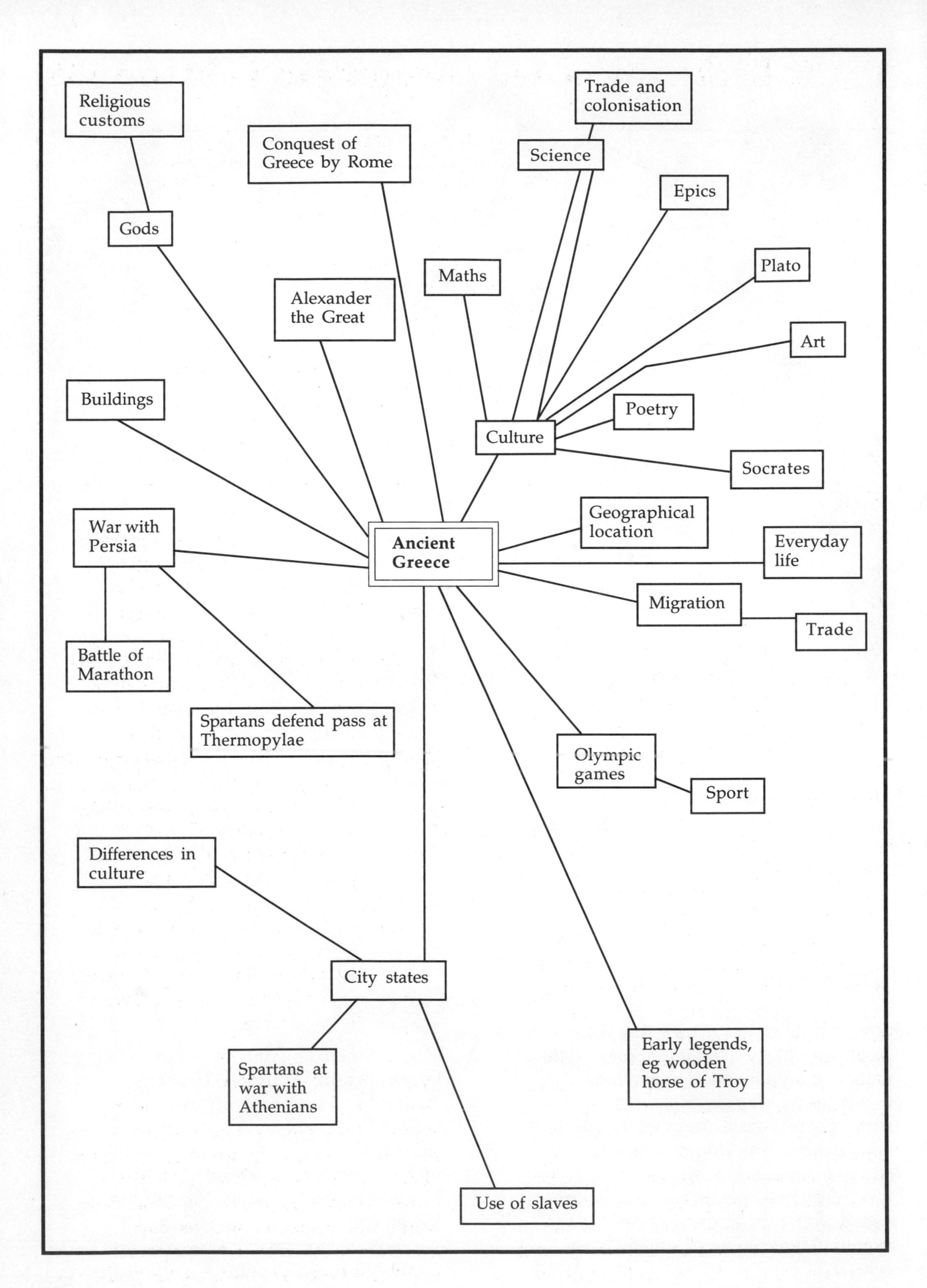
Religious customs
Gods
Conquest of Greece by Rome
Trade and colonisation
Science
Epics
Maths
Alexander the Great
Plato
Art
Buildings
Poetry
Culture
Socrates
Geographical location
War with Persia
Ancient Greece
Everyday life
Migration
Trade
Battle of Marathon
Spartans defend pass at Thermopylae
Olympic games
Sport
Differences in culture
City states
Spartans at war with Athenians
Early legends, eg wooden horse of Troy
Use of slaves

CSU6: Exploration and encounters 1450 to 1550

	Pupils should be taught about:
voyages of exploration	• descriptions and maps of the world in the late fifteenth century the search for a route to the Spice Islands, including Columbus's voyages navigation on trans-oceanic voyages life on board ships on trans-oceanic voyages
Aztec civilisation	• Montezuma and the Aztec Empire the Aztec way of life Aztec gods and religious practices Aztec crafts and technology Aztec art and architecture
the Spanish conquest	• differences between European and Aztec civilisation motives for the expedition of Cortes the Spanish conquest of the Aztec Empire the legacy of the Spanish conquest of Mexico the creation of the Spanish American Empire the growth of trade between the Old and the New World

Starting points

Pupils will need briefly to revise the work they undertook in the earlier unit CSU1, Invaders and settlers. They will need to recall the voyages of exploration of the Vikings and then compare these with the Europeans' lack of nautical exploration before 1422 when Henry the Navigator of Portugal began his programme of exploration. The children will need to understand the advances made in European exploration in the next 100 years, the period during which the globe was circumnavigated.

A very large wall map would be useful for pupils to plot the journeys they study. It should show Spain and Portugal, West Africa and Central and South America, including the West Indies. This could be drawn by photocopying or tracing a suitable map on to an acetate sheet, projecting it to a suitable size and drawing over the projection first with pencil and then with a felt-tipped pen.

The children will also need to study maps available to sailors at the time of Henry the Navigator, such as the Catalan Atlas of 1375 or the globe made by Martin Behaim in 1492. Pupils could be set the task of identifying which countries are not shown on the old maps, which countries are shown in the wrong place, and which countries have a recognisable outline.

It has been suggested that medieval sailors did not venture far out to sea because they had insufficient knowledge of astronomy and mathematics; indeed, they knew less about these things than the ancient Greeks. However, ancient Greek knowledge, translated into Arabic by Muslims, gradually became available as the Christian conquest of Muslim Iberia progressed, and was used by European Christian scholars. Ptolemy's work, *Geography*, was translated into Latin and made available in the early fifteenth century.

People still believed the world was flat, and fear of the unknown coupled with a lack of navigational skill still discouraged sailors from undertaking long voyages, despite the new learning.

Navigational aids

Magnetic compasses were available at this time, but little was known about magnetic variation. The Pole Star would indicate north at night, and the sun at noon showed south, with a shadow stick used to ascertain midday. Time-keeping was important for dead reckoning the position of ships at sea, and hour-glasses were used until mechanical clocks became reliable enough to use at sea. The marine chronometer was not invented until 1761.

Longitude, the measure of distance travelled from east to west or west to east, had to be worked out by calculating the speed of the ship, the length of time taken and the direction of travel. Latitude, the distance travelled north to south, could be worked out in theory by measuring the angle of the Pole Star above the horizon. Mariners used an outstretched arm to estimate this angle at first, reckoning that if the distance between star and horizon was one finger wide, this represented two degrees, while if it was as wide as the wrist it was equal to eight degrees, and if as wide as a fist it represented eighteen degrees.

Direction and time

What you need

A steel nail, a strong magnet, cotton, a compass, a shadow stick, an hour glass.

What to do

Let the children try to make their own compass by stroking a steel nail in one direction only with a strong magnet. They could then find the point of balance and tie a length of cotton to this point, allowing the magnetised nail to dangle from the thread. Ask the children to test the accuracy of their compass against a modern one.

Set two groups of children the task of telling when it is midday without using a watch or clock. Start both groups off at 9am on a sunny day, and ask one group to use a shadow stick and the other group an hour glass. Ask the groups to report to you when they think it is midday, and then they can compare and analyse the accuracy of each method. You will need the co-operation of the rest of the school in not giving the time away!

The new explorers

Prince Henry, the third son of John I of Portugal, was known as Henry the Navigator. He is credited with giving impetus to extended nautical exploration. He did not become an explorer himself, but planned and organised explorations, training promising sea captains at his school of navigation at Sagres on the extreme south-west promontory of Portugal. As each voyage brought back new information, Henry ordered existing charts to be upgraded. Master Jacome of Majorca was employed for this task, as well as for making navigational instruments.

The development of the caravel coincided with Henry the Navigator's desire to promote Portuguese exploration. The caravel was a light, broad ship, capable of carrying a heavy load, with triangular lateen sails for tacking and square sails for moving fast before a following wind.

After Henry died in 1460, King Alfonso V did not pursue the idea of supporting exploration for exploration's sake. In 1469 Alfonso entered into an agreement with Ferdinand Gomes. Gomes agreed to explore 500 miles of unknown African coastline each year for five years, in exchange for exclusive trading rights.

In 1488 Bartholomew Diaz sailed around the most southerly tip of Africa, now known as the Cape of Good Hope.

The voyages of Columbus

It is well known that Columbus discovered America (or rediscovered it if pupils remember Leif Erickson's voyage) whilst seeking a westerly passage to the Spice Islands. It may not be so well known that he believed that six sevenths of the world was made up of land and only one seventh of water. This theory was based on a passage in the Apocrypha concerning the creation. It is thought that Colombus believed that the earth was round, and because he thought that there was so much more land than sea, he would have predicted that the Atlantic Ocean was not very large and that the eastern shores of Asia could be reached by sailing westward less than 3,000 miles.

Colombus, a Genoan, failed to convince King John of Portugal that his plans were viable. His terms were extreme and included the demand of a knighthood, being appointed admiral, being made viceroy of all the land he discovered and having a tenth share of all profits. He took his plans to King Ferdinand of Spain, who, celebrating his defeat of the King of Granada, eventually agreed to back the expedition.

Two small caravels, the *Pinta* and the *Nina*, and one larger caravel, the *Santa Maria*, were equipped and prepared for sea at the small Spanish port of Palos. They sailed on August 3, 1492. Columbus had the same kinds of navigational aids that sailors in Henry the Navigator's time used, although by this time the angle of the Pole Star was fixed with a quadrant rather than by rule of thumb.

During the crossing, the crews became concerned about the wind always blowing from west to east. They were not sure that they would be able to return, and there was almost a mutiny.

They reached Watling Island in the Bahamas after a voyage of 37 days. During their exploration of the surrounding islands, Colombus and his men made contact with native Americans. Some gave him nuggets of gold which led him to hope that great riches waited to be discovered.

During the voyage, the *Santa Maria* was shipwrecked when all hands except the ship's boy were asleep. The ship's timbers were used to make a kind of fortification on the island of Hispaniola for the 39 men that Columbus had to leave behind. After a dangerous voyage home through one of the worst winters of that time, and surviving an enforced period of shelter in hostile Portugal, Columbus and the *Nina* arrived back in Palos in March 1493.

Columbus made a second voyage to the New World in 1493, only to find that none of the men left behind on Hispaniola had survived. The Indians had killed them in revenge for the sailors' theft of gold and women. This abuse of the native population was repeated only too frequently by subsequent Europeans.

Columbus sailed to Jamaica and then back to Spain. His third voyage of 1498 was fraught with problems. He had been made responsible for governing the new colony of Hispaniola, but a revolt against the authorities broke out, and Columbus handled this very badly. News of his incompetence and cruelty reached the King, who sent out agents to arrest Columbus and bring him back to Spain in chains. He was later pardoned, and undertook a final voyage in 1502. Because of his earlier mistakes he was forbidden by the King to visit Hispaniola, and so he sailed down the coast of South America. Until the time of his death, Columbus believed that he had found a westerly route to Asia, and therefore to the spice-producing countries.

Voyages of discovery

What you need

Time line, large world map, bread and butter, a range of spices, craft materials, writing equipment, biscuits, bread, fruit, vegetables, water, pieces of wood, sacking and crockery.

What to do

- Ask pupils to mark the voyages of Columbus on the time line and on the map.

• Ask the children why spices were so important to people in the fifteenth century. Encourage them to consider the use of spices to preserve food and hide any rotten taste, linking this with the difficulty sailors would have had in keeping food edible on a long journey. Pupils could try tasting a selection of spices sprinkled on bread and butter to find out if they recognise any of the flavours, and to see if they like the tastes. The children need to know how prized spices were, and that explorers would hope to make a fortune out of finding a quicker route to Asia. A study of the medieval trade in spices should be undertaken to give pupils supporting information about Columbus' voyages westward.

• If pupils have looked at the navigational aids available to sailors during the time of Henry the Navigator, they will have some understanding of the technical problems which Columbus faced. They could be asked to design and produce a quadrant for measuring the angle of the Pole Star. It could involve the use of a plumb line to show the user the vertical position, as it would be used on the rolling deck of a ship.

• Several aspects of the essential information for this unit could be brought together at this stage, by setting pupils a piece of serial writing in the form of a log of Columbus' first voyage. We suggest that the pupils are asked to write one entry a week for five weeks during the topic, each representing one week of the five-week outward voyage. The entry writing task should follow the teaching and research done for the topic work, so that factual information is included in the fictional log. It could start with a list of the provisions and equipment needed for the voyage. Pupils could let their fictional character bemoan the prevailing westerly wind and the difficulty of steering an accurate course. The construction of navigational instruments would give further authority to the story.

This piece of serial writing could provide a focus for a study of the following items of information: technical problems of trans-oceanic voyages; life on board ships on trans-oceanic voyages; and European artefacts connected with voyages and exploration.

• Consider the impact that the arrival of Columbus and his men had on the native Indians, and discuss how such a small group of Europeans managed to dominate the Indians.

• Biscuits, bread, fruit, vegetables and water could be kept over a five-week period in containers made of wood, sacking or pottery, to see how fresh they remained. Obviously, hygiene in the classroom would have to be taken into consideration.

Cabot

An explorer who sailed under a British flag on his voyages of discovery was John Cabot. In fact, like Columbus, he was born in Genoa. He was originally named Giovanni Caboto. He was a spice dealer in Mecca, and became curious as to the origins of the spice. The traders thought they had been brought to Mecca on caravans from the south-east. Cabot, like Columbus, reasoned that it might be quicker to sail westward. Backed by the merchants of Bristol and with the King's consent, Cabot set sail on May 2, 1497.

He sighted land on June 24 of that year. It was probably Newfoundland or Nova Scotia, but no records have survived to make it certain.

Magellan

After Vasco da Gama reached India by sailing round the Cape of Good Hope and then eastward, the origin of spices was known in more detail. Like Columbus and Cabot, Magellan thought that it would be quicker to sail westwards rather than take the long and dangerous eastwards route. He believed there was a gap in the American land mass that could easily be sailed through, and that the Pacific Ocean was only 600 miles across instead of the 11,000 miles from South America to the Molucca Islands.

Magellan had lost favour in Portugal, since he argued with his superiors in the navy, and annoyed the king by demanding a new commission, which was turned down. Consequently, he took his idea to Spain. He was provided with five old and leaky ships, crewed by 234 men, most of whom undertook the voyage to escape a prison sentence. His ships sailed on September 20, 1519.

Magellan survived not only the disappointment of not finding an easy passage through the land mass, but also a mutiny. On October 21, 1520, the four remaining ships entered the channel joining the two oceans, now known as the Strait of Magellan. After five weeks of battling through this passage, the crew of the ship carrying most of the provisions, the *San Antonia*, mutinied and turned back. After further hardships caused by lack of food, they made landfall on the Islands of Marianas, where they found fresh food and water.

Magellan and many of his men were later killed by natives in the Philippines and the survivors fled. They reached the Moluccas at last, and loaded up with the precious spices. By now only 101 men out of the original 234 survived. The *Victoria* set sail with 47 of the survivors, while the *Trinidad* remained behind for repairs. The *Victoria* reached Spain in 1522 crewed by the 18 sailors who survived, and the cargo of spices made a huge profit for the backers of the expedition. This was the first circumnavigation of the globe.

The Conquistadores

Many explorers followed Columbus to America. Men such as Ponce de Leon enslaved the native Indians and worked them to death in gold mines. Other Europeans who came for easy fortune justified the mass murder of the Indians by arguing that they were cannibals, or that they were not Christian. A Spanish priest, Bartolome de Las Casas, encouraged this mass killing. The Indians could not counter the Spaniards' hand-guns, cannon, armour, crossbows and metal weapons.

Cortes led the conquest of Mexico in 1519. He had 11 ships and 600 men. He also had 16 horses, which the Indians had never seen before. Cortes was helped by a legend believed by the Aztecs' priests and the Emperor Montezuma, that one day white-faced, bearded gods would come to wreak vengeance on the Aztec people. Cortes won thousands of Aztecs over to his side by promising to free them from the rule of Montezuma. He marched into the capital, Tenochtitlan, pretending friendship, and then seized the emperor and held him hostage.

Some Aztec leaders did not believe the Spaniards were gods, and led an uprising. Montezuma was told to persuade the people not to attack, but they stoned him to death. The Spaniards had to flee for their lives. Cortes later laid siege to the city and it surrendered on August 13, 1521.

The Incas were conquered in a similar fashion by Pizarro, using 180 soldiers and 27 horses. The Inca emperor, Atahualpa, had entered Pizarro's camp for negotiations. When the emperor refused demands to surrender and become a Christian, Pizarro's men opened fire on the Inca leaders. In under half an hour 4,000 Incas were killed. After this it was a simple matter for the Spaniards to plunder the country of gold and silver. Pizarro promised that he would release Atahualpa in return for a room filled with gold. As the Incas brought in the gold, the Spaniards removed it, making it impossible to fill the room. The emperor was put on trial and sentenced to be burned at the stake. He was told that if he converted to Christianity not one drop of his blood would be shed. He accepted these terms and was baptised, and was then strangled to death.

The Aztecs

The Aztecs were a wandering tribe who settled on a small island in lake Texcoco in 1345. There they founded their capital city, Tenochtitlan. The lake was no more than four metres deep, and it was very swampy. The Aztecs extended the island by reclaiming plots of land, which they did by first pushing poles into the lake bed and stringing rush mats between them to mark out an enclosure. They they wrapped bundles of reeds and mats around stones and sank these between the poles. They then dredged up mud from the bottom of the lake and piled it into the middle of the enclosure until the mud was higher than the water level. These reclaimed plots were called *chinampas*.

The mud was very fertile, and the Aztecs worked it with wooden digging sticks. Among the crops they grew were likely to have been squashes, carrots, sweet potatoes, tomatoes and maize.

Canals were dredged between the plots to provide routes for transport. The Aztecs did not have horses or wheeled vehicles. Three causeways connected the city to the mainland, and an aqueduct brought fresh water to the city.

As well as the vegetables they grew on the chinampas, the Aztecs lived on frogs, newts and fish, which they bartered for wood with neighbouring tribes. With the help of three other tribes the Aztecs finally managed to defeat the Tepenec tribe, to whom they had been forced to pay tribute. The Aztecs then went on to conquer the whole of the Valley of Mexico.

When Cortes reached the Valley of Mexico in 1519 the Aztecs ruled an empire which stretched from the Gulf of Mexico to the Pacific.

Studying the Aztec empire

What you need

Reference books on the subject, a tank or deep tray, water, clay, dowel, net curtain, pebbles, garden soil, mustard and cress seeds.

What to do

Teachers will be able to match the presentation of this information to their pupils' needs. The children will have to study the growth of the Aztec empire before it was overthrown by the Spaniards. They will need to compare the Aztec domestic and military technology with that of the Spaniards, and study various aspects of Aztec life, including religious worship, art, architecture and the impact of the Spanish conquerors.

Ask the children to imagine how difficult it would be to move loads overland without pack horses or wheeled carts. They could make a copy of a chinampa by lining the bottom of a tank or deep tray with a layer of clay about 2cm thick. Thin sections of dowel could be pushed into the clay at intervals of about 1cm, to enclose a

rectangle, and the children could weave strips of net curtain in and out of the dowel to imitate the rush matting. They could place some pebbles along the inner bottom edge of the netting and add some water to just below the tops of the posts. Garden soil could then be used to fill up the enclosure, and then after the top of the soil has dried out a little, cress or mustard seeds could be planted on the surface.

Aztec society

The Aztecs had a very rigid social class system. Dual rulers, the emperor and the Snake Woman (in fact a man), shared power. The emperor was responsible for foreign affairs and war, while Snake Woman was responsible for city law, taxes, food and buildings. Four military commanders advised the emperor, and below them were chief officials, lesser officials, craftsmen, merchants, ordinary people, peasants and slaves. It was against the law to wear clothes or jewellery not allocated to your social class. The higher up the social ladder you were, the nearer you lived to the centre of the city.

Although the Aztecs took parenthood seriously, pupils may be interested to know that punishments for Aztec children included pricking the child with thorns and holding the child over a fire of burning peppers to make their eyes sting.

The art of the Aztecs involved geometric designs and stylised drawing.

Encourage the children to make patterns based on Aztec designs, using squared paper. The pictures could be used to make glyphs, the Aztec method of writing using pictures.

Organise the children into groups to research aspects of Aztec life such as domestic life and housing, farming, buildings, religion, art, military and civil technology, clothing, Aztec legends and writing. Ask each group to make a presentation to the rest of the class using paintings, drawings and handouts typed on the computer and photocopied. Teachers could follow up the presentation with a quiz.

Religion

The Aztecs worshipped many gods, and lived in fear of them. As they conquered more tribes, they adopted the gods of those tribes.

They believed that the gods had sacrificed themselves to create the sun. They sacrificed human offerings to the sun god Huitzilopochtli to give him strength to rise each day. The most important festival, the New Fire Ceremony, took place every 52 years.

Temples

What you need

Reference books on the period.

What to do

Many text-books have good illustrations of Aztec temples. The children will probably note the similarity with the Egyptian pyramids.

Ask the children to find out about the temples, and speculate on the methods which might have been used in their construction by a people who used stone-age technology for building and had no metal tools.

The decline of the Aztecs

After the conquest, the Aztecs were treated with contempt by the victorious Spanish. They were deprived of any rights or freedom and their land and wealth was taken from them. With no immunity from European diseases, and under harsh treatment from the Spaniards, the Aztec people declined in number.

Books

Christopher Colombus, G Duchet-Suchaux (Hart Davies).
Man Explores (pack) J Platts (Macmillan).
The Aztecs, J Crosher (Macdonald).
The Aztecs, L Watson (Wayland).
The Great Age of Exploration, D Castlereagh.
The Voyages of Discovery, G R Crone and A Kendall (Wayland).

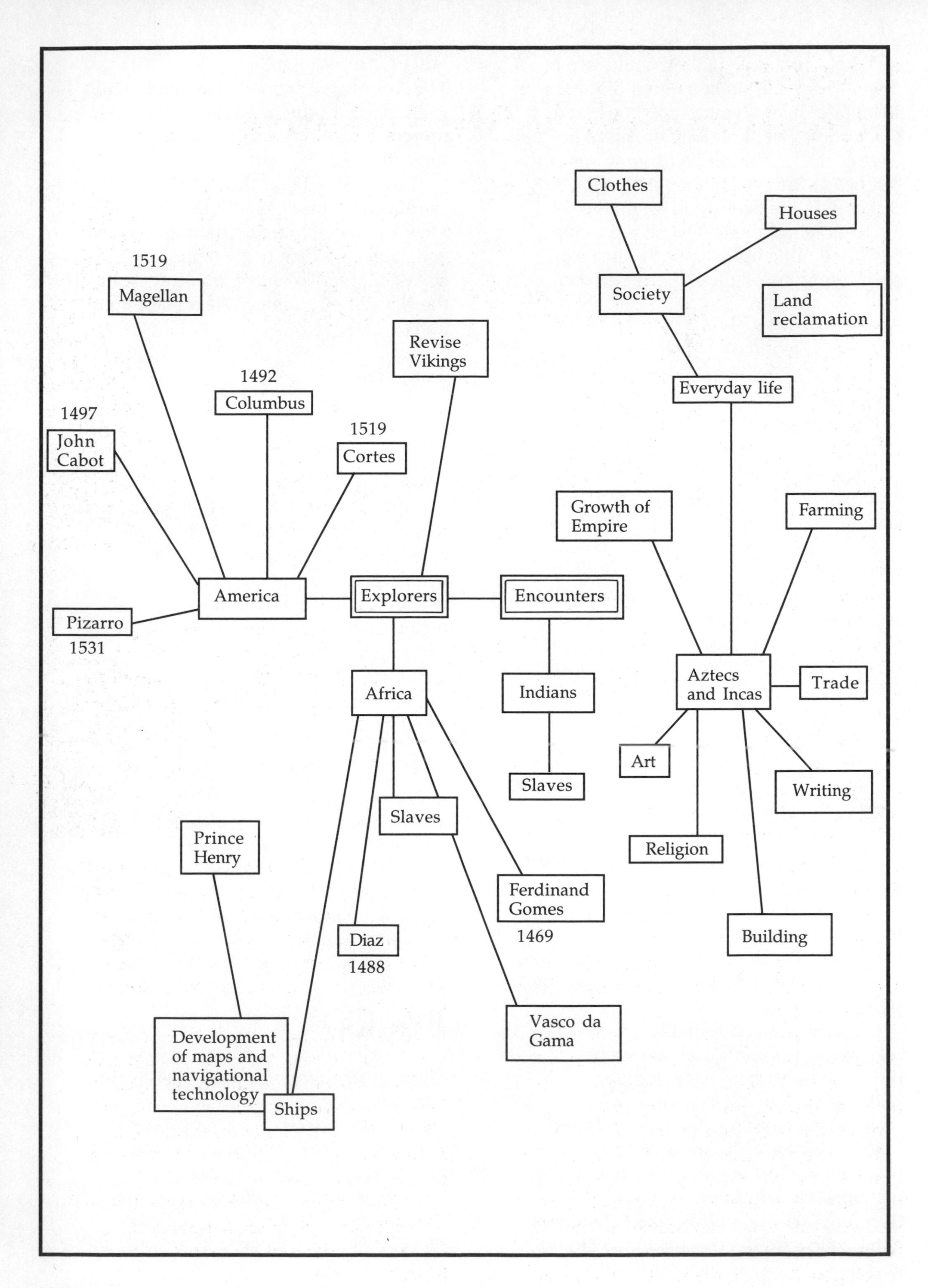

Clothes
Houses
Society
Land reclamation
1519
Magellan
Revise Vikings
Everyday life
1492
Columbus
1497
John Cabot
1519
Cortes
Growth of Empire
Farming
America
Explorers
Encounters
Pizarro
1531
Africa
Indians
Aztecs and Incas
Trade
Art
Slaves
Writing
Slaves
Prince Henry
Religion
Ferdinand Gomes
1469
Building
Diaz
1488
Vasco da Gama
Development of maps and navigational technology
Ships

Chapter 4
Supplementary Study Units

Children should be taught three or four of the Supplementary Study Units (SSUs) with at least one unit from each of the categories A, B and C.

The SSUs offer the opportunity to link aspects of history that have already been studied, and can help to reinforce the concept of chronology. We feel strongly that these units should be undertaken after the Core Study Units, so that they can build on work already done rather than exploring entirely new information.

We suggest that each child has a ring file of work from Y1, Y2 and Y3 that relates to the SSUs. When a piece of information is studied again with relevance to an SSU, the earlier work can be reviewed and developed. Keeping the work in a ring file allows it to be filed in chronological order, and means that changes and additions can easily be made. Pupils will be able to see how their learning has developed when they look at work done in earlier years. Teachers can also use this collection of work for assessment.

On page 173 we have included a chart which can be used to record each pupil's progress through the nine units taken at Key Stage 2. The Attainment Targets are listed down the left hand side and the school will need to fill in the Study Units undertaken across the top.

In this chapter, the SSUs are dealt with in the order in which they appear in the National Curriculum documents for history.

Supplementary Study Units – Category A

The purpose of this category is to study a theme over a long period of time. Units chosen from this category should:

- involve the study of important historical issues;
- cover a time span of at least 1,000 years;
- compare developments in different periods;
- show links between local, British, European and world history.

Ships and seafarers

Starting points

The children should already have undertaken a great deal of work concerned with ships and seafarers in the Core Study Units. We feel that it makes sense to follow up the core units with this optional unit so that the core work can be reviewed, developed and placed in a chronological sequence over a very long period of time.

A time line from 5000 BC to the present would allow pupils to locate their work in a time context. If the classroom layout allows, the time line could be placed along the top of some frieze boards so that illustrations and writing can be placed near to the point in time to which they refer. Coloured wool could join the work to the appropriate point on the time lines.

Once the work saved from earlier years has been filed, we suggest that pupils make a study of the history of ship-building from earliest times to the end of the sailing era.

The following is a list of suggestions for relevant areas of study and linked activities. Teachers may wish to allocate these to groups, asking them to report back and give demonstrations.

Dug-out canoes

Pupils could model dug-out canoes from balsa-wood and test out their sailing properties.

Egyptian rush canoes

From about 2,500 BC, the Egyptians developed rush canoes. Pupils could model these canoes using long art straws, sealing the ends with PVA adhesive.

Sea-going Egyptian ships

The Egyptians used ships for coastal trading. An example of this would be the 60 ships dispatched by Pharoah Seneferu in 2,700 BC which brought back timber. They were over 150 feet long and were propelled by oars and sails, and had strong rope running above decks connecting stem to stern.

Fishing and trading

Cretan merchants were trading by sea before 3,000 BC and the Phoenicians by 2,000 BC. The city of Carthage could be studied as an example of a city growing wealthy because of sea trade.

The use of oar-power

Pupils will have studied Viking ships in some detail, and could compare this boat-building and rowing technology to that of Greek and Roman galleys. Pupils should be familiar with the Roman and Greek ships from their earlier studies, but may not have detailed knowledge of them.

The use of oared galleys continued until the latter part of the sixteenth century. Improvement in square-rigged sailing technology, a shift of trade to ocean routes and the development of shipboard cannons combined to make the galleys obsolete. The last major sea battle dominated by galleys was between the Venetians and Turks at Lepanto in 1571.

Improvements in sailing technology

The provision of a square sail to be used with a following wind was common to Egyptian, Phoenician, Greek, Roman and Viking ships. Arab sailors introduced the triangular or lateen sail into the Mediterranean. This enabled the ship to be sailed across or even against the wind. As ships grew bigger, the long yard of the lateen sail became unwieldy, and the sail area was divided between two masts. These caravels, as they became known, should have been studied when pupils researched the period of Henry the Navigator in CSU6.

Three-masted ships were built in the early part of the fifteenth century, at first with only one sail to each mast. A top sail was added to the middle mast and then to the front mast. The rear mast carried a triangular sail. The first English four-masted ship, Henry VII's *Regent*, was built in 1487. During the same century, clinker-built ships with overlapping planks were replaced by ships built with butt-jointed planks.

Pupils could experiment with sail designs using balsa-wood hulls, dowel masts and manila card sails. A hair drier held in a clamp can be used to give a constant range of wind speeds and the children could use a large tank or tray to sail the models on. The models may have to be weighted underneath to keep them upright. As well as sail design, pupils could experiment with sail angles, sailing across the wind, tacking and rudder design.

Military developments

The open platforms built on to the front and rear of the hulls of ships became the fore- and aftercastles, and were integrated into the design. Until the fifteenth century, kings had requisitioned merchant ships in times of war. Small cannons could be fired from the aftercastle of these merchant ships, but over the next 100 years cannons grew in size, and had to be placed in a special gun deck. Kings then had to commission specially built warships. The lofty fore- and aftercastles were reduced by some ship designers to improve the sailings qualities of the ships.

Pupils could revise the differences in design between the Spanish ships and English ships at the time of the Armada.

Mapping and exploration

In CSU6, pupils will have studied mapping, exploration and navigational aids from 1450 to 1550, and may have looked at voyages of discovery within CSU2 when Tudor and Stuart history was investigated. CSU3 requires pupils to research Victorian exploration, but this focuses mainly on travel in Africa. This work can be revised and extended where appropriate. Further study of nautical exploration and mapping could include the voyages of Vitus Bering (1680–1741) and Captain James Cook (1728–1779).

The effect of imports

Pupils will have studied the spice trade in detail in CSU6. This work can be revised and extended, and further study undertaken to research the impact of imports such as potatoes, tobacco, sugar, tea, coffee, chocolate, cotton, tinned meat, dairy products, fruit and petrol. The shortages caused by wartime should be researched, from the Napoleonic Wars to the Second World War.

Ports and fishing communities

Pupils could research the specialised shops, industries and services that would support a fishing fleet or a port. Pupils could consider the specialised shore-based workers, such as chandlers, ship repairers, fish wholesalers, dockers and warehouse workers. The threat of the press gang should be investigated, as well as the reasons for the cosmopolitan nature of the population in ports such as Bristol and Liverpool.

Life on board ships

Pupils will have researched this area in detail, and should have considered life on board a Viking ship, life on board one of Columbus' ships and life as a galley slave. This work can be revised and extended. New information could be added, such as a study of the life of a sailor aboard HMS *Victory* or the *Cutty Sark*.

The children could learn the actions that go with sea shanties. Some are capstan shanties, to encourage a continuous effort, others are halliard shanties which encourage a series of rope pulling efforts.

Design and decoration

Pupils will have studied the ornate carvings on Viking ships. The highly decorated sterns of Dutch men-of-war in the seventeenth century and the ornate decorations of the French fleet at Trafalgar could be studied through contemporary illustration. The figureheads of sailing ships could be imitated in models carved from balsa, then painted and varnished. The models could be stuck to a two-dimensional picture of a ship's bow, and could be used to decorate related pieces of work.

Ships and fleets in war and peace

Pupils will have looked at naval battles such as the Greeks' defeat of the Persians, Alfred's Saxon navy defending against the Vikings and the English defeat of the Spanish Armada. The children will need to be taught that the possession of a powerful fleet by a country sometimes acted as a deterrent. The Victorian naval reviews could be looked at as a display of naval power. The use of navies to defend trade routes should be studied, along with the design of armed merchantmen for particular trade routes. The Battle of Trafalgar should be studied in detail.

A visit to Greenwich or Exeter Maritime Museum, or to the Portsmouth collection of ships which includes the *Victory* and the remains of the *Mary Rose*, would be a valuable experience.

Food and farming through history

Schools may wish to choose this optional unit because it explores a great deal of information not covered in the core units. If the Roman period was studied in CSU1, 'Invaders and settlers', then pupils may have learnt how towns could develop if food could be easily transported to them. However, much of the history study undertaken in the core units will not be appropriate to this unit. Moreover, the Neolithic and Medieval periods and the eighteenth century will not have been studied. Because this unit involves so much new essential information, we feel that schools should be aware of how much planning will be required.

Schools could, however, consider the history of food production as part of a unit from Category B based on local history, taking into account local resources, such as farming museums, specialised museums such as Cadbury's World, field study centres, archive material showing the changing boundaries of fields, pictures of old farming methods and talks by elderly agricultural workers who could give a first-hand account of recent changes in farming methods.

Starting points

Pupils could find out if there are people in the world who still live by hunting and gathering. They could try to make replicas of the hunting tools used by Stone Age people, such as the bow, the harpoon, the pick and the adze.

The development of farming, when people began to stay in one place to grow crops and look after cattle, could be charted on a large map showing North Africa, Europe and the Middle East. From 7,000 BC, herding and grain harvesting had developed in the lands now called Israel and Iraq. By 3,500 BC, farming had spread to most of Europe, including Britain but excluding the north of Scotland and the north of Ireland. Wild wheat may have been harvested even earlier. Remains of crop plants found in Thailand have been carbon-dated to about 9,700 BC. This predates Middle Eastern farming by several centuries. Pupils should consider why ancient people chose this way of life.

The following areas will be useful topics of study.

Changes in food production in Neolithic times

Pupils should study the methods used by Neolithic or New Stone Age men and women who, like their forebears, used wooden ploughs. In addition they used flint sickles to harvest the wheat and barley, red deer antlers to dig the soil and shoulder blades of cattle as shovels. The changes also included a move towards the specialisation of labour, with the development of trades such as pottery, mining and flint tool making.

The development of cities, states and empires

The stability of a farming population made political development easier. Pupils will have learnt how the farming communities of Egypt and Greece, with their slave and peasant workers, produced a surplus of food that allowed a complex society to emerge because the whole of the population did not need to work on the land.

Early technological developments

A study of the development of wheat hybrids may be appropriate for some pupils in Y6. The chance crossing of wild einkorn with another grass in Western Asia more than 10,000 years ago resulted in wild emmer. The cultivation of wild emmer gave rise to other forms, such as emmer and durum. Bread wheat is thought to be descended from emmer crossed with a second wild grass. The first known farming of the following cereals could be plotted on a time line: barley grown in Egypt about 4,000 BC, maize grown in Mexico about 5,000 BC, millet first grown in China about 2,700 BC, oats first cultivated in Asia and Europe about 500 BC, rice first grown in India about 3,000 BC, wheat first grown in parts of the Mediterranean Middle East about 9,000 to 8,000 BC.

Religious and social life based on the farming year

Pupils will have learnt how important a successful harvest was to most civilisations, and how certain gods were allocated to the weather and the fields. Bronze Age and Iron Age fertility gods could be studied, and modern festivals with agricultural origins could be investigated.

The manorial system

After the Norman Conquest, the existing feudal system in Britain became more organised. This system continued up to the Wars of the Roses. The king owned all of the land, and let out the parts he did not wish to keep for his own use to the barons, in return for their support. The barons let out land to knights in return for military service, and villeins leased land from the lord of the manor in return for two or three days' work a week on the lord's farm. Serfs, who made up about ten per cent of the population, worked in return for food and lodgings. Serfs were the property of the lord, and could be bought and sold like cattle. Small farmers who worked their own land were called yeomen, and owed allegiance to the king only.

Comparisons could be made between the English feudal system and those of mainland Europe.

Medieval technological developments

A visit to a museum showing replicas of medieval ploughs and detailing developments in horse-breeding and harnesses which allowed for greater efficiency would be most suitable at this point. Also valuable would be visits to mills to find out how water and wind power were used to grind grain, and how wind power was used to reclaim wetlands.

The roles of men, women and children in agriculture

Pupils could investigate the history of gender roles. Have men always undertaken the heavy work? Have women and children always tended the animals and undertaken lighter work? Pupils will have learnt that this was not the case in all cultures. Viking women, for example, sometimes managed farms themselves. Pupils could explore the roles of children by empathising with their historic counterparts. How would they like to spend a long, cold day stone-picking or bird-scaring?

Cooking and eating

Pupils will have studied ways of cooking and eating in the core units. Greek, Roman, Aztec, Celtic, Saxon, Viking, Tudor, Stuart, Victorian and modern food and cooking methods will have been explored and, in some cases, tried out. If medieval and eighteenth century methods are examined, with special emphasis given to bread, then pupils will have studied the history of food over a very long period.

Enclosures and clearances

During the fifteenth century the demand for wool led to some common land being enclosed by lords of the manor and other rich farmers. Peasants lost their small plots of land and grazing rights and, as sheep farming required less labour than arable farming, many jobs were lost. Further enclosure took place during the sixteenth century, until the Duke of Somerset, the Protector of England, banned further enclosure.

Towards the end of the eighteenth century, when Britain was at war with France, the need for higher food production led to larger and more productive farms. Special acts of parliament allowed wealthy farmers to enclose village common land. At the same time thousands of Scottish families were cleared from the Highlands. This was partly as an act of revenge by the British Government for the uprising which led to the battle of Culloden in 1745, but also because the wealthy landowners wanted the land for sheep farming.

English landlords evicted Irish tenants and destroyed their cottages during the nineteenth century. Pupils should know that one of the consequences of the clearances was the emigration of large numbers of Scots and Irish.

Eighteenth century husbandry

Public figures such as George III led the way with their enthusiasm for new farming methods. Windsor Park became a model farm visited by thousands.

Jethro Tull wrote *The New Horse Hoeing Husbandry*, which explained how the fallow period could be abandoned. He also invented a deep-penetrating horse-drawn hoe and a horse-drawn seed drill. Because seeds could now be sown in straight rows with a covering of soil protecting them from birds, and as hoeing destroyed weeds, grain production increased greatly. The growing of root crops not only restored fertility to the soil but meant that animals could be fed in the winter rather than slaughtered.

Thomas Coke, a landowner in Holkham, Norfolk, insisted that his tenants used the new crop rotation method, planting root crops and grain alternately.

Art and agriculture

Pupils could make corn dollies from art straws, gather a collection of food advertisements, and visit a modern farm if possible. Some authorities run educational farm centres, and rural schools may be able to visit a local farm.

Houses and places of worship

Starting points

If the children have undertaken the Core Study Units they will have studied buildings in many shapes and forms. A starting point could then be a revision of the types of buildings looked at in previous units. Pairs or groups of pupils could draw to an agreed scale an example of a house from each unit studied. These could be displayed along a time-line, and each group could make a presentation to the class about the use and construction of its own building.

A visit to a museum of buildings is highly recommended, or to a town or village containing a range of original buildings. One very good museum is Avoncroft, in Bromsgrove, to the south of Birmingham (see page 60). Many other open air museums either specialise in restored buildings or have some on their site as part of their theme. Further details are given in the section on resources (see page 185).

Classroom follow-up

The amount of follow-up work which can be developed from such a visit is enormous. However, even if a visit is not feasible, it is still possible to undertake a lot of interesting work in this unit. Pupils could work in groups to make large scale models of a range of houses. One group could weave sections of wattle from twigs, raffia, art straws or narrow strips of card. These could be designed to fit a frame made from thick beams of balsa-wood. The corners of the frame could be butt-jointed using right-angled triangles of card to brace the joints. The wattle sections could be pinned to the frame and a thin layer of clay or plaster spread over the wattle to represent the daub. The building could be thatched with reeds, straw or art straws. A collection of buildings to the same scale could be laid out to represent a village, and the pupils could research and make appropriate artefacts to go with them. Other buildings such as a church, a mill or a barn could be added to the village.

Staying on the theme of timber-framed buildings, some pupils might like to construct a model of the type of frame used by Tudor builders. Again, balsa-wood is ideal for this. The uprights can be set in Plasticine on a modelling board. Quite intricate frames can be made by pupils of seven years and above.

This theme can also be used in art work. If a Tudor street scene is drawn on to a piece of manila card and decorated using felt-tipped pens, then strips of balsa can be added to the buildings to give a partial three-dimensional effect. The buildings can be cut out and raised on thin strips of balsa to enhance this effect.

A dramatic corridor display can be made by drawing and painting large pictures of historical buildings. Cardboard packing from around washing machines or other large items is ideal for this. If the paintings are done to a consistent scale, then visitors and other classes can gain an impression of the compact size of a Stone Age hut compared with a Georgian mansion, for example. Well known local houses could also be accurately represented. Other classes could co-operate to add houses from the periods they are studying.

The study of houses from a range of periods in history can be easily linked to a study of the lifestyles of those who originally lived in them. Pupils could research domestic life in various periods and report back to the class and/or make a wall display of their findings. This will obviously link to CSUs 1, 2, 3, 4 and 5. Alternatively, groups of pupils could research themes related to domestic life and housing such as cooking, furniture and linen, sanitation, degrees of privacy, lighting, heating, slaves and servants, household gadgets and the difference between wealthy homes and poor homes within a specified period of history.

Science and technology

A great deal of technological or scientific work could stem from this research. Pupils could compare the effectiveness of different roof coverings for heat retention and waterproofing. Systems for channelling water into a dwelling could be designed using plastic flexible tubing and containers. A car windscreen cleaning system rescued from a junkyard would be a cheap and useful resource for this. In the same way, a system for removing waste liquids could also be designed.

A large model house, perhaps based on a late Victorian design, could have an electric lighting system added and perhaps a telephone system could be installed.

A comparison of the strength of beams of wood and steel could be made. Pupils could be asked to set up a test rig as a design task, including a means of evaluating the results.

Model bricks could be moulded from self-hardening clay. It would help if a wooden box mould was made and a specific amount of clay used each time. A size of 9cm long by 4cm wide by 3cm deep would give a scale replica of a building brick. A model wall could be built by pupils using a baseboard and a pack of ready-mixed mortar. They could reproduce brick patterns observed in real buildings and in drawings, such as English bond, Tudor herringbone or modern simple bonding. Thin slices of brick could be made in the same way, and these could be stuck on to painted backgrounds to give a textured finish to a picture of a brick building.

English work

Much of the programme of study for English in the National Curriculum will be covered as pupils discuss work at the planning and evaluating stage, read for information, make notes and compile reports for a presentation. Imaginative work could be based on a building topic if pupils are shown either a real building or a video, a set of slides or a photograph of one, and asked to use this information as the basis for a story about the original inhabitants and their way of life. Children could be encouraged to use a suitable degree of historical accuracy in their stories.

These stories could be used as the starting point for role-play, with the pupils researching as much information as possible about the likely lifestyle of the characters involved. A degree of conflict in the story-line is necessary to develop dialogue that goes beyond the descriptive, but when the children have come up with a satisfying drama, they could perform it for the rest of the school and the parents in an assembly.

Places of worship

This unit is concerned with places of worship throughout history, as well as with houses. In Britain we are fortunate in having many excellent examples of church architecture from a wide range of periods. Stained glass windows, brasses and effigies in old churches may give pupils clues about the types of clothing worn at various times in the past, and headstones can give evidence about life expectancies in different centuries. Pupils will be able to compare the construction methods and materials used in churches with those used in houses of the same period. They will need to think about why so much time and money were invested in building a church. A single church will often have sections dating from different periods, such as a Norman tower, a medieval nave and a Victorian screen.

Other sacred buildings in Great Britain, such as mosques, synagogues and temples, will probably date from fairly recent times. It may be possible to arrange a visit to a religious building where its layout and use can be explained to the children in terms of the history of the faith to which it is dedicated.

It would probably be sensible to link part of this study unit to a wider study of world religions.

Roman and Victorian households

This subject may already have been undertaken if the Romans were the invaders studied in detail in CSU1 and the Victorian Core Study Unit was selected.

The medieval parish church

Pupils may have followed the suggestion for using the local church as a resource in Key Stage 1.

The mosque

Many children attend a mosque, and if you have pupils who do so, they may be prepared to explain how the building is used. Organise a visit to a mosque if possible. Pupils should not gain the impression that a mosque is a curiosity, but rather the centre of worship, educational and social life for those who attend.

Styles and decorations

Pupils will have investigated the design and decoration of temples in Ancient Greece and Aztec Mexico, and looked at the design and interior decoration of the domestic buildings of the Greeks and Aztecs, as well as the Romans, Celts, Anglo-Saxons, Vikings, Tudors, Stuarts and Victorians, and/or those prevalent in Britain since the 1930s. This work could be revised and developed to a level appropriate to the pupils' current ability.

Domestic service

This will also have been studied in depth, and could be revised.

Local church and parish government

Ask the children to find out details of how a local parish council works.

Laws concerning houses

The following are examples of laws that related to housing:

- the Public Health Act of 1875;
- the Housing of the Working Classes Act 1890;
- the Housing and Town Planning Act 1919;
- the Chamberlain Housing Act, 1923.

Pupils would need to have the implications of such acts explained to them.

Writing and printing

Starting points

By the time that Y3, Y4, Y5 and Y6 are all following the History National Curriculum, pupils will have completed a great deal of investigation and practical work related to writing in the Core Study Units. Pupils will have studied the Greek alphabet, Aztec picture writing (glyphs), Roman writing using waxed boards and Viking runes. When pupils studied the life of King Alfred, they may have noted the advantages that writing gave him when communicating with his troops. This will have to be revised as essential information for this unit.

When pupils studied the Roman and Aztec road systems they will have learnt that written messages could be quickly carried along them. The use of royal and government seals to authenticate such messages should be studied as essential information.

Pupils will have covered the period of history when monks devoted their entire lives to copying manuscripts, and the period when Caxton introduced printing into this country. Schools may have decided to save detailed investigation of these areas until this unit is taken.

The role of Greek, Roman and Aztec scribes and the various ways of teaching children to read in these periods will also have been studied, along with the implements used. Pupils should have tried out for themselves some early forms of writing. This information should be revised and developed to include the role of women in teaching children at home and the role of the scribe, both female and male, in history. This could be compared with the need for handwritten documents today.

Pupils will have investigated the influence of religions on everyday life in the Core Study Units, and this will have included the control of writing by Aztec priests, as well as the fact that the early monks and priests in Britain formed the nucleus of the literate population. This information will need to be extended to include the role of the Church in preserving literary skills, knowledge and traditions and maintaining libraries. The

elaborate illuminated manuscripts should be studied. Pupils could illuminate their own initials in the same style as these ancient manuscripts.

Pupils will have investigated the oral tradition of the Vikings, and will have made up sagas themselves. This can be extended by looking at the history of writing as a whole, including the ways of recording and communicating used by pre-literate cultures, such as cave painting, the quipu knotted cord records of the Incas, the wampum belt of the North American Indians, Australian Aboriginal picture messages and the use of the wooden tally. (Incredibly, the method of keeping tally of money lent to the Exchequer was changed from these wooden tally sticks to paper records as recently as 1834. Instead of giving the vast number of old tally sticks to the poor for firewood, they were burnt in a stove in the House of Lords. This fire got out of control and the Houses of Parliament were burned to the ground.)

Pupils should learn how Chinese and Japanese writing developed from picture writing, and about the difference in the way the symbols are used: one character can represent a syllable in Japanese script, but each Chinese character represents a whole word.

Cuneiform writing, which was used in ancient Assyria, has only been deciphered within the last two centuries. The wedge-shaped characters were impressed into damp clay with the end of a reed.

Our own alphabet uses classical Latin capital letters and early Roman cursive small letters.

Pupils could investigate the history of writing implements and writing surfaces. They could attempt to paint on a paper-covered wall in the style of cave paintings using feathers and hammered stick ends. They could try out different kinds of writing media, and write with a stylus on a wax-covered board, make and use a quill pen, scratch on a slate, write in sand trays (a method used in schools during World War Two because of paper shortages) and make a collection of modern writing implements.

The history of printing should be studied from Chinese block printing through to Gutenberg and Caxton. The advantages of moveable type should be discussed. Pupils could also investigate the extension of literacy from the clergy and royal clerks to a wider section of the population following the development of printed books in English rather than handwritten ones in Latin.

The development of literacy in Britain should be considered. Much of this took place in the Victorian era. The subsequent developments up to 1930 should be studied, and those after 1930 if CSU4 has not been taken, or Victorian educational developments if CSU3 has not been taken.

The history of freedom of the written word in newspapers and books should also be investigated.

Land transport

Starting points

The following areas should have been researched in previous work, and can quickly be included in the file. Pupils will have studied how the Roman road system was used to move troops around quickly in order to maintain political control and to facilitate communications. Pupils will have compared the time it took for Harold's army to march north to Stamford Bridge with the time it took Roman legionaries to march the same distance. Pupils will need to understand that the total mileage of Roman road in Britain suitable for fast wheeled transport (approximately 5,000 miles) was not matched until about 1780.

Pupils will have studied the use of cavalry by the Greeks and the fact that the terrain meant that it was quicker to send messages by runner (for example, news of the victory at Marathon).

The study of Aztec society during CSU6 will have revealed that they did not use the wheel, and pupils will have considered the implications of this. Despite the lack of wheeled transport, the Aztecs used a system of good roads to send messages quickly via runners from town to town, and this reinforced their control over subject peoples and enabled their rigid system of tax-gathering to be implemented. Pupils will probably find it interesting that the emperor was carried in a litter by teams of eight men who could take over the litter from each other without slowing down.

The children will have studied the way in which Britons used the chariot to oppose the Romans, and how post-Roman Britons used cavalry to oppose the Saxons. The study of the Vikings will have concentrated on their sea-going skills, but the children might like to know that it is thought that the Vikings introduced the Britons to the use of the stirrup for horse-riding and the breast collar and shafts for draught horses.

The study of the Tudors and Stuarts will have included work on towns, markets and transport. Pupils will have learnt that pack horses were used because wheeled transport was very difficult owing to the poor condition of roads.

If CSU3, 'Victorian Britain', has been studied, then pupils will have researched road, rail and canal transport of this era. Further study will be necessary as much of the history of canals, railways and bicycles predated Queen Victoria's reign.

We suggest that the following areas are investigated to supplement previous work.

Travel by foot

This could include looking at the litter, the ice skate and the ski.

Transport using draught animals

This could include looking at the horse, the mule, the ox, the dog and the reindeer. The technical developments which allowed the power of the animal to be used more efficiently should be considered. For example, the Roman method of harnessing horses to a cart was not very efficient, while the introduction of surplus bloodstock horses as stage coach teams raised the speed of coaches on British roads from about 1780 onwards.

The history of horse-riding

Horse-riding could be considered as a military and civil form of transport, including the use of the pack horse.

The history of the bicycle

This could range from the first appearance of two-wheeled, man-powered devices, up to the Macmillan Hobbyhorse bicycle.

The history of road-making

Pupils will have researched the Roman methods of road-building. They can compare the political control that these roads allowed the Romans with the attempt to counter Jacobite attacks after the 1715 rebellion. Between 1726 and 1737 General Wade was ordered to supervise construction of many new roads and bridges in Scotland. The government hoped that this would enable troops and guns to be moved quickly in an emergency.

The government subsequently realised that a good system of roads was important in England as well, and the Great North Road was rebuilt. The turnpike system of roads is worth studying because the roads were built using finance raised by turnpike trusts, which charged tolls for travellers using them. Pupils should study the technology that Telford and Macadam used to build and resurface roads.

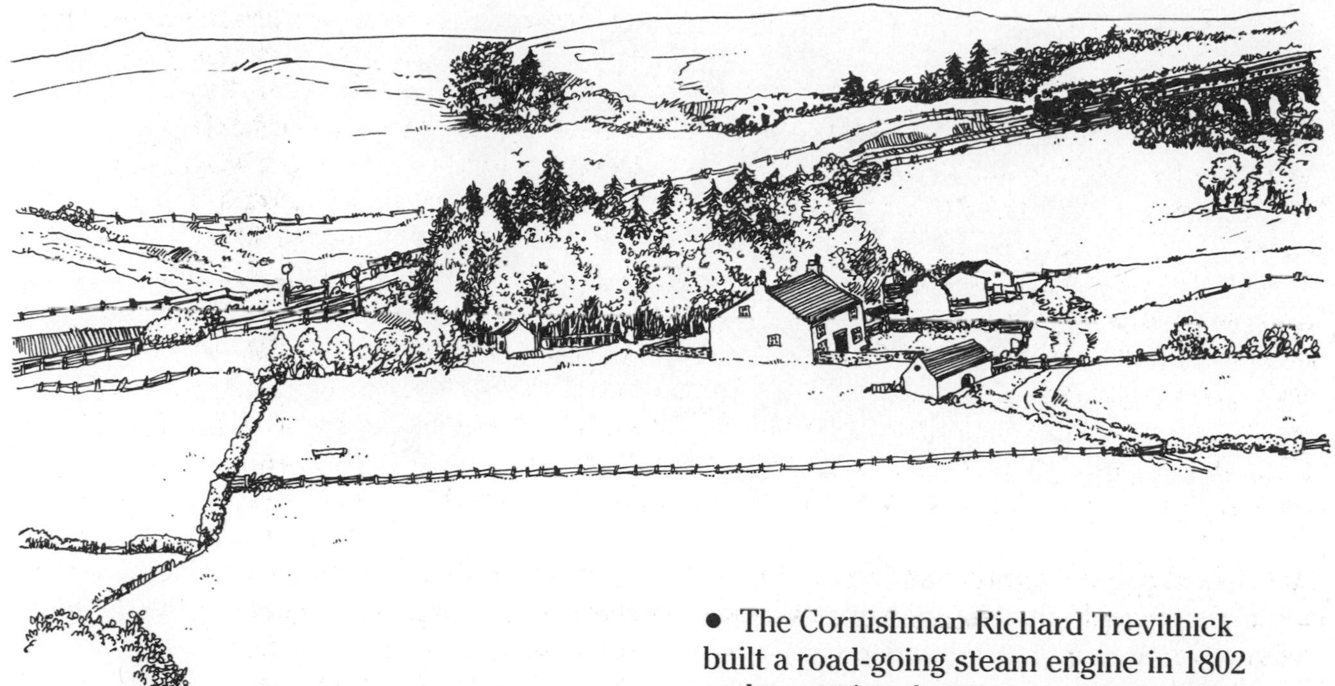

The history of canals

Some work in earlier units will have dealt with Aztec, Roman and Victorian canals. To supplement this work, we suggest that pupils research the canals of China from 219 BC and the canals of medieval Europe. The history of British canals should be researched from the Duke of Bridgewater's canal in 1761 to 1830, when canals started to face competition from the railways.

The history of railway transport

The beginning of the railway age came before the reign of Queen Victoria commenced in 1837. The following information should be included in an investigation of the early development of the railways:

- The Frenchman Nicolas Joseph Cugnot built a road-going steam engine in 1771.
- William Murdoch built a model of James Watt's self-propelling steam engine in 1784, and managed to make it run along the road. Watt was not pleased with his pupil Murdoch, because he did not think boilers were safe enough for mobile steam engines.
- The Cornishman Richard Trevithick built a road-going steam engine in 1802 and an engine that ran on rails in 1803.
- The Stockton to Darlington Railway was opened in 1825.
- The Rainhill trials involving Stephenson's *Rocket* were held in 1829.
- The Liverpool to Manchester Railway opened in 1830.

Purposes of travel

Children could undertake research into what it was like to travel for business, pleasure or because of a religious conviction. This aspect could include research into pilgrimages made by people of all faiths, journeys to escape religious persecution and what the job of stage coach driver or bargee must have been like. Pupils could use information gained from reproductions of paintings and line drawings and from passages in literature such as Chaucer's *Canterbury Tales*.

Architecture

Pupils could look at examples of canal and railway civil engineering and architecture that have survived from 1759 to 1850. It may be possible to get to local aqueducts, viaducts, tunnel entrances, canal locks and railway embankments that survive from this period. Photographs will provide excellent material for visual displays.

Domestic life, families and childhood

We suggest that this unit could be used to pull together all of the history work undertaken at Key Stages 1 and 2. If a school has a well-defined history plan, then pupils could keep a selection of their work related to domestic life from all the other units that they have undertaken. Teachers will need to make sure that these files are passed on from year to year, so that by Y6 pupils have a selection of their history work related to domestic life which they can revise and develop.

Starting points

The National Curriculum requires that this unit covers a period of at least 1000 years. We suggest that pupils consider a period from the Roman invasion of Britain to post-war Britain. The Romans, the Tudors, the Stuarts, the Victorians and Britain from 1930 onwards could be taken as periods on which to focus much of the work, as they will already have been studied in depth. Other information, such as the domestic life of Medieval Britons and Georgian Britons, could be included if teachers felt that new ground needed to be covered. The inclusion of a European and worldwide dimension to this unit will require pupils to supplement their original findings.

To illustrate the work to be undertaken in this unit, draw up a grid divided into historical periods one way, and showing the 13 areas of research we suggest the other way.

These 13 areas of research could be tackled as a series of group investigation topics, so that groups of between two and four pupils spend one lesson undertaking research using reference material, writing up a presentation, creating domestic role-play and making illustrations. A second lesson could be given over to the presentations and mounting some of the work on a frieze. This sequence could be repeated for subsequent lessons with groups taking on further research topics.

The grid, which could be a single large poster or one A4-sized sheet for each group, would then be used to organise which group undertakes which research topic. Pupils could be given some choice in the matter. They could review the work kept in folders from earlier years to see if it could be developed for this unit.

Display the new work in a long frieze corresponding to the planning grid. Some of the work could be summarised and kept in a computer database such as *Grass* or *Our Facts*.

Encourage the children to construct word sketches of characters based on research material. These could be saved on databases and classified by using fields such as PERIOD (Roman, Tudor, Victorian etc), AGE (adult, child), CLASS (royalty, middle class, poor), LOCATION (town dweller, country dweller), STATUS (freeman, serf, slave, servant), LIVING CONDITIONS (castle, cottage, hovel, slum, mansion), WORK (working conditions) and PLAY (leisure opportunities, toys, sports).

The following areas of research could be covered in the topic.

Laws affecting the family

Roman marriages were monogamous, but divorce was easy and common among the wealthy. The lower age limit for marriage was 14 for men and twelve for women. Upon her marriage the bride would have been provided with a dowry and would move from the authority of her father to that of her husband.

A medieval heiress whose father had died would have become the King's ward. He would have sold the right to marry her to the highest bidder, or given her in marriage to a loyal servant.

Victorian property law endowed the husband with his wife's property until the Married Women's Property Act of 1900. Many of the laws studied in CSU3 which ended child labour and restricted women working down pits had an effect on the lives of poor families.

Domestic utensils and appliances

Mass production brought some appliances within the price range of working people. Roman, Tudor, Victorian and twentieth century kitchens and utensils can be compared in wealthy homes and poor homes. Museums are an excellent source of domestic appliances.

Toys and leisure activities

Pupils should consider which class of children would have had leisure time and expensive toys in each historical period. Let the children research the origins of skipping rhymes and children's songs which are still sung today. Home made toys such as hoops and spinning tops could be made and used.

A medieval pastime enjoyed by the children of the gentry was to sit in a circle and compose a verse in turn. Each verse had to rhyme with that of the previous speaker. Ask the children to try this out for themselves.

Authority and gender roles

Throughout the ages it has been common for the children of wealthy families to have little contact with their parents. Slaves and servants were often used to rear such children, with contact between children and their parents, especially their fathers, being formal. Some late medieval parents believed in beating their children once a week to keep them in their place.

The children of the Duke of Somerset (died 1748) were not allowed to sit in his presence. One daughter who did so was cut off without a penny. He may have been an extreme authoritarian, but strict discipline was the order of the day in the 1700s, when corporal punishment for children was a common practice.

In some levels of Victorian society the father expected to be obeyed in all matters. He may have been addressed formally by his wife as Mr —. Victorian mothers were often concerned with running the household, and because large families were common, they may have been constantly pregnant throughout their childbearing years.

Families

Babies were always born at home until hospital maternity wards became common during this century. Mothers in the medieval period would have wrapped their babies tightly in swaddling clothes. Until recently child mortality was high, and it was not uncommon for fifty per cent of the children in wealthy Roman families to die in infancy. The child death rate for most of the nineteenth century was about fifteen per cent.

Large families were encouraged in some phases of Roman history. The Emperor Augustus granted privileges to parents of three or more children. Victorian families were also often very large.

There will be plenty of photographic

evidence of domestic life in Britain since 1930. Some of this could come from the children's older relatives. Many photographs have survived from the late nineteenth century which depict the Victorian family at home and at play. Not all the photographs show wealthy families. Pupils will have to rely on drawings and paintings for evidence about images of family life from earlier periods.

Women's roles

Many mothers in poorer Victorian families had to work, which sometimes meant that their children were neglected. Older brothers and sisters had to look after the younger ones as best they could, and the extreme poverty of such families often resulted in women having to take on low-paid and dangerous work.

Class differences

The difference in lifestyles between the classes should be studied. Some Roman craftsmen and Victorian clerks could afford a slave or a servant. The dependence of various cultures throughout history on low-cost or free labour should be investigated.

Food and festivals

The types of food eaten by the Romans, the formal eating habits of the wealthy and middle classes and Roman festivals will have been studied in CSU1. This work should be revised and expanded to cover holy days throughout history which allowed poor people some opportunity to feast and enjoy themselves.

Interior decor and furniture

The information for this will be derived from contemporary art work and, in the case of the nineteenth and twentieth centuries, photographs. Many textbooks give artist's impressions, which pupils need to realise are based on informed knowledge.

Sanitation

Sanitation and water supply systems throughout the ages could be compared. Pupils will recall the unsanitary conditions of cities in the 1660s which led to the Plague. Were Victorians who lived in slum conditions any better served than middle-class Romans?

Housing

The size and density of poor people's housing could be compared with that of wealthy people during the periods studied. Information in the SSU on houses and places of worship may be useful here. Pioneer housing such as log cabins could be compared to contemporary European housing.

Books

Changing Society in Victorian England, I Doncaster (Longman).
Children in the War, E Merson (Longman).
Clothes in History, C Sewell (Wayland).
Everyday Life in Roman and Anglo Saxon Times, M Quennell and C H Quennell (Batsford and Putnams).
Growing up in the Middle Ages, P Davies (Wayland).
Growing up in the 13th Century, A Duggan (Faber and Faber).
Growing up in Victorian England, S Ferguson (Batsford).
How We Used to Live, F Kelsall (A & C Black).
Puritan Times, A Clarke (Batsford).
Roman Britain, R R Sellman (Methuen).
The Georgian Child, F Gordon Roe (Phoenix House).
The Tudors, C Morris (Batsford).

Supplementary Study Units – Category B

Schools are advised in the History National Curriculum that they should undertake a unit based on local history which should involve an investigation of an important historical issue, relate local developments to national trends and involve the study of one of the following types of local history:

- an aspect of the local community over a long period of time;
- an aspect of the local community during a short period of time or the local community's involvement in a particular event;
- an aspect of the local community which illustrates developments taught in other study units.

If two units are chosen from this category, they should cover different types of local history.

Starting points

Many schools will be fortunate enough to have a particular industry, building, local feature, specialist museum or other resource within easy reach. In our area we could choose such subjects as canals, the car industry, jewellery-making, the Industrial Revolution, nail-making, chain-making, needle-making, the growth of a city and the development of shops as well as investigations based upon local environments around the school.

Before undertaking a local investigation, a large map of the appropriate area will be required for plotting information. The following areas of investigation could be undertaken.

Political developments

- How did the laws relating to common enclosures affect the development of the village in the eighteenth century?
- How did laws relating to public housing and health affect the village in the nineteenth and twentieth centuries?
- Are there any new or current laws proposed that will affect your area? Encourage the children to write to the council to ask this question. Such proposals should be marked on the large map.

Economic, technological and scientific changes

- When did specific factories open and specific agricultural areas become built over?
- When was the railway built?
- When was the canal built?
- Have any cottage industries such as weaving or nail-making existed in your area?
- A local resident could explain how the prosperity of the area has changed, and give views on changes in personal prosperity.
- The local hospital or health centre could be asked to provide a speaker to talk about the changes in medical science.

Social and religious aspects

- On the large map, chart the building and use of places of worship in the local area. Invite speakers from each to tell the pupils about their place of worship.
- Use census material to see how the local population and the jobs available for them have changed.
- Look at ordnance survey maps from 20, 40, 60, 80, 100 and 150 years ago to find out when local buildings were erected, when roads, canals and railways were built and when agricultural land was built over. Pupils could try to confirm this information from other resources, including field work.
- Chart the location and uses of community centres on the large map.

Cultural and aesthetic aspects

- Interview library workers about the use of their resources.
- Visit a collection of paintings and antiques in a local stately home.
- Ask a speaker from the local art society to talk to the pupils about the history of local artists.
- Chart any schools of music and dance in the area on the large map.

Local knowledge

- Invite pupils and their families to share any knowledge they have of local history. Family photographs and newspaper clippings would provide useful information.
- Ask the local newspaper to allow pupils access to archives or microfiches.
- Research the history of the school. Invite ex-pupils to tell the present pupils how the school has changed.

Books and resources

The 'History Around You' series, edited by A Waplington (Oliver and Boyd).
Investigating Census Material, D Lee (Arnold Wheaton).
Additional information can be gained from any local history book, local history societies, library archives and local museums.

Supplementary Study Units – Category C

This unit involves the study of a past non-European society, chosen from:
- Ancient Egypt
- Mesopotamia
- Assyria
- The Indus Valley
- The Maya
- Benin.

This unit should:
- involve study from a variety of perspectives: political; economic, technological and scientific; social; religious; cultural and aesthetic;
- introduce pupils to the uses of archaeological evidence;
- cover key features, including the everyday lives of men and women.

Ancient Egypt

Starting points

Pupils will need to be taught where Egypt is, how far away it is and that many objects and much architecture survives from ancient Egypt.

Make a time strip showing the great length of the Egyptian period compared with the Greek and Roman periods. Britain in the post-Roman period could be placed alongside.

Pupils will need to understand that ancient Egyptian agriculture relied upon the flood waters of the Nile covering the bank with rich mud. Melting snow and heavy rains in the Ethiopian mountains sent muddy floodwater down the Nile causing it to overflow its banks. This was known as the Inundation. As it receded, a layer of fertile mud was deposited along the narrow strips of flat land alongside. During the period of the Inundation there was little for the farmers to do, and many worked on building projects. Once the waters subsided, farmers had to work quickly to break up the heavy soil and then plough it with wooden ploughs pulled by oxen. The seeds were sown by hand and pushed deep into the damp soil by the passage of animals' feet. Irrigation channels were dug between the rows of crops.

The complicated systems of dykes and channels, which were used to retain as much of the flood water as possible, required a great deal of upkeep. The shaduf came into common use sometime during the New Kingdom (1567 BC to 1085 BC). This was a counterbalanced pole with a rope and bucket on one end and a weight on the other, which made the job of pouring water into the irrigation channels much easier.

Farming by the Nile

What you need
Containers, clay, water, filter paper, mustard and cress seeds, seed tray, 1cm dowel, string, yoghurt pots, Plasticine.

What to do
Ask the children to mix clay and water and see how long it stays in suspension when left still. Muddy water could be poured through a filter to imitate the action of the Nile washing mud on to its banks. Seeds of mustard or cress could be planted before the mud hardens.

A seed tray could be used to create a model field dependent upon irrigation channels for water. This could be set as a design task, so that rows of seeds are grown between miniature ditches that carry water to them from a main channel.

Pupils could be asked to construct a working shaduf using only 1cm dowel, string, a yoghurt pot for the bucket and some clay or Plasticine for the weight.

Paper

Many papyrus scrolls have survived, and from them scholars have learnt a great deal about Egyptian life. Papyrus is still made using the ancient method.

Layers of the core from papyrus were laid in alternating layers of vertical and horizontal bands. These were pressed, and the juice stuck the strips together. More and more sheets were stuck on to make a roll. Pupils should note the derivation of the word paper from papyrus.

Making papyrus

What you need

Sugar paper, polythene sheeting, wallpaper paste, brush, wooden board, bricks, paint.

What to do

Ask the children to tear strips of sugar paper approximately 2cm wide and 20cm long, then lay them in vertical strips on top of a sheet of polythene. Ask them to brush wallpaper paste on top of the strips and stick another layer horizontally on top. A third and fourth layer could be added, each time with a coat of paste in between. Finally, place another sheet of polythene on top and weight down the whole arrangement with a board and some bricks. After a week or so the paste should have dried and the strips bonded into one sheet. This sheet can then be used for painting copies of hieroglyphs or tomb paintings.

Friezes

Almost all children's books about ancient Egypt contain pictures of tomb scenes and tomb models. Pupils could be asked to study such pictures, and look at the stylistic features which Egyptian artists used. They should note the sideways stance of the figures, the relative sizes of people of different social status, the geometric border on many friezes and the styling of hair, make-up, clothing and jewellery.

A frieze stretching around as much of the classroom as possible or along a corridor could be used as a focus for all the work about Egypt. The class could be divided into groups, and each group asked to research an aspect of Egyptian life in detail, then draw and paint their findings on the frieze. For example, the group studying tomb building might depict a lot of small figures moving stones, together with much larger overseers and the details of how the stone was moved. Each part of the frieze could include some hieroglyphs related to the scene.

Hieroglyphics

Because the kingdom needed to keep records and accounts, a method of recording was needed, and picture writing was used at first. The next development was to use the same picture consistently to depict an object. Eventually these pictures were used to represent sounds. This kind of writing is called hieroglyphic.

Training to be a scribe was a long, hard process. The twelve years of training started at the age of five for selected boys. Because paper was so expensive, the boys would have practised on bits of stone or broken pottery. They sat cross-legged and dipped reed pens in ink, writing from left to right, right to left or in vertical columns as they desired. The animal head characters pointed to the start of the row. Hieroglyphs continued to be used for sacred inscriptions, even after a simpler form of writing known as hieratic script was used for everyday purposes.

Many textbooks give examples of hieroglyphs, and pupils could attempt these using pencils and felt-tipped pens at first, and then a replica of an Egyptian reed pen made from reed or balsa wood.

Mummies

The Egyptian practice of mummification is directly related to their belief in the afterlife, regulated by a whole range of gods. The elaborate tombs were connected to their belief that they would live on in their tombs as well as in the Field of the Blessed, but to live for eternity after death, it was essential that the body did not decay.

The early Egyptians buried their dead in the sand. The hot, dry sand dried out and preserved the body. When the practice of burying the dead in pits lined with bricks or wood became common, bodies decayed. During the succeeding centuries the art of embalming mummies was perfected.

Teachers may not wish to dwell on the details of mummification, such as the brain being removed through the nostrils, and organs removed and mummified separately. Facts such as the body having toe and fingernails covered in gold and being adorned with previous jewels, being carefully bound in twenty layers, with resin coating every few layers and having magic amulets called shabtis tucked between the layers, might be more appropriate for this age group to study.

Pupils would need to know that a portrait mask was added to enable the soul to recognise the corpse if the preserving process did not work. A collection of spells or instructions for coping with the afterlife was buried with the body. This was known as the book of the dead. A coffin or nest of coffins, each elaborately painted, was used to contain the mummy. Magic spells were painted on the coffins.

Make a mummy

What you need

An old doll, strips of fabric, latex adhesive, Plasticine, paper, felt-tipped pens, papier mâché, petroleum jelly, craft knife, paint, gold spray.

What to do

Wrap an old doll in long strips of fabric, using latex adhesive every few layers as a resin substitute. Make small 'shabtis' from Plasticine and place these inside the layers of material. Give the model mummy a final coat of petroleum jelly, then build a papier mâché coffin around it.

When the papier mâché is dry, cut it with a craft knife around the sides to give a

top and bottom to the model coffin or sarcophagus. Clean away the petroleum jelly and add a face mask made of papier mâché.

The coffin could be painted in an appropriate style, and the model could serve as a centre piece for a model tomb. Ask the children to write a book of the dead, giving their own version of good advice for dealing with the afterlife. Place the book of the dead in the coffin with the mummy. Pupils may like to make an inner and an outer coffin, rather like a nest of Russian dolls. The inner coffin could be sprayed gold in the style of Tutankhamen, and the outer painted with hieroglyphs.

Gods

The Egyptians were a very religious people whose lives were ruled to a large extent by their beliefs. The origins of Egyptian worship may be too complicated for pupils to understand in great detail. In early ancient Egypt there were three schools of religion, one based on a belief that Thoth, the scribe to the gods, had created the world; a second based on the sun god Ra as creator; and a third based on the belief that Ptah was all-powerful. The worship of Ra came to dominate all Egypt, partly due to the priests of Ra maintaining that Horus, the *alter ego* of every Egyptian ruler, was a personification of Ra. Thus the worship of Ra was firmly linked to the rule of the pharaohs.

The pharaohs were worshipped as gods, and were perceived as having a duty to liaise between gods and men. They were believed to be the sons of Ra, the sun god, and when they died they became Osiris, the god of the underworld.

The Egyptians believed that after they had died their soul was judged by the gods. The trial took place before Osiris and his wife, Isis, and Anubis weighed the heart of the dead man against a feather. Thoth wrote down the verdict of the court.

Pupils could make an illustrated chart to show which gods had which power and responsibility. They could learn about the gods through stories which were told in ancient Egypt.

Ask the children to research the story of Isis and Osiris and to retell it as an Egyptian-style frieze.

Tomb building

Tombs were built in the desert where the land was of no use for farming. In early times bodies were wrapped in reed mats and buried in a hole in the ground, but over the years graves became more complex, especially those of the rich and powerful. They were lined with boards or bricks and covered with a mound faced with bricks. These graves with rectangular covers are called mastabas. Soon it was thought that even an elaborate mastaba was not grand enough for a king.

The mastaba of King Zoser (c. 2660 BC) at Sakkara was enlarged several times, and ended up as a six-step pyramid. The next architectural development was the smooth sided pyramid. This was a stepped construction like King Zoser's mastaba, but the outside was smoothed off. Perfect symmetry was achieved in the building of the Great Pyramid of Cheops at Giza.

Pupils will need to know that the method of building the pyramids is still not fully understood. Most theories suggest that massive earth ramps were used, and the stones pulled up on rollers. Some theories favour a straight ramp while others favour a ramp that spiralled upwards.

Mastabas and pyramids

What you need

Heavy block, tray of sand, dowel, string, pulley, weights, card, map of Egypt, cardboard box, paint, sugar paper, model-making equipment.

What to do

Ask the children to devise a fair test to see how much effort is needed to move a heavy block on sand and how much effort is needed to move the same block on a series of rollers. A length of string passing over a pulley attached to the edge of a table and tied to a container with a range

of weights would be one way of testing the effort required.

Let the children construct pyramids out of card. These could be painted and set in a large tray of sand to form the basis of a model.

Pupils could mark on a map of Egypt the location of the tombs of each dynasty.

Show the children how to make a model tomb by cutting the flaps off a large cardboard box and laying it on its side. The inside could then be painted to show the burial chamber of a pharaoh. Cut sugar paper to size and paint it like a tomb frieze before sticking it like wallpaper to the inside of the box. A model mummy could be placed inside with tiny Plasticine figures and balsa-wood model furniture, based on pictures of the inside of royal tombs.

Pharaohs and laws

Pharaohs were not idle rulers, but were expected to be law-givers, administrators, priests and skilled warriors. It was their duty to oversee the irrigation system and to defend the country against attack. Only a pharaoh could confirm a death sentence or grant mercy. The royal line was passed down through the queen, and her eldest surviving son was the heir. Because of the high mortality rate all royal princes were trained to be pharaoh. A pharaoh could only marry his sister, as she would also be descended directly from the gods.

Pupils could read well known Bible stories which refer to pharaohs, such as the story of Joseph and his coat of many colours and the flight of the Children of Israel from Egypt led by Moses.

Land transport

Although most transport was undertaken by boats on the Nile, war chariots have been found in tombs. These were light, strong and very manoeuvrable.

Leisure

Many tomb paintings show scenes of men hunting fish and fowl on the Nile. Wrestling and swimming were popular sports, as was a form of fencing using sticks. Gaming boards have been found in tombs. The rules are lost, but the games were probably similar to chess or draughts.

Children's toys have also been found in tombs, such as a wooden horse on wheels and a lion that snapped its jaws. It is thought that boys and girls did not play together.

Mesopotamia

Starting points

The name Mesopotamia means 'land between two rivers', and it is the land between the rivers Tigris and Euphrates with which this unit is concerned. This unit could cover a period from 10,000 BC to the conquest by Alexander the Great in 334 BC. This long period would take in the very early history of the region.

The change of Stone Age people from hunter-gatherers to settled farmers took place in the area about 12,000 years ago. There was a highly developed civilisation in Mesopotamia more than 6,000 years ago. The Sumerians, Babylonians, Assyrians and Persians were the dominant forces at different times, and their cultures influenced the Greek and Roman civilisations that followed them.

It would be unrealistic to expect a class to cover this huge time-span, and teachers may wish to choose just one civilisation that developed in Mesopotamia. The technique of splitting the class into four groups, each studying one aspect of the period, should be considered if teachers feel that they want to cover more than one civilisation. In that case, the discussion and reporting back to the class will be a valuable way of developing the skills of speaking and listening. We suggest that the groups research one of the following civilisations: the Sumerians, the Babylonians, The Assyrians and the Persians.

Because under the History National Curriculum the Assyrians can be studied as a unit in their own right, details of this period are given in a separate section on page 145.

You could organise a class quiz, in which each group makes a verbal as well as a written and drawn presentation to the class, and draws up a set of 30 questions about their work. Assume the role of quiz-mistress/master and ask each group questions about the other teams' work.

A time-line will be essential to support the period covered.

Political aspects

Historians surmise that great co-operation would have been needed to irrigate the dry land and to control the flood waters of the Tigris and Euphrates. Leaders would have been necessary, to direct these co-operative endeavours. It would be a natural development for a society that accepted leaders of local projects to accept leaders with more and more authority, and eventually to accept kings as rulers. By 4,000 BC Mesopotamia comprised a peasant economy whose farming produce supported large villages and even small towns. This progress continued in Mesopotamia, and cities grew up whose citizens were proud of their culture, their writing, their architecture and their mathematics.

The Sumerians became a dominant civilisation in the Mesopotamian area from about 3,500 BC. Their main city was Ur, which is mentioned in the Old Testament as the city of Abraham (Genesis 11.31).

The centre of the Babylonian civilisation was the city of Babylon. This civilisation became important in 2,000 BC when Semitic Amorites overcame the Sumerians and settled along the Euphrates.

The King and his officials were the rulers of Babylonian society. The King who brought Babylonian society to a peak was Hammurabi (from about 1,800 BC to 1,760 BC). Under him the old Sumerian laws were collated and turned into an elaborate and just legal system.

The Assyrian Babylonian civilisations overlapped, with Babylon being under Assyrian domination for long periods. After the Chaldeans had defeated the Assyrians in 612 BC, Nebuchadrezza II (604–562 BC) came to power. This is described in the Book of Judith in the Apocrypha. He extended his empire from the Persian Gulf to the Mediterranean and Egypt. It was Nebuchadrezza II who conquered the Hebrews and brought them back as captives to Babylon (2 Kings 1.7–9). Here they would have seen the very tall ziggurat he had built for his queen, which was the Tower of Babel in the Old Testament (Babylon in Hebrew is Babel). They would also have seen the ziggurat planted with trees and bushes along its terraces. This was one of the wonders of the ancient world, the Hanging Gardens of Babylon.

The Persians had been allies of the Chaldeans at the time of the capture of Nineveh in 612 BC. After the death of Nebuchadrezza II they captured Babylon, and the rise of the Persian empire began. Cyrus the Great (550–529 BC) not only conquered the Babylonians and their neighbours the Medes, but he marched into Asia Minor, defeated Croesus, King of the Lydians, conquered the Greek cities on the Mediterranean coast and reached as far east as India.

He is remembered in the Old Testament as the King who allowed the Hebrews to return to Jerusalem (2 Chronicles 36.22 and Ezra 1.1–4). This seems to have been typical of his tolerant attitude to different religious beliefs and customs.

Cyrus was succeeded by his son Cambyses, who conquered Egypt. Cambyses was succeeded by Darius I (522–486 BC) who was a superb administrator of the empire. Pupils will be familiar or will become familiar with King Darius when they cover CSU5, the Ancient Greeks. In 490 BC, he dispatched a force which was beaten at the famous battle of Marathon. Darius' successor Xerxes sent a force which won the land battle at the Pass of Thermopylae. This was the battle in which the Spartan soldiers fought to the last man.

The Persian empire lasted until Alexander the Great overthrew it in 334.

Economic history

The Sumerian economy was based on agriculture.

The Babylonians had no coinage as such, and barter was used for the trading of goods. A standard weight existed for metal. This was known as the talent and weighed 60 pounds. Rich merchants and priests acted as money lenders or credit arrangers, which assisted trade.

Organise role-play to help the children understand the concept of barter. Toy animals, old clothes and imitation food could be used to represent the goods exchanged.

The Persians divided the empire into provinces, each under a governor called a satrap. They collected taxes and administered justice. Uniform coinage was used throughout the empire.

Technological developments

Early Sumerian houses were huts built from bundles of reeds. Let the children use long art straws to make a replica of a hut, following the process illustrated in Figures 1 to 3.

Later, sun-baked mud bricks came into common use. This was possible because of the dry climate, but meant that buildings did not last longer than a lifetime. Because of a shortage of stone, even important buildings like temples were built in this way. They were often built on a raised mound to protect them from floods.

The Babylonians also used dry mud bricks for building, but richer people used kiln-baked bricks for their houses.

Let the children try to make sun-dried bricks from clay, and then devise and conduct fair tests to compare the strength of a kiln-baked brick to a sun-dried one.

The Persians continued to build temples in the same style, but they used stone rather than brick. They built many long roads, some more than 1,500 miles long, which aided trade and troop movements.

In the early period Sumerians would have ploughed with stone ploughs and cut their crops with clay sickles. As they acquired metal-working skills they developed metal ploughs. They used a method of sowing and ploughing at the same time. A funnel filled with seed fed the seed into the furrow.

The Sumerians discovered how to use the wheel, which was made from solid wood at first.

Pupils could attempt to make and use a clay sickle if there are firing facilities available. We imagine that a stone would constantly be needed to sharpen the cutting edge.

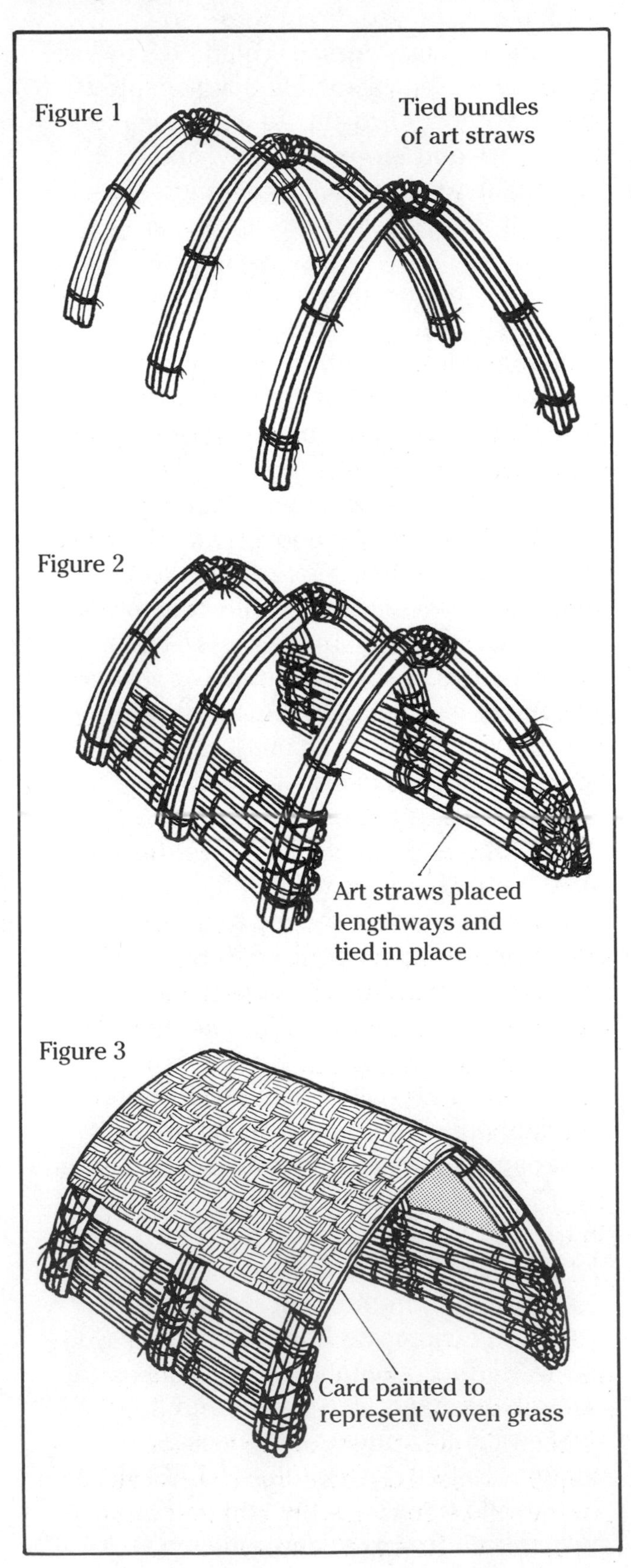

Social aspects

The Sumerians were ruled by kings who took advice from priests and councils. There was a degree of democracy as well. Free adult males decided when to make peace or war.

The upper class of Babylonian society was made up of the King and his officials, rich merchants and priests. A lower order was made up from workers and farmers.

Ask the children to research into the differences between the lifestyles of these two social classes.

Religious beliefs

The most powerful Sumerian god was Anu, who represented authority. Other gods were worshipped such as Inanna, goddess of love and war. The Sumerians believed that they had a duty to feed and shelter their gods. The temples were a home for the gods to live in. They were built in stages, each stage smaller than the one beneath it. The mounds of these temples still exist.

The Sumerians believed that they were responsible for their own fortune and would pray to the gods for intervention or relief.

Babylonian priests tried to foretell the future by examining the offal of slaughtered animals. The priests were skilled in astronomy and believed that the gods revealed messages to them in the movements of the stars and planets. The Babylonian religion held that when people died they descended to a cave where they lived a gloomy existence. This belief made them want to live as happy a life as possible on the earth. Their chief god was Marduk.

There are opportunities for art work and dance drama based on interpretations of this gloomy cave.

The religious beliefs of the Persian people changed as the empire grew and prospered. At first they worshipped many gods, but in the sixth century BC a religious leader, Zoroaster, questioned why the strongest of the gods did not overcome the weaker gods, thus resulting in the dominance of one god. He believed that there was one supreme god, Ahura Mazda, who constantly fought against evil.

Cultural and aesthetic life

The invention of writing is credited to the Sumerians. At first their script was a collection of pictures, but the pictures later came to represent words and then syllables. The wedge-shaped end of a reed was pressed into soft clay to make this cuneiform writing.

Rich Sumerian boys would have been sent to school to study reading, writing, mathematics and the stars and planets.

This would be one area that pupils may study in the supplementary unit on writing and printing. Care will need to be taken so that work is not duplicated.

Babylonian literature contains many epic poems about real or imaginary heroes. The epic of Gilgamesh is the best known of these.

The Persians placed great emphasis on their children learning to ride, shoot and tell the truth.

The Babylonians were highly skilled weavers of linen and wool, skilled furniture makers, jewellers and potters. Although they were skilled sculptors, their best work was done in miniature.

Pupils should examine illustrations showing Sumerian statuettes, gold ornaments and jewellery, cylinder seals and pottery.

Pupils could attempt to copy miniature statuettes in clay or Plasticine.

Books

Ancient Mesopotamia and Persia, C A Robinson (Edmund Ward).
Early Mesopotamia and Iran, M E L Mallowan (Hudson).
Everyday Life in Babylon and Assyria, H W F Saggs (Batsford Putnam).
The Assyrians, R J Unstead (Ward Lock).
They Lived Like This in Ancient Mesopotamia, E Warboys (Parrish).

Assyria

Starting point

From about 3000 BC a people who became known as Assyrians settled and defended an area called Assur, straddling the River Tigris. This is now in the modern state of Iraq.

The Assyrians had to fight to hold on to this land, as the peoples of Akkad and Ur in the south and the Hittites and Mitanni to the north-west were hostile to them. During the period from 3000 BC to 612 BC when the fall of the city of Nineveh marked the end of the Assyrian Empire, a huge area stretching from the Mediterranean Sea to the Caspian Sea and from the Persian Gulf to the Red Sea had been captured by the Assyrians.

This was the largest empire in the world at the time. The rise and fall of this empire can be linked to six Assyrian kings who were willing and able to wage war.

We suggest that the class is divided into six groups, each of which researches the life, times and achievements of a particular king. Their findings could be presented as a six-panelled frieze.

Ashurnasirpal II (883–859 BC)

Ashurnasirpal had many temples and palaces built, and decorated them with wall sculptures showing court and battle scenes. He defeated tribes to the north and east, the Babylonians in the south and the Arameans in the west. His chief city was Nimrud, known as Calah in the Bible. A stone carving showing King Ashurnasirpal has survived from Nimrud.

Shalmaneser III (858–824 BC)

Ashurnasirpal's son Shalmaneser carried on his father's policy of expansionism. He claimed that he defeated a coalition of Syrian and Palestinian forces comprising 2000 chariots and 10,000 infantry. He subjugated Palestine and made King Jehu pay homage, according to Assyrian records (the Black Obelisk at Nimrud). The city of Damascus was so strongly defended, however, that Shalmaneser had to withdraw. Towards the end of his reign, there was a rebellion when it is thought that the great cities of Assyria and Babylon revolted against the King. The revolt was put down, and Shalmaneser was succeeded by his heir, Shamshi-Adad V (823–811 BC).

Tiglath-Pileser III (745–727 BC)

The entire Assyrian royal family was murdered in 746 BC during a revolt in the capital city of Calah. The next king was Tiglath-Pileser who rebuilt and reformed the army into a powerful permanent force. He did not intend to invade other territories just for plunder and tribute, but to occupy them. He restarted the policy of expansionism and captured Babylon in the south, some Syrian kingdoms in the west, including Damascus, and Uratu in the north. Tiglath-Pileser III is remembered for his extensive administrative reforms.

Sargon II (722–705 BC)

Sargon II continued the expansion of the empire until it covered most of western Asia and included 70 provinces. He built a new city called Sharrukin to the north of Nineveh. A vast new palace was built in this new city. It is thought that Sargon II had a liking for poetry, because many of his records are written in a verse form.

Sennacherib (704–681 BC)

Sennacherib continued to enlarge the empire, capturing the Phoenician Mediterranean ports and reaching the borders of Egypt. His siege of Lachish in Palestine is described in Kings and Isaiah in the Old Testament, as well as the saving of Jerusalem by a heaven-sent plague on the Assyrian army. The city of Babylon rebelled again during Sennacherib's reign, and he flattened the city. It was rebuilt because of its commercial importance.

Sennacherib undertook new building in Nineveh rather than Sharrukin, and had walls, palaces, temples and gardens built. The aqueduct bringing water to these gardens (the Jerwan Aqueduct) was the first of its kind. Tribute flowed into Nineveh along the new roads from the Empire, which was ruled with an iron hand by King Sennacherib.

Ashurbanipal (669–631 BC)

Ashurbanipal advanced into Egypt as far as Thebes, which was the capital at the time. It had become policy to bequeath Assyria to one of the King's sons and Babylonia to another. Ashurbanipal became involved in a civil war against his brother which temporarily weakened the empire, but when he captured Babylon in 648 BC, the empire seemed to recover.

Ashurbanipal was a scholar as well as a soldier. He built up a library of thousands of clay tablets recording the history, scientific knowledge and literature of his time. He celebrated his success in battle with stone carvings on the walls of his palaces.

The fall of the empire

Little is known about the period following Ashurbanipal's reign. It is known that, surprisingly, the Egyptians became allied with the Assyrians against the Medes and Chaldeans, but their support came too late. The Assyrians had become hated for their greed and their cruelty to the subjugated people. Peasants who would rather be tending their fields were pressed into the army, as were thousands of foreign troops. This seriously weakened the army. The Assyrians were threatened by Medes and Persians from the north-east and by the Chaldeans from the south-east. In 616 BC Babylon was captured by the Chaldeans, and in 614 BC Assur was captured by the Medes. The Medes and the Chaldeans combined to capture Nineveh in 612 BC.

Technological developments

A great deal of Assyrian technology was devoted to military matters. Heavily-armed infantry used iron spears and swords as well as shields. Light infantry used bows and arrows and slingshots. The archers

were famous for their accuracy, and the slingers could hurl heavy stones a long way. Horse-drawn chariots were also used. Sappers were trained to dig under city walls, and battering rams were used to complete the demolition. The Assyrians' siege machines included wheeled platforms to roll against the walls.

Ask the children to design and build working models of siege machines and to experiment with slingshot using lumps of Plasticine as missiles. This should be done under close adult supervision.

Scientific achievements

The Assyrians seem to have taken over ideas from the peoples they conquered, rather than making scientific discoveries themselves. They would have known about casting techniques, soldering, riveting and annealing in metal work. They would have known how to produce coloured glassware, but glass-blowing was unknown at this time.

Social aspects

The lives of ordinary people have to be surmised, because written records relate only to deeds of state and people of high office.

An Assyrian official might have come from a family which had served the kings for generations. The family land would be granted back to the family by the king each time the owner died, provided that substantial payments were made to the king.

The family might have owned a communal burial ground. Rituals respecting the dead would have been carried out, as would magic rituals for other features of family life such as birth. A child born to that family, whose father may or may not have been monogamous, would have been suckled for two years. If the child was male he would have been encouraged to learn to ride and shoot a bow. At the age of about ten he would have been taught to write using the cuneiform script.

Religious beliefs

As one might expect, the most important Assyrian god, Ashur, was a cruel and warlike figure. There were thousands of other gods, but ordinary people would not have worshipped all of them. Five or six would have been chosen to protect the worshippers from demons, witchcraft and bad luck.

Because the records were written by priestly scribes they tell us more about the official religion than about the religion of ordinary people. The priests watched the stars, looking for eclipses which were believed to be messages from the gods.

Priests would also have given advice about when to undertake important missions.

The New Year festival was the principal religious feast of the year.

Cultural and aesthetic life

We know that the Assyrians were a cruel race who ruled by terror, torture and destruction, because they boasted about it in the written records.

The Assyrians had a good supply of stone to use for building and carving. They recorded many of their deeds on stone reliefs, some of which can be seen in the British Museum.

Let the children make facsimiles of the sculptured reliefs by cutting figures out of large polystyrene tiles with a hot wire cutter, sticking the figures on to flat tiles and assembling the set of tiles into a frieze. Light grey water-based paint mixed with PVA adhesive could be painted over the whole frieze to give a stone-like colouring.

Encourage the children to find out more about Assyrian clothing, hairstyles, architecture and artefacts by examining pictures of the carved stone friezes or bronze plaques.

The Assyrians used cuneiform writing, in which symbols were shaped by pressing the end of a reed or stylus into a tablet of soft clay. The symbols could stand for either a whole word (an ideogram), a syllable or a letter. Some Assyrian texts used a combination of these, and signs could have a different meaning according to their position in a word.

The Assyrian number system also used the impressed reed mark. It was based on the Sumerian number systems which uses bases of 60 and 100. These seem to have been used in conjunction without any more confusion than we have experienced using metric and imperial measurements for different purposes. There was no zero in the system. Let the children try out simple calculations using the Assyrian number system as in Figure 1.

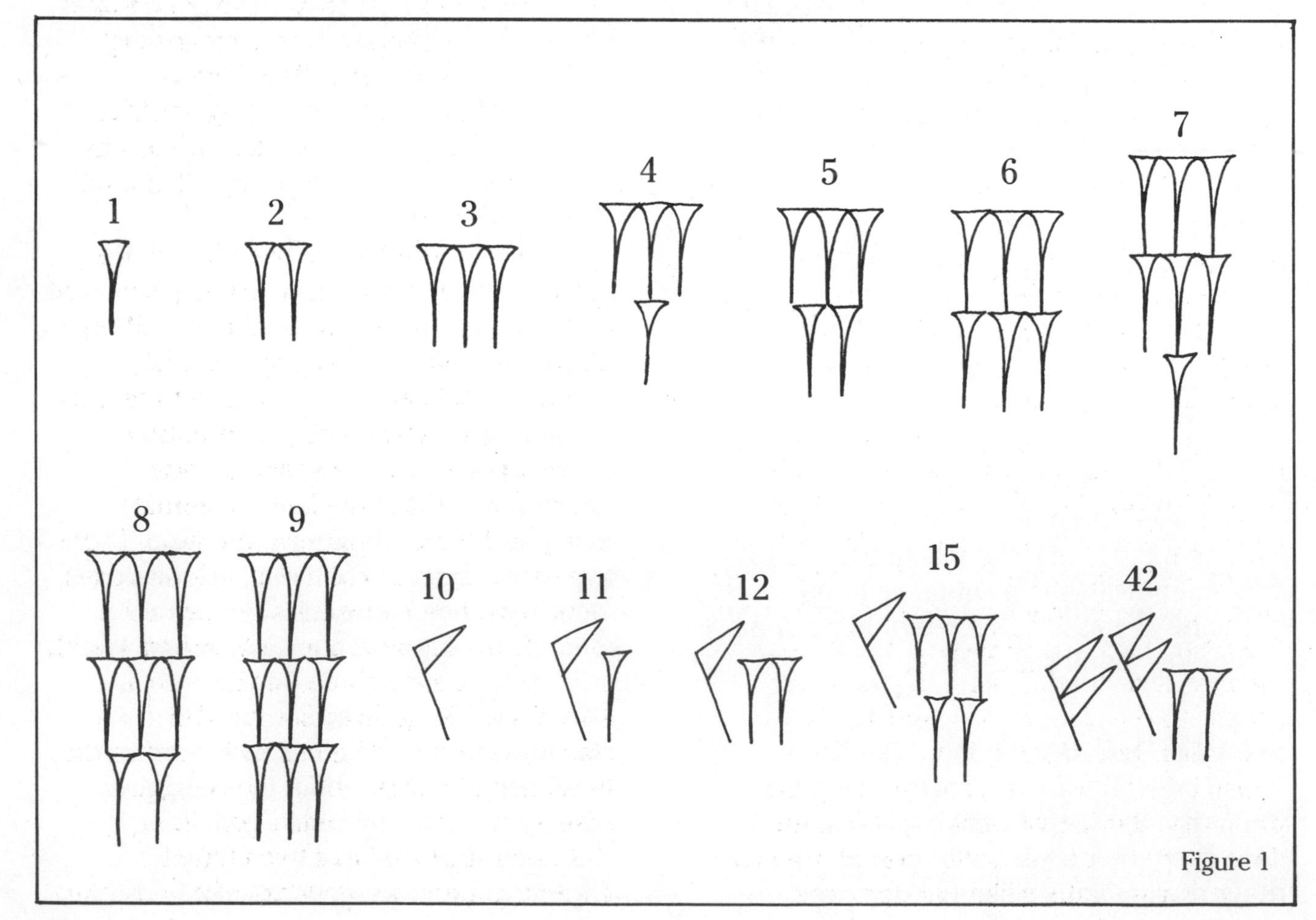

Figure 1

The Indus valley

Teachers should be aware that, at the time of writing, little is available in the way of pupils' resource books on this subject, which will make research difficult for children.

Starting points

The Rivers Indus and Ravi flow from the mountains out to the sea, through a valley which is part of modern Pakistan and India. Let the children try to locate the Indus valley on a modern map.

Over 4,000 years ago, in about 2500 BC, the Indus valley was the home of a great and mighty civilisation. Mystery surrounds the origins of the people and of the two important cities of Harappa and Mohenjo-daro. Archaeologists have dug on the sites of the cities, and other historians have tried to trace their growth, but these attempts have not been successful. The few written remains of the Indus people are in a language that, as yet, no one has been able to decipher. It is difficult to find out how the cities were ruled and what gods the people worshipped. There are, however, clues which have helped archaeologists to build up some kind of picture of what life might have been like.

Harappa and Mohenjo-daro were both built in the same way. They had wide straight streets with drains running alongside them. Buildings were constructed of brick, and the most important ones, such as the rulers' palaces, were built on high mounds overlooking the cities. Each city had a huge granary where barley and wheat were stored. These granaries were built on high platforms near the river. This was to protect them from the frequent flooding and to give them access to the river for transport. The granaries were wood and brick constructions with air vents to keep the grain dry. Studies of remains at Mohenjo-daro show that there were special areas in the granaries rather like parking bays, where farmers could back up their carts to unload the wheat and barley brought in from their fields around the city. It is likely that the grain was stored like this in good summers so that there would be sufficient grain for everyone when the crops failed. It is possible, on the other hand, that the grain formed taxes or gifts to kings or priests.

Archaeologists have discovered over 60 Indian cities built at the same time as Harappa and Mohenjo-daro. These are built on the same pattern with the same wide streets. The similarity of the writing and the weights and measures used in all these cities suggest that they might have been ruled by one king. One of the cities, Lothal, seems to have been a port, and archaeologists found there the remains of a warehouse which burned down thousands of years ago. Many pieces of clay were found in the ruins, and one theory is that these were pressed over the ropes which tied up bundles of goods. The merchants may have stamped their seals on top of the clay. Some of these seals have been found far away in Sumerian cities, suggesting trade with these cities. This idea is reinforced by Sumerian writing about a land they refer to as Melukka, which was reached by a long sea journey. That land could have been India.

The seals which have been found are very decorative, with lifelike images carved on them and names or messages written on top in the Indus language. Danish archaeologists are currently attempting to decipher this script using a computer.

The animals on the seals provide information about the kind of animals living in the Indus valley at the time. There were long-nosed crocodiles, rhinoceroses, elephants, tigers and bulls. Some of the animals depicted on the seals are mythical, such as a strange three-headed beast. These may be gods or spirits. The seals also show a horned goddess lurking in the branches of a tree, and a cross-legged figure similar to the Hindu god Shiva.

Several statues have been found depicting a mother goddess who may have been thought to protect women and children. The absence of huge statues of gods and kings suggests that, if these ever existed, they were probably carved in wood and have consequently rotted away. Small beautifully carved statues of metal and stone have been found. One particularly fine example depicts a dancing girl. Items of jewellery have been found which suggest that rich women wore necklaces, bracelets, earrings and rings of gold, jade, agate, onyx and other stones. Some beads were carved in the shape of tiny monkeys and squirrels. Some statues show men wearing jewellery. Indus craftsmen also made a variety of interesting toys such as clay whistles shaped like birds and monkeys. Toy carts had movable wheels, and a clay cow has been found with a movable head which bobbed up and down when a string was pulled. Dice and figurines rather like chess pieces have also been found.

Pupils could tackle a study of the Indus valley by attempting drawings of the buildings and considering how they were used. They could model some merchants' clay seals, and reconstruct some Indus Valley toys in clay and wood. They could also make models of the jewellery using scrap material. Pupils could try to seal string-tied parcels using clay tablets.

The decline of the Indus civilisation

In about 1500 BC invaders destroyed Mohenjo-daro and Harappa as well as other Indus towns. Skeletons showing signs of sword cuts have been found in rooms. It was probably the Aryans who settled in India who had attacked the cities of the Indus.

It is generally believed that the cities were decaying before the invaders attacked them. The decline may have been brought on by the cutting down of trees along the rivers for building and fuel. This may have made the floods more severe, which could have rendered the soil infertile. It must be said that the growth and decline of the ancient civilisation in the Indus valley still remains a mystery.

The cutting down of the trees could be compared to present day 'slash and burn' deforestation in the Amazon.

Books

Discovering the Ancient Past, M Gibson (Macdonald Educational).

The Maya

This unit could be chosen to complement and extend the work undertaken in Core Study Unit 6, Exploration and Encounters 1450 to 1550. Once that unit has been completed, pupils will have studied the Aztec way of life and the impact of the Spanish Conquistadores upon them. Pupils will also study the Ancient Greeks at some point, and the Mayan city states provide an interesting parallel.

On the other hand, schools may feel that within the four years of Key Stage 2 there is not enough time to study two American Indian cultures at the expense of another historic culture from a different part of the world.

If this unit is selected, we suggest that schools plan to retain some of the work on the Aztecs from CSU6. Pupils could then compare the Aztec and Maya cultures. A chart could be displayed to illustrate the differences and similarities.

Starting points

From about 2000 BC, the Maya lived and developed their civilisation in the part of Central America now known as Guatemala, Belize and the South Mexican Yucatan Peninsula. They became skilled farmers and builders, constructing flat-topped pyramids and working out complex calendars. Their cities became city states with the Halach Uinic, a godlike figure, at the head. He would have had a council of state to advise him.

Although Mayan soldiers seem to have been well-trained and disciplined, there was probably no standing army as such. Battles ended at night-time, when each side retired to eat. The soldiers tended to pack up and go home when they were needed to work on the land. The Mexicans' use of the bow and of thrown spears against the Maya decreased the length of time spent fighting hand to hand. The Maya responded by making quilted armour for protection.

In about AD 900 the Maya abandoned their cities in the Guatemalan jungles and migrated to the flat Yucatan Peninsula. At this point the great civilisation seems to have declined. No one knows for sure why this happened, but one possibility is that the soil became exhausted through the over-use of 'slash and burn' methods of agriculture. After this decline the city states of the Yucatan engaged in ceaseless war. The Spanish commander Martin de Ursaa captured Tayasaal in 1697 and ended centuries of Mayan independence.

Pupils could write an account of the first sighting of the Spaniards by the Maya.

Economic aspects

The Maya were great traders. They had a well-constructed system of roads and also used river transport. They traded with the Mexicans in the north-west and the Panamanians in the south. All goods had to be carried, as they had no wheeled vehicles or beasts of burden. Pupils could conduct an experiment to see how long it takes to carry heavy sacks on their backs over 100m and how long it takes to move the same load over 100m using a wheeled trolley.

Cocoa beans may have been used as a form of currency. Feathers, jade, copal (hard resin used as incense) and cocoa beans were imported and salt, dried fish, animal skins, sea shells and honey were exported. Slaves were also traded.

Technological and scientific developments

The Maya calendar was as accurate as the modern calendar, using 365 days (a *haab*). However, it was divided into 18 months (*uinals*) of 20 days (*kins*) each. The five days left over were an unlucky period called the *uayeb*. The Maya used two other ways of reckoning the years. A sacred 260-day calendar (*tzolkin*) was used to calculate religious feast-days, and the Maya also counted back every day to the beginning of their history, which seems to have been in about 3111 BC by Mayan calculations.

The Maya had a Stone Age culture. They did not know how to make bronze, although copper and gold artefacts were imported. This makes the building of the huge stone pyramids even more impressive. Weapons were made of stone, often set into wooden handles. The Maya never used the wheel to any great purpose, neither did they discover how to make a true arch in architecture.

The Maya system of counting used base 20, and they had a sign for zero (see Figure 1). Let the children undertake calculations using base 20.

The hunting tools of the Maya were very primitive. Dogs, clubs, blow-pipes and snares were the only aids up to AD 1000, when bows and arrows were introduced from Mexico. Ask the children to design protective bodywear based on known Mayan materials.

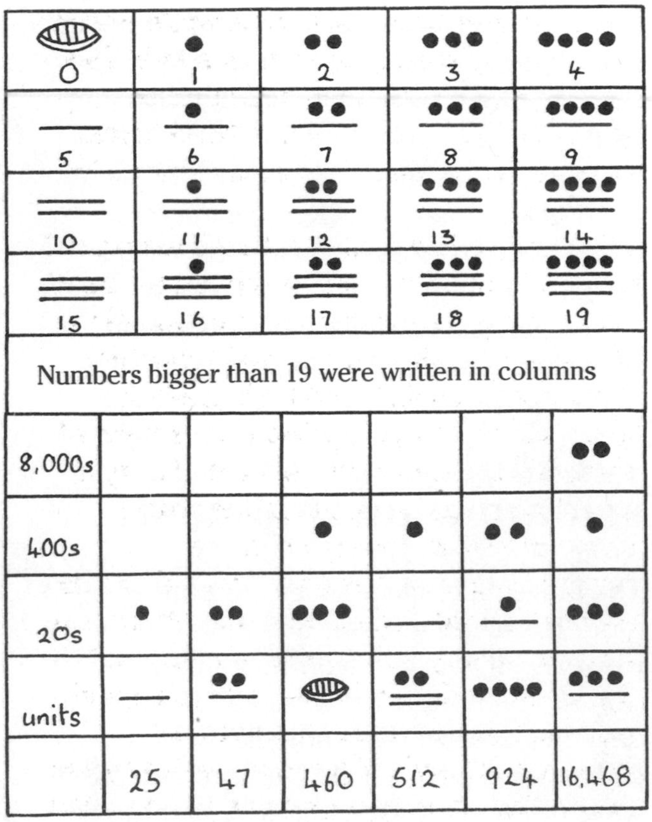

0	1	2	3	4
5	6	7	8	9
10	11	12	13	14
15	16	17	18	19

Numbers bigger than 19 were written in columns

8,000s						
400s						
20s						
units						
	25	47	460	512	924	16,468

Figure 1

Social aspects

The Maya were able to grow several crops. Maize was the most common, and formed their staple diet. Beans, sweet potatoes and squashes were grown for food, and cotton and sisal were grown for making cloth or for trading.

The Mayan method of slashing and burning new areas for farming each season can be contrasted to the Aztec floating gardens. It can also be related to the present methods of clearing rain forest for cattle grazing in South America.

The Maya supplemented their edible crops with meat which they hunted, such as venison, large rodents called agouti, armadillos, wild pigs and tapirs. Turtles and iguanas were prized as delicacies. The Maya kept few domestic animals, which meant that they had to clear land by their own efforts. Dogs were kept and used in hunting, and a hairless breed of dog was reared for eating. Ducks and turkeys were also domesticated.

Fish were caught for food, sometimes by the unusual method of damming a river and placing drugs in the water so that the fish floated to the surface.

The most common item of food was the tortilla, a flat, savoury pancake made from maize. These were cooked on a platform of clay supported over a fire by stones. Let the children try to make these by pounding some sweetcorn kernels in a bowl so that they form a dough. A large frying pan or wok would have to substitute for the clay platform.

The Maya used honey for sweetening food and for making a mead-like drink. Many homes would have a hollowed out tree trunk outside in which to keep bees. The Maya were fortunate in having a variety of bee that was stingless.

A popular drink was cocoa, which was not the milky drink that we know but a concentrated liquid with spices added. Visitor to Cadbury's World in Bournville, Birmingham, are given a sample of this spicy drink.

There would have been little privacy in

the home of the poorer Maya. The houses were built of local materials such as wood, woven withies or stone. Houses were often built on a low platform, and the high pitched roofs were thatched with palm or grass. There would have been no doors and the house would have been divided by a screen into a kitchen and sleeping quarters. It is thought that the Maya were used to a community life and so stealing from open homes was rare.

The Maya were not ruled as one nation but as independent city states. The ruler of each state was the Halach Uinich or true man. This office was hereditary.

Although towns were not built on a mathematical plan, the temple would be in the centre with the priests living nearest to it. The lower the social status of the Maya, the further away from the centre they lived.

The same distinction applied to clothing. The higher the social rank, the more elaborate the clothing and accessories. Some historians believe that the wearing of cotton was reserved for the priests and nobility. Peasants would have worn simple clothing. Men wore loincloths while women wore a simple dress known as a kub. This was made from a folded and stitched length of cloth with arm and head holes. Both men and women wore a cloak called a manta.

Let the children cut out two-dimensional figures from thick card, and paint the head, arms and legs. Ask them to find out about the style of body-painting and tattooing the Maya practised, and then dress the figures in the Maya fashion from scraps of material. If groups were allocated a style based on social status then the whole range of Mayan society could be represented. The class would need to make a priest, a lord and his wife, an official and his wife, a very rich couple, a respected merchant and his wife and a peasant and his wife. Pupils would also need to research the style of jewellery worn by the Maya. The set of figures could be mounted on a frieze showing a Mayan temple and other buildings as a background.

Religious beliefs

The Maya believed that the afterlife was made up of 22 different horizontal layers. Thirteen were above the earth and nine below the earth. Although these corresponded to heaven and hell, Mayan souls were allocated a layer of the afterlife according to social status rather than because they led a good or bad life. Pupils could try to represent this concept diagrammatically.

The supreme god was Hunab Ku, but he was so remote that he was seldom worshipped. Itzamna, his son, was the god of night and day. He is often depicted as an old man in a lizard's body. As with other ancient civilisations, each aspect of nature had its own god. The Mayan peasants would worship the gods more out of fear of crop failure or natural disaster than out of piety. The priests were a very important class to the Maya. They had the knowledge to forecast the right time for planting crops and holding festivals. Human sacrifice formed part of the Mayan religion, as it did with the Aztecs.

Cultural and aesthetic life

Religion seemed to play a dominant part in the long history of the Maya. Their stone-built pyramids were at the centre of each city. These were constructed from a core of earth and rubble, clad with cut stone and cemented with mortar made by burning limestone.

The priests also served as the scribes. The Maya wrote accounts of their history and their legends using the glyph form of picture writing. Paper was made from the inner fibres of certain trees. The Mayan writing is still not fully understood. Show the children examples of these glyphs and then ask them to design their own glyph in the Mayan style to represent an idea or an object.

The Maya were skilled potters. They did not use the wheel for throwing pots but made coil pots which were smoothed out.

Let the children try this technique using clay or Plasticine. Pupils could also research the style of Mayan pottery figures and attempt to reproduce one.

Sport

The ball court would have been a feature of most Mayan cities. A rubber ball about six inches across was used, and the players had to use their fists, elbows and buttocks to hit the ball. A goal was scored by hitting the ball through a ring set 20 or 30 feet high in a wall. Pupils could try this game for themselves if you can set a ring high enough. It must have been a rare occasion when a goal was scored.

Books

Everyday Life of the Maya, R Whitlock (Batsford/Putnam).
The People Who Came, A Norman (Longman).
What Became of the Maya, P Francis (Wheaton).

Benin

Although we can understand that teachers may wish to undertake this unit to develop pupils' understanding of African history and culture, we must advise that at the time of writing there is not a wide range of material available for KS2 pupils related to the Benin. This will make pupils' research difficult.

Starting points

Pupils will be able to find the Republic of Benin on a modern map of Africa. It is west of Nigeria and east of Togo. The ancient Benin kingdom covered an area approximate to the Benin division of modern Nigeria, about 100 miles south east of the kingdom of Ife. Benin was one of West Africa's foremost states. It only became known to Europeans in any detail in AD 1600. Ask the children to draw two maps comparing modern West Africa with the territory of the Benin.

Political aspects

The kingship of Benin was established about AD 1000. There is evidence that there had been a number of dynasties before that date. It is believed that by the end of the thirteenth century these dynasties had collapsed and that the elders or noblemen sent messengers to the ruler of the Oba kingdom asking him to send them a strong ruler. The ruler sent his son who, though he only stayed for a short time, married a Benin princess who bore his son. The son became the founder of the new dynasty and was known as the Oba Ewuare.

The next Oba Ewuare reigned from about AD 1440. He added 201 neighbouring towns to those already controlled by his people. He is said to have constructed good roads in Benin City and to have been a skilled healer. Although the Benin rulers were not actually worshipped as gods, they were thought to have divine elements as the representatives of the Most High. The Obas had enormous prestige in the community, but they were not despots; their status seems to have been roughly comparable to that of the Tudor monarchs in England. They ruled through chiefs and sub-chiefs who were organised into rival groupings so as to complement each other's rights and duties and to place limits on the power of the King.

In AD 1600, a Dutchman, Dierick Ruiters, went to Benin as a merchant. He reported that Benin was a city with broad straight streets. Before entering the gates of the city, Ruiters observed a large suburb outside it. He described the houses as being large and fine and the King's palace as having many courtyards and galleries, which were always guarded by sentries. The King made an annual 'public progress' around the exterior of his palace, riding a richly ornamented horse and followed by a train of 300 or 400 gentlemen, horses and musicians.

The 'public progress' would make a good starting point for role-play. Pupils could reconstruct costumes to wear. Musical instruments could be made as a design and technology task. Drums, stringed harps, percussion instruments and flutes could be included. These instruments could be used to make music for the procession.

Cultural and aesthetic life

The Benin kingdom came into prominence largely because of the Iron Age culture persisting in much of Africa, and the Benin kings commemorated their triumphs with statues, artefacts and jewellery of bronze and brass. Many examples of these remain in existence today. There are also paintings by contemporaries such as seventeenth century Dutch artists, showing the Oba's annual progress, and written accounts of their culture, some of which were commissioned by the Obas themselves. These were written in the Edo language as well as the Dutch of Dierick Ruiters' accounts.

Visitors from Europe were impressed by the social discipline and civic order of the Benin, and by the general stability and self-confidence of the people. They were surprised, however, by some aspects of Benin life, such as the fact that the Oba had 1,000 wives! The Dutch traders were received by the Benin people with much civility, and even before trading began the Portuguese had visited Benin as missionaries. They had been allowed to build a church in Benin and bring priests from Portugal. Ambassadors had been exchanged between Portugal and Benin, and the two peoples discovered much about each other's homeland.

Discuss with the children the image of Africa and Africans held by Europeans at that time. Ask them how the Benin civilisation might have challenged that image. The slave trade was important at this time. Pupils could discuss the implications of slavery for such a sophisticated culture.

Religious beliefs

The Benin religion was a complex system of beliefs and practices. They believed that man was composed of three distinct parts, as exemplified by the objects of worship, which were the Head, the Hand and the Spirit of the worshipper himself. The Head represented personal luck and fortune, the Hand physical strength and the Spirit the distillation of soul and mind as opposed to the physical.

The worship of three parts of the body could provide a starting point for poetry, using the following format:
My Hand is . . .
My Head is . . .
My Spirit is . . .
These poems could be read at the end of the role-play, which could be used as the basis for an assembly.

Books

Benin Studies, R E Bradbury (Oxford University Press).
The Story of Africa, B Davidson (Mitchell Beazeley/Channel 4).

Chapter 5
History assemblies

Much of the historical work undertaken by the pupils could be presented as an assembly. This can act as a focus for the work, as well as providing the children with an audience.

Teachers will have used the children's sense of audience to develop their writing for a purpose, and we feel that the idea of presenting findings to the school through an assembly can give purpose to the art, music, drama, photographs, videos and writing that stem from historical research. The anticipation of presenting work to parents, relatives, staff and fellow pupils often adds a sense of excitement to the activities.

Clearly, the objectives will be slightly different for each Key Stage, but the broad aims will be the same:

- to enrich and reinforce the children's learning in history;
- to show that knowledge of the past is a necessary background to, and support for, what we try to understand about the present;
- to involve parents, grandparents and the wider community in the children's learning.

Key Stage 1

At Key Stage 1 we feel that assemblies should be designed as a class project, and undertaken with the children who are currently working on a particular main topic. Each assembly in this chapter, therefore, relates to one of these main topics. It is suggested that each assembly lasts about 20 minutes, but that visitors remain behind afterwards for coffee and to look at the displays, with the class who have held the assembly acting as hosts and guides.

Assembly 1: Families

Objectives

- To give the children experience in understanding growth and change in themselves and their families, noting that adults change even if they do not grow.
- To become aware of the links formed through time by family relationships.

Preparation

Parents, grandparents and others should be invited to the assembly well beforehand. Involve the children as much as possible in the writing and decoration of the invitations. The hall should be arranged with semi-circles of chairs for visitors and room for the action to take place in the centre. A large time-line should be set up (see page 36), and a similarly enlarged family tree (see page 18). There should be a display of pictures and photographs showing different generations of one family, and photographs of people as babies or children as well as recent pictures. Wedding groups and old school photographs could be included.

A particular family could be asked to provide the focal point for the assembly. Of course, this does not necessarily have to be a traditional family of two parents and children; a single parent family is equally valid so long as several generations can be represented. In such a case, though, the family tree (page 18) might need some adaptation.

Introduction

Song: 'Love Somebody' (from the *Tinderbox Song Book*, A & C Black).

The teacher leading the assembly could start by explaining that they are going to think about families, and how everybody is part of one. We all start as babies, develop into children and grow up into adults, probably becoming parents ourselves, then grandparents and often great-grandparents. A distinction would need to be made between growing and changing, pointing out that people change even if they do not grow (changes in hair colour and the need to wear spectacles, for example).

Members of the family forming the focal point of the assembly could be introduced one by one and their names written on the family tree. They could be asked to say when they were born, and their names could be written on the appropriate section of the time-line. Each adult could be asked to recall something that has changed since he or she was small.

Development

Children in the class could be invited to hold up paintings of their families. The children could say the poem 'The End' by A A Milne (from *Now We Are Six*, published by Methuen).

Story

'Milly-Molly-Mandy Goes Errands' from *Milly-Molly-Mandy Stories* by Joyce Lankester Brisley (Puffin) is a good illustration of different generations and the role each member of the family plays in the pattern of family life.

Prayer

The following prayer could be used if it is appropriate to the group. Other prayers can, of course, be substituted.
'Thank you, God, for making us all part of a family. Help us to take care of each other and to listen to each other. When we grow up we shall have stories to tell about when we were small. Our Mums and Dads, Grannies and Grandads all have stories to tell about what life was like before we were born. Thank you God for the gift of memory.'

This assembly could end with a hymn or song chosen by the family who are helping.

Assembly 2: Old things

This is an assembly that could be prepared by a class working on 'Suitcase in the attic' (see page 28). As well as writing invitations to parents and grandparents, the children could produce an illustrated catalogue of the items used in the assembly, and a short explanation of what the assembly is to be about.

Objectives

- To give the children experience in explaining ways of finding out about the past.
- To demonstrate how certain artefacts can tell us about the past, showing where there are differences from and similarities with our own times.

Preparation

Visitors' chairs can be arranged as for Assembly 1, with the children who are taking the assembly sitting in the front in two diagonally arranged groups. The children and the teacher could dress up in Victorian or Edwardian costume. In the centre there should be a display of 'old things'. These could be selections from the suitcase or collected from staff, parents, grandparents and children. They could include the following:
- a baby's christening robe;
- an old book of children's stories;

- a flat iron;
- a Victorian sampler;
- an old doll;
- a chamber pot;
- a few old picture post cards;
- a jug and wash basin.

The children should select the objects, choosing the things about which they feel they know the most.

Introduction

Hymn 'He gave me eyes so I could see the wonders of the world' (from *Someone's Singing Lord*, A&C Black).

One of the children could explain that some of the wonders of the world we sang about are the old things that people keep which help us to find out about history. The teacher should then explain that the class has been finding out about history and ask them to tell the audience about some of the ways they have discovered of finding out about the past. Hopefully the children will answer that they have looked at old toys, books, clothes, letters, postcards and pictures, listened to old people's memories and visited different kinds of museums. Pairs of children could introduce each object and, with the teacher's help, explain its function and how it helps us to understand how people used to live. For example, when looking at the jug and wash basin we could tell that very few people had bathrooms in their houses 100 years ago and someone would have had to carry a pail of water upstairs so that people could wash. If they lived in the countryside they would have had to carry water from a well (think about 'Jack and Jill'). If the water needed to be warm it would have had to have been heated in a kettle over the fire.

Story

The teacher could tell the following story while a few of the children mime it.

'At school, Sally had been finding out about history all week. Her class had been thinking about a family who lived about 100 years ago, and Sally had decided that she would like to have been a Victorian girl, especially if she had been able to sleep in a big brass bed, wear a long dress and a frilly pinafore and sit by a roaring coal fire.

As she was going to bed that night she folded up her track suit and thought how much more fun it would have been to wear a long rustly grey silk dress with purple ribbons on it, like the one she had tried on in the museum that day. She gave a big, big sigh as she snuggled down under her duvet and thought, "of course, I would ride in a carriage instead of going to school in the car . . .", then she seemed to drift into a sound sleep. She was very tired after the day in the museum and her class was going to act a play about it on Monday.

Suddenly she woke up. It was morning and she felt very cold. She was wearing a big white cotton nighty instead of her own red pyjamas. The duvet had gone and she was covered with a thin cotton sheet and a very rough tickly blanket. But that wasn't all – sleeping next to her were her two sisters, Jane and Joy, and there wasn't much room in the bed because they were both bigger than her!

Sally rubbed her eyes and found the room looked completely different. There was cold shiny stuff on the floor, a big chest of drawers and nothing else. It was still dark but Mum called them all to get up and they tumbled out of bed rubbing their eyes and shivering. Jane went downstairs and came back with a bucket of cold water in which they all had a wash. They dressed in thick, rough black dresses and white pinafores, but Sally didn't feel nearly so comfortable as she usually did. Joy plaited her hair so tightly that it hurt.

Jane helped Mum to cook the porridge over the coal fire, and their brother Tom cleaned everyone's boots. Sally and Joy washed up in water that had been heated over the fire in a big black pan, and then Mum gave them a slice of bread and lard each, with a spreading of jam, for their dinner at school.

Then Mum went to work. She wasn't a

school dinner lady any more – no one seemed to know what dinner ladies were! Mum was going to scrub the kitchen in the big house up the hill where the doctor lived. Dad had gone to work ages ago to the factory where buttons were made.

The children set off for school with shawls round their shoulders and horrid stiff boots on their feet. Tom's boots had paper stuffed in them to keep out the rain. Sally's were too big for her but Joy said she shouldn't complain because hers were too small and Jane's hadn't any laces. It was cold and still quite dark, but they had to hurry because it would take an hour to walk to school and if they were late they would all get the cane.

As Sally walked along in the grey gloom of the morning she began to dream of a day when all houses would be warm and all children would have comfortable boots and lovely things to eat – and she began to feel sleepier and sleepier and sleepier.

"Wake up, Sal! You were talking in your sleep. Joy and I could hear you from our room. It's bacon and eggs for breakfast and then we are all going to Sainsbury's in the car. Don't forget it's Saturday!"

Sally was very relieved. She was glad to feel her duvet, to feel the soft carpet on the floor and to know she could go into a warm bathroom for a shower. She was very glad to be living now.'

Prayer

After the story has been discussed, the following prayer could be said where appropriate.

'Thank you, God, for helping us to understand about history through all the old things that people have kept. Help us to be glad we live now, but to remember all the people who lived long ago and who helped to make our world. Amen.'

Conclusion

Hymn: 'Stand up, clap hands, shout thank you Lord'.

Assembly 3: Schooldays

This assembly is intended to link with the work in Topic C, 'Going to school in Great-Grandma's day'. However, in this assembly it is intended for the whole school to join in the work on the history of the school. Even a modern school will have a history, and it has to be remembered that most children in Key Stage 1 will have been born since their school was built. This assembly should be seen as the culmination of all the work done on the history of the school and would, of course, be particularly fitting if it happened to coincide with a special anniversary of the school.

Objectives

- To enable children to understand something of the history of their own school.
- To compare the past of the school with its present.

Preparation

The hall should be arranged as for the previous assemblies, with an exhibition facing the audience. This could consist of old school log books, punishment books, old school photographs, photographs of the area as it once was and plans of the school from education office records. Older people from the area (former pupils and parents of former pupils) could be invited into school in the weeks beforehand to share their earliest memories of the school. These could be written (or typed on the computer) and mounted as part of the exhibition. A large flip chart and the time-line (see page 36) should also be available.

Introduction

Hymn: 'The ink is black, the page is white' (from *Someone's Singing, Lord*, A & C Black).

The teacher taking the assembly should explain that we have been thinking about all the things we enjoy doing in school. The children should be invited to say what their favourite aspects of school life are, and these should be written on the large flip chart. The teacher should then point to the exhibition and say that children have been doing some of these things in this school for X number of years. The children could be asked to suggest where this would fit on the time-line. A discussion should follow in which all the audience are asked to say what else was going on in the world at that time. Some of the ideas put forward could be considered in a little more detail.

Development

The teacher could point out and discuss some of the items in the exhibition, and children and visitors could be allowed an opportunity to look at the exhibits more closely later in the day. A former pupil and a former teacher could talk to the children recalling one or two memories of the time they were at the school. They could be asked to recall the lessons, the building, the people, playtimes and dinner times. Emphasis should be placed on:

- things that have changed;
- things that have stayed the same.

Story

David's First Day At School by N Snell (Hamish Hamilton).

Prayer

'Thank you, God, for our school. Help us to remember the children and teachers who worked here together in years gone by, especially those who remember the past and are able to tell us about it. Bless all the people who are here now and give us the will to go on making our school a good place where people can live and learn with each other. Amen.'

Conclusion

Hymn: 'Hands to work and feet to run, God's good gifts to me and you' (*Someone's Singing, Lord*, A&C Black).

Key Stage 2

Schools may need to reconsider their policy concerning class assemblies. In many schools these are already planned to follow on from normal class work. In others, class assemblies take up a great deal of time in terms of preparation and rehearsals, depriving pupils of time to spend on other things. With so many demands being made upon already crowded timetables, the one-off class assembly may seem rather a luxury. We have noticed that sometimes class assemblies become competitive, and this in turn leads to far more time being spent on preparation than is necessary.

We feel that the school ethos should encourage pupils to present their normal, planned curriculum work on a regular basis to other children, both in the classroom and in school assemblies. One assembly per class per term may no longer be adequate. Schools will need to consider how the notion of a predominantly Christian assembly can be reconciled with pupils presenting work. The usual format is to include a selection of relevant hymns and prayers at the beginning or the end.

In our experience a 20- to 25-minute presentation is long enough to maintain interest if there is a variety of content. Any longer, and the younger pupils watching will not be able to concentrate. All the pupils who wish to take part should be allowed to do so. It is tempting to use star pupils to do all the reading, but this gives a clear message to pupils who are not selected. The process of taking an active part in a presentation is more important than the actual presentation as a product.

It would be possible to give pupils the task of designing their own assembly based upon their work, handling the publicity and writing the invitations. This would form links with the Technology National Curriculum programme of study at Key Stage 2, developing artefacts, systems and environments. If this approach is used, teachers will need to make sure that dominant characters do not prevent other pupils from playing an active part in the assembly.

One way of presenting work as an assembly would be to plan a 25-minute sequence that gives examples representing the chronological breadth of the unit and the variety of media that pupils have used to record their research. A range of presentation methods helps maintain interest for those watching.

Assembly 1: Ancient Egypt

An assembly based on SSUC might focus on the Egyptian period. Pupils could start by reading a summary of what they have found out, such as the flood waters making the soil fertile, how irrigation was developed, the lifestyle of the peasants and the lifestyle of the royalty, the religious beliefs that prevailed, and so on. One child could explain how the hieroglyphic system of writing developed, while another could draw an example of a hieroglyph on an overhead projector transparency.

Examples of paper made using the papyrus method could be shown, with an explanation and perhaps a quick demonstration.

A long frieze showing aspects of Egyptian life could be walked across the front of the hall or displayed as a backdrop to the assembly. If pupils have made replicas of Egyptian head-dresses and jewellery, these could be paraded. A parody of a fashion show ('and here we have Sally wearing the latest style in mummy masks') might amuse the people watching.

A reading from the Bible about the exodus of the Israelites from Egypt or Joseph in Egypt can be included, with an explanation of the chronological context.

The pupils could write a piece of dramatic prose on the theme of the harsh life of a slave building a pyramid. This could be read out in the assembly as choral speaking. The script could be divided into sections to be spoken by individuals, groups and the whole class.

A song ends an assembly very well. Although no genuine ancient Egyptian songs are readily available, there are several spirituals which tell the story of when the Children of Israel were enslaved in Egypt. These were written by slaves in North America who identified themselves with the oppressed Israelites. Two of the best known are 'When Israel was in Egypt's Land' and 'There was a Man come into Egypt'.

Work from the project should be displayed around the front of the hall for parents, visitors, fellow pupils and governors to view before and after the assembly.

Sample programme

The programme might look like this:

- Hymn and prayer, introduced by class members (five minutes).
- Presentation of various aspects of the work (five minutes).
- Paper-making and letter-writing demonstration (five minutes).
- Fashion show (three minutes).
- Bible reading (two minutes).
- Choral speaking (three minutes).
- Song (two minutes).

Assembly 2: Puppets

An unusual assembly that we remember used craft work as much as historic work and was based on puppet-making. The much-used method of blowing up a balloon and covering it with papier mâché was used to form the puppet heads. The papier mâché was allowed to dry and the balloons were carefully burst. Noses and ears were stuck on and the whole face given a layer of tissue-paper to finish it off before painting. Thick dowel rods were stuck to the heads, a cross-piece of dowel firmly fixed across for the shoulders, and two short sections of dowel with flexible wire joints were added for each arm. Thick card hands were stuck on, and the puppets were then painted. Wool was cut to length and stuck on for the hair. The pupils then cut out and sewed the costumes.

The particular assembly that we are thinking about was set in the time of King John, but pupils can use their research into costumes as part of any Study Unit to inform the costume design. Thin dowel rods were connected to each puppet's hands, and these were long enough to work the arms with when the puppet was held above the pupil's head.

A screen was made for the pupils to hide behind and work the puppets. It was roughly 10cm taller than the tallest pupil. Corrugated card was used for the screen, which was arranged in a zigzag to enable the card to stand unsupported. The front of the card was painted as scenery, and each end of the screen had a built-up section to allow the puppets to enter and exit the stage.

A long piece of twine was stretched across the hall about one and a half metres behind the screen and one metre higher. A backdrop painted on sheets of kitchen paper was hung from this line. The puppets were worked above the front screen and in front of the backdrop, one pupil holding the main dowel while a second pupil worked the arms. The dialogue was worked out by the pupils and recorded on tape, and suitable dramatic music was added. This recording allowed the pupils to

concentrate on working the puppets, and also provided a consistent set of cues.

This assembly could be adapted to tell stories such as:

- Roman troops on Hadrian's Wall facing attacking Picts;
- Aztecs meeting Spaniards;
- Greeks defending passes;
- Londoners during the Blitz;
- Saxons facing a Viking raid;
- King Alfred fighting the Vikings.

As a bonus, the puppets can form part of a classroom display afterwards.

Other ideas

Other assemblies might lend themselves to:

- drama;
- tableaux of historical scenes, with a narrator;
- slide shows;
- video shows, with drama by pupils in costume representing the lives of people they have studied.

A quick method of making background scenery for drama is to photocopy or trace an appropriate picture on to an overhead projector acetate sheet, and then project this on to a wall behind the actors.

Chapter 6
Assessment

The question of assessment is at the forefront of many teachers' minds at present. The extra time which appears to be needed seems impossible to find, but assessment is not a new demand; teachers have always assessed children and evaluated the success of work undertaken. The National Curriculum, with increased emphasis on formal assessment procedures, is merely seeking to make explicit that which was once implicit. It has, in fact, served to concentrate the minds of many people on the question of what and how we should assess and what we should do with the information once it is gathered together. History, no less than other areas of the curriculum, should undergo a process of assessment, even though there is no statutory obligation to do this. We should attempt to assess what we have taught for the following reasons.

- We need to know how much of what we have attempted to teach has in fact been learned (summative assessment).
- We need information which enables us to formulate future plans based on the children's current level of knowledge and understanding (formative assessment).
- We need to test and monitor the materials and methods we are using.

Planning a programme of assessment

What do we need to assess?

We could base our assessment on knowledge and understanding, attitudes and the acquisition of historical skills.

Photocopiable pages 171 to 173 offer examples of assessment sheets. The examples for Key Stage 1 use the themes and topics suggested in this book, but can be adapted to suit the individual teacher's needs.

Knowledge and understanding

Knowledge and understanding could be assessed through the work suggested on the Key Elements in the programmes of study. Linking it to these Key Elements, we can use the following criteria:
1. Thorough understanding.
2. Fair understanding.
3. Needs further experience.

(See photocopiable page 171.)

Attitudes

Consider what attitudes the child has shown towards work in history. This could also be expressed on a three-point scale, using the following criteria:
1. Positive and enthusiastic.
2. Varying according to the task in hand.
3. Still not fully engaged; needs further stimulation.

(See photocopiable page 172.)

Historical skills

What historical skills has the child gained? This again could be expressed on a three-point scale, using the following criteria:
1. Able.
2. Becoming able.
3. Needs more help.

(See photocopiable page 172.)

This assessment should consider to what extent the child can respond to a range of historical questions, can ask historical questions and can identify differences between primary and secondary sources.

How do we assess work in history?

- We can assess children's understanding by asking them some of the questions suggested in the course of each topic and recording some of the answers they give. To do this effectively we need to talk to the children in small groups, or occasionally as individuals. This makes it necessary to enlist the help of volunteers, who must be adequately and correctly briefed. It is also important to note the questions the children themselves raise, and the questions their comments give rise to.
- We can assess by observing the children as they work in small groups, noting such activities as role-play, art and craft work and practical activities in history-related areas of maths, science and technology.
- We can assess by looking at the quality of children's writing and drawing and noting the details they have observed, remembered and recorded.
- We can assess by using videos and sound cassettes to record the children's responses. This can be particularly useful in assessing children's levels of social interaction as they are working.
- We can assess by asking children what they think they have learned, what they find most interesting and what they have enjoyed. This is probably the most important and the most neglected aspect of assessment.

It would be pointless and unrealistic to attempt assessment at every stage of the work, although a great deal of informal assessment will be going on for much of the time. On the other hand it is important not to put the children into a test situation, with the accompanying stress and strain for all concerned. A sensible arrangement would be to undertake a structured assessment of each of the main topics, recording the results for inclusion in the child's profile.

How do we record the results of assessment?

A clearly designed record sheet for each child with space for each topic would seem to be a straightforward way of tabulating information. Page 173 gives an example of a record sheet for the assessment of children's historical skills at Key Stage 2. It must be emphasised that teachers will need to adapt any record-keeping system to the needs of their own approach.

What use can we make of the information?

Assessment is only worthwhile if we make positive use of the information we collect. We need the information to inform our judgements about the level of work children are ready to attempt in the next stage. We shall be making decisions not only for a class as a whole but for individual children, since the contributions made by each child will depend on motivation, level of maturity and overall ability. In all the themes and topics, a measure of differentiation will need to be worked out by each teacher to give all the children opportunities to learn.

We need the information which arises from assessment to gain insight into the materials and methods we are using, and we will have to adapt, adjust and, where necessary, reformulate our plans as we gain feedback. Some of our resources may need rethinking, and we might become aware of needs we had not anticipated.

Finally, assessment confronts us with the need to review and revise our school's history policy regularly, providing evidence of how it is working in practice.

Record of progress in history at Key Stage 1

Name ....

Place the appropriate number in the box and add a comment if needed

Criterion for assessment	Topic A My story	Topic B Suitcase in the attic	Topic C School in Great-Grandma's day
Knowledge and understanding of:	1. Thorough understanding 2. Fair understanding 3. Needs more experience	1. Thorough understanding 2. Fair understanding 3. Needs more experience	1. Thorough understanding 2. Fair understanding 3. Needs more experience
Concepts of time: past, present, year, seasons. Why changes have taken place			
Importance of stories and oral history to give differing views of the past (eg, a rich and a poor child)			
Importance of deriving knowledge from old artefacts			
Importance of expressing understanding in different ways (eg, talking to grandparents, making models, drama, writing)			

Record of progress in history at Key Stage 1

Name ....

Place the appropriate number in the box and add a comment if needed

Criterion for assessment	Topic A My story	Topic B Suitcase in the attic	Topic C School in Great-Grandma's day
Attitude to history	1. Positive and enthusiastic 2. Varies according to task 3. Still not fully engaged	1. Positive and enthusiastic 2. Varies according to task 3. Still not fully engaged	1. Positive and enthusiastic 2. Varies according to task 3. Still not fully engaged
Historical skills:	1. Able 2. Becoming able 3. Needs more help	1. Able 2. Becoming able 3. Needs more help	1. Able 2. Becoming able 3. Needs more help
Able to respond to a range of questions			
Able to ask historical questions			
Able to differentiate between primary and secondary sources			

History record for individual pupils at Key Stage 2

Name ....

The nine Study Units to be undertaken

L2	Place familiar objects in chronological order									
	Suggest reasons why people in the past acted as they did									
	Identify differences between past and present times									
	Show an awareness that different stories about the past can give different versions of what happened									
	Recognise that historic sources can stimulate and help answer questions about the past									
L3	Describe changes over a period of time									
	Give a reason for an historical event or development									
	Identify differences between times in the past									
	Distinguish between a fact and a point of view									
	Make deductions from historical sources									
L4	Recognise that over a time some things changed and others stayed the same									
	Show an awareness that historical events usually have more than one cause and consequence									
	Describe different features of an historical period									
	Show an understanding that deficiencies in evidence may lead to different interpretations of the past									
	Put together information drawn from different historical sources									
L5	Distinguish between different kinds of historical change									
	Identify different types of cause and consequence									
	Show how different features in an historic situation relate to each other									
	Recognise that interpretation of the past may differ from what is known to have happened									
	Comment on the usefulness of an historic source as evidence for a particular enquiry									

Chapter 7
Setting up a school resource bank

The teaching of history, like any other curriculum area, demands the provision of carefully planned and organised resources, many of which can be gathered together to form a permanent school resource bank. The responsibility for co-ordinating such a bank would need to rest with a particular person, but many other people, such as staff, children, parents, grandparents, school governors and members of the local community, could be asked to help in assembling it. Many of the resources suggested for each of the topics and themes would be gathered together for one particular occasion and then returned to their original source, but the provision in school of a permanent stock of historical resources would make for good starting points for historical topics and help teachers to plan ahead with greater confidence. A collection of items for role-play would also be useful.

Human resources are extremely important, and they will be considered separately, with some discussion of the different ways in which other people's experiences can be used and incorporated in the school's plans for work in history.

Resources

The most valuable resources would fit into one of the following categories.

Visual resources

Photographs

Old photographs of the local area, old school photographs and pictures of family events such as weddings showing people dressed in the fashions of former times can be copied by most modern photographers in either black and white or sepia tint. Occasionally old photograph albums can be picked up in antique shops or will be donated by individuals.

Modern photographs of places and things of historic interest such as old buildings, or photographs recording reconstructions of events, could be taken by teachers and children specially for the resource bank.

Pictures

Illustrations cut from books and magazines and large posters and pictures from back copies of magazines such as *Child Education* are a useful resource. Members of staff could be asked to look back through their old copies to extract all the pictures relating to history. Greetings cards with reproductions of historical scenes are another useful source, as are reproductions of famous paintings.

Written resources

Books

A good selection of reference books should be included, both for children and for teachers. Examples of these are listed in the references section on page 185, as well as in the lists of resources at the end of each topic and theme. Teachers will have to make provisional decisions as to which books they would choose to buy, and which they would borrow. If possible, the collection should include examples of old cookery books, children's books (such as 1930s comic annuals), Bibles, school books and books published to celebrate national events such as the coronation of George V.

Old postcards

These can be a valuable source of information because they comprise a picture, some hand-written text and a date. Postcards can be acquired from personal collections or from antique fairs and specialist shops or stalls, but they are becoming increasingly expensive.

Old newspapers and magazines

Old newspapers reporting important historical events are useful, even if they are only copies. Women's magazines from former years (increasingly available from junk shops) give much information about domestic life, fashion and food. Old copies of publications such as *Radio Times* are also worth collecting.

Back copies of modern educational magazines such as *Child Education* and *Junior Education* are valuable because many issues contain accounts of work in history.

Posters and programmes

A few posters advertising household goods, soaps and clothes would be useful, together with some posters advertising plays and concerts. Try to obtain some old theatre programmes which also contain advertisements.

Artefacts

Household objects

The term 'artefacts' clearly covers a wide range of things, but some objects worth collecting for a school resource bank include old lamps, vases or ornaments, wartime souvenirs, a Victorian chamber pot, an old flat iron, a dolly maid and a collection of bottles and jars.

Coins

Coins from the pre-decimal era are useful, since they show the dates and heads of reigning monarchs. Coins might come from personal collections, but they can also be bought from collectors' fairs.

Toys

Old dolls and teddy bears might be donated to the resource bank, along with Dinky and Matchbox toys. A collection of old jigsaw puzzles would also be useful.

School memorabilia

Of particular interest are log-books, punishment books, exercise books, reports and everyday objects such as geometry sets.

Clothing and furnishings

Old clothes

Genuine old clothing is quite difficult to acquire permanently, but people are often happy to lend it. If the school makes it known that it is interested in acquiring old clothing, however, items will occasionally be donated when an old person dies and their effects are being disposed of. Many a relative would be happy to think that Grandad's old trilby hat or Grandma's old blouse were to be cared for and appreciated by the younger generation. Children's clothing such as old-fashioned items of school uniform may be offered, as well as the odd item of military uniform.

Role-play

Simple costumes can be made, such as Victorian pinafores and Eton collars. Fringed table cloths and lace curtains which tie back can convert the home corner into a parlour. Wartime siren suits can be made from track suits, and rolls of corrugated card can serve as Anderson shelters.

Display

Lengths of Laura Ashley or William Morris-type fabric and wallpaper make wonderful backgrounds for displays. The good-tempered aspidistra can add atmosphere to a Victorian or Edwardian display.

Audio resources

Cassettes, records and videos

The following recordings would be useful:

- sounds such as air raid alerts, the 'all clear', an old chiming clock;
- recordings of people's accounts of events or personal reminiscences (see 'Human resources', page 179);
- music relating to a particular topic or theme, or which would be appropriate for an assembly;
- videos of visits or activities.

Human resources

The human resources are probably the most valuable of all, and they have been mentioned frequently in the topics and themes dealing with more recent history. Older people in the community, ranging from children's grandparents in their 50s to people in their 90s, all have a part to play. As well as inviting them to school to take part in the work, their memories and accounts can be recorded and stored. All members of the school community can be asked to take part, including dinner ladies, caretakers, crossing wardens and the school nurse and doctor. Parents of both sexes should be encouraged to help in the classroom and on visits, along with students, governors and helpers from the local secondary school. Everyone who participates must be properly briefed as to what is going on.

Creating history for ourselves

As we are trying to demonstrate to children that people and events in the past are real, we might attempt to show them that what is happening to us now will one day be history and will be of great interest to people who live after us. An interesting activity to be undertaken by children at any stage, and certainly at Key Stages 1 and 2, would be the creation of their own school history book and time capsule. This could be seen as a direct primary source to be used by future children when they come to investigate what the school was like in the 1990s. We suggest that schools might like to try keeping a school history book for a year, and then consider whether it should be an ongoing thing or something undertaken from time to time.

Keeping a school history book

The school history book could be written by the children themselves, with their contributions pasted into a large, durable hardback book. We feel that all the classes in a school should take turns in being 'history writers' for the week or however frequently the book is to be written. The advantage of a weekly book would be that the pattern of a school year would emerge in a very fresh and immediate fashion. If a rota system were worked out, the onus would only fall on each class and teacher perhaps once or twice each half term. Teachers who feel that weekly writing is too much of a strain will obviously work out their own pattern.

The ideal way of organising this activity would be for all the children together to choose what they consider to be the most interesting thing that has happened in school during that week, decide how it could best be recorded (by writing, drawing, graphs, collage or a combination of these).

The decision as to whether the work should be handwritten or typed on the computer could also be taken by the children. The youngest children in the school might need the teacher to act as scribe for their entries. Since only one main written entry and one other type of contribution would be required per class, the teacher and children would need to decide whether one or two people could be delegated to be scribe and artist, transcribing everyone's ideas.

The following sorts of school events could be recorded:

- a special assembly;
- a class outing or visit;
- a visiting theatre group;
- Harvest Festival;
- Diwali;
- bonfire celebrations;
- Christmas activities;
- the leavers' concert;
- sports day;
- new children starting school;
- a visit to or by another school;
- a games match;
- musical activities.

It would be equally valid, however, to record very simple events in the life of the particular class whose turn it happens to be, such as the bringing of a new baby sibling into school, or the fact that one of their number has left to go to another school. Whatever is selected should have some significance for all the class.

A time capsule

The time capsule would be something related to the school history book, but different in form. It could consist of a durable box, placed in a safe place in school and labelled 'TO BE OPENED IN THE YEAR 2021' (or whenever). The box could contain items discussed and agreed by all the children and teachers. These items could include:

- photographs of children, teachers and the building;
- a letter written by the head and signed by the staff;
- a piece of writing by a child;
- a child's painting;
- an exercise book for mathematics or English;
- a maths scheme book in current use;
- a reading scheme book in current use.

All of these activities would be useful for work in English as well as in history.

Chapter 8
Conclusion

As we reach the end of our book we would like to explain the reasons for what we have chosen to include, comment on some areas where we feel we have not given a great deal of guidance and restate some points that we wish to emphasise most strongly.

We have attempted to gather together a core of information that teachers can use as starting points, whilst giving them opportunities to research further afield and organise the material to suit their own children in their particular schools. At Key Stage 2 it has been necessary to give a somewhat greater emphasis to facts than at Key Stage 1, because of the requirements of the National Curriculum itself. Nevertheless, we have tried very hard to avoid writing a text book. We have tried to treat Key Stage 1 as a valid learning stage in its own right, whilst being aware of the need to lay foundations for Key Stage 2.

This need to lay foundations for the next stage applies equally to Key Stage 2. We have born in mind the 'spiral' approach mentioned in the Final Report of the National Curriculum working group of history ('Structure of the History Course' 2.6), where it states that 'The general philosophy underlying our proposed structure can be described diagrammatically (Fig 1) by means of the 'cone' and 'helix'.

In this diagram (which is purely indicative, and not an attempt to depict a set of precise geometrical relationships) the cone represents the broadening and necessary accumulation of historical information as a pupil moves from age 5 to age 16 through the four key stages. A pupil's growing understanding and skills are represented in the diagram by the twin helix. One helix represents increasing understanding and conceptual sophistication and the other helix represents increasing refinement and competence in performing historical tasks.

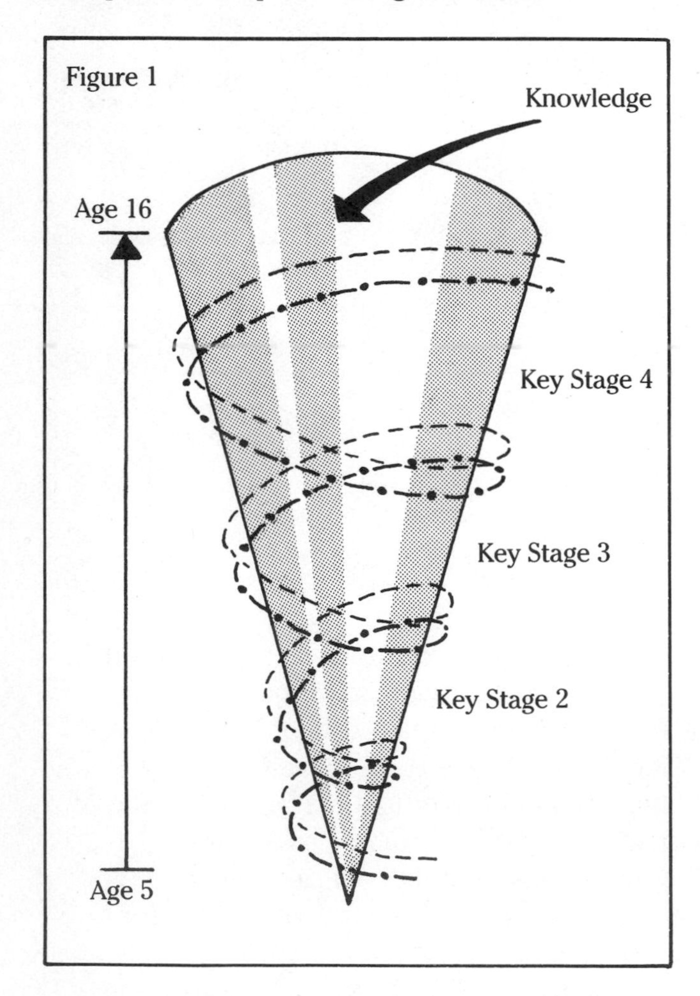

The twin helix and the cone are inter-dependent and of equal importance; no more should be read into the diagram than that.'

Multicultural dimensions

The need to consider the question of delivering a multicultural curriculum has exercised our minds throughout, but we have not designed our themes and topics specifically with this need uppermost in our minds, for two important reasons:

- the format of the National Curriculum itself;
- our own particular fields of experience and expertise.

Having worked through our suggestions carefully, however, we feel that many of them (by no means all!) could be adapted to fulfill the needs of children whose roots lie outside Britain. Much of the work involving parents and older people, in particular, could include the memories of African or Asian people. In several instances we have pointed out the opportunities for work of this kind and hope it will be taken up by teachers. There are certainly other people who will produce work which meets the needs of ethnic minorities more fully than we have been able to in this book.

Some important points

The points we wish to restate are as follows:

- The cross-curricular nature of all the work suggested is very important. If teachers attempt an 'end-on' type of approach to the National Curriculum, overload will become so serious that complete breakdown will be inevitable. In this book we have attempted to cover most of the English attainment targets through history, as well as some of those for science and mathematics. Opportunities for art, craft, technology, geography and music are many. Teachers can themselves devise ways of enriching this cross-curricular mix, bringing in their own local resources.

• The value of using parents, grandparents and other older people in the neighbourhood cannot be stressed too strongly, since eye-witness accounts from people who were 'really there' not only bring history to life but demonstrate how different people see the same event from different points of view. It also helps children to differentiate between what was real and was was fictional, legendary or mythical.
• The importance of getting to know your own local museum is also a feature we wish to emphasise, along with liaison with your local advisor for history.

We wish all those who attempt to teach history to primary children good luck and many interesting and stimulating experiences. To the children we send the wish that history will become a rich and meaningful part of their lives.

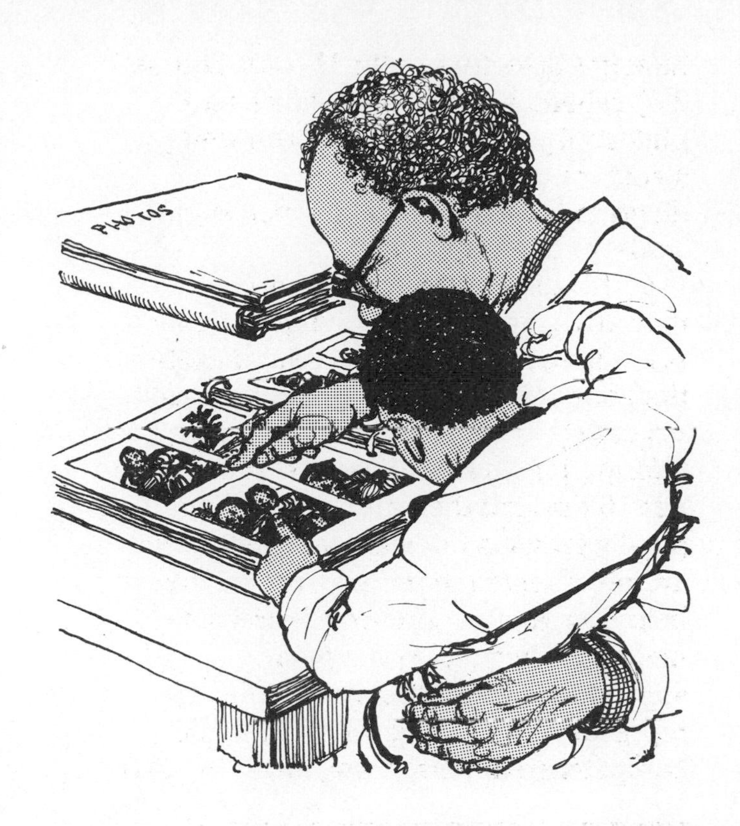

Chapter 9
References and resources

We have included lists of resources at the end of each topic and theme at both Key Stage 1 and Key Stage 2. In 'Setting up a school resource bank' (page 175) a number of suggestions have been made for selecting materials that a school might wish to possess as a permanent resource. At this stage we would like to refer to and recommend many of the resources that we have used ourselves, have been used by colleagues or have been recommended to us through reliable sources. We need to emphasise once again that we do not pretend that our list is in any way exhaustive and we hope that teachers will keep, in their school resource banks, careful accounts of books, articles, pamphlets, places to visit and other information so that there can be a pooling of experience. Computerised information would clearly be ideal since once a disk had been started it could be added to and edited regularly.

In attempting to suggest resources we decided to categorise them in the following way:

- publications, including books, periodicals, specialist journals and articles;
- museums, including specialist museums of buildings and those containing a Victorian or Edwardian school room;
- sites;
- associations and organisations;
- other resources.

Publications

Books

A Chronicle of The Twentieth Century, conceived and co-ordinated by Jacques Legrand, editor in chief Derrik Mercer (Longman).

A Child's History of Britain and Ireland, Christopher Wright (Derrydale Books, New York).

Under 5s and Museums: Guidelines for Teachers (The Ironbridge Museum, Telford, Shropshire).

In Touch with the Past: A Practical Approach to Primary History (Avon Resources for Learning Development Unit, Bishop Road, Bishopstone, Bristol BS7 8LS).

Where's the ME in Museums? – Going to Museums with Children, Milde Waterfall and Sarah Crusin (Vandermere Press, Arlington, Virginia, USA).

The Cambridge Guide to the Museums of Britain and Ireland, Kenneth Hudson and Ann Nicholls (Cambridge University Press).

A series of books we found helpful for pupil and teacher reference was the 'Into the past' series published by Longman. The six titles are as follows: *At home in 1900*, Sallie Purkiss; *In the street in 1900*, Sallie Purkiss; *In the country in 1900*, Elizabeth Merson; *Entertainment in 1900*, Stephen Attmore; *Transport in 1900*, Elizabeth Merson.

Periodicals

Various copies of *Child Education* are most helpful. These are as follows: May 1982 for work on Mums, Dads and Grandparents; March 1985 for a project file on ageing; June 1990 for work on history. Write to Scholastic Publications, Westfield Road, Southam, Warwickshire CV33 0JH.

Packs

The 'Starting History' series (Scholastic Publications) includes packs on 'Transport' and 'Homes' which contain photocopiable worksheets, posters, photographs and teachers' notes.

Specialist journals

GEM (Group for Education in Museums) publishes *JEM* (Journal of Education in Museums) annually and back copies may be obtained from the Museum Education Service, Liverpool Museum, William Brown Street, Liverpool, L3 8EN.

Remnants – Journal of English Heritage Education, Keysign House, 429 Oxford Street, London W1R 2HD.

Historic Houses, Castles and Gardens in Great Britain and Ireland, published annually by ABC Historic Publications, Oldhill, London Road, Dunstable, Bedfordshire.

'History Project Kit: Man Explores', by John Platts (Macmillan).

Museums

Specialist museums of buildings and industrial and rural history

Avoncroft Museum of Buildings, Stoke Heath, Worcestershire B60 4JR. This museum runs a membership scheme with free access to the museum, extensive reference materials, notification of lectures, courses and visits and a regular newsletter.

North of England Open Air Museum, Beamish Hall, Chester-le-Street, Stanley, County Durham DH9 0RG. This is primarily a museum showing many aspects of the everyday way of life of people in north-east England in the last century.

Wigan Pier: 'The Way We Were' Wigan, Lancashire WN3 4EU. An open air museum showing life in north-west England in the last century.

Weald and Downland Open Air Museum, Singleton, West Sussex PO18 0EU. This museum shows aspects of Sussex rural life in the last century.

Welsh Folk Museum, St Fagans, South Glamorgan CF5 6XB. This is a museum showing a range of old buildings from different parts of Wales and from different periods.

Ironbridge, Telford, Shropshire TF8 7AW. This museum stands at the site of the world's first iron bridge, where the industria revolution was born. It is a World Heritage site and has been created around a series of industrial monuments over some six square miles of the Ironbridge Gorge.

The Black Country Museum, Dudley, West Midlands DY1 4SQ. This is a museum showing Black Country life in the last century, including some specific trades such as chain making and rope making.

Museums of science and industry

The Science Museum, South Kensington, London SW7 2DD, contains, among other wonders of science, an excellent exhibition of old bathrooms.

Birmingham Museum of Science and Industry, Newhall Street, Birmingham B3 1RX, is described in its brochure as 'An Aladdin's cave of inventions, machines, technology, and demonstrations from the industrial revolution to the present day, many of which can be seen in action. Explore a Victorian machine shop, trace the development of steam power, the history of the motor car and much more.'

The Mining Museum Trust, Chatterly Whitfield Colliery, Tunstall, Stoke-on-Trent, Staffs, ST6 8UN traces the history of the mining industry through a particular colliery.

Transport museums

The Lock Museum, Walsall Street, Willenhall, West Midlands WV13 2DA.

Darlington Railway Centre and Museum, North Road Station, Darlington DL3 6ST, is run by Darlington Railway Preservation Society and provided by Darlington Borough Council. It is housed in a historic station and shows many old locomotives, lovingly restored.

Birmingham Railway Museum, Warwick Road, Tyseley, Birmingham B11 2HL.

The Severn Valley Railway, The Railway Station, Bewdley, Worcestershire DY12 1BG. This is not strictly a museum, but a restored steam railway. It can give children an experience of travelling through the countryside as their ancestors may have done in order to get to school or work.

Midland Air Museum, Baginton, Coventry.

The Midland Motor Museum, Stanmore Hall, Stourbridge Road, Bridgnorth, Shropshire WV15 6DT.

Museum of British Road Transport, St Agnes Lane, Hales Street, Coventry CV1 1PN.

The Patrick Collection of old motor vehicles, Lifford Lane, Birmingham B30 3NT.

The Beaulieu Abbey and Palace House National Motor Museum, near Lyndhurst, Hampshire.

The National Motor Cycle Museum, Coventry Road, Bickenhill, Solihull B92 0EJ.

The Norton Collection, Davenal House, Bromsgrove, Hereford and Worcester. This is a bicycle collection.

The London Transport Museum, Covent Garden, London WC2E 7BB. This includes an interesting new exhibition commemorating the centenary of the opening of the tube (1890–1990).

The National Maritime Museum, Romney Road, Greenwich, London SE10 9NF.

Exeter Maritime Museum, The Quay, Exeter, Devon EX2 4AN.

Victorian schoolrooms

These are now opening in many parts of the country and will probably increase in number as buildings and old educational artefacts become available. Some of the museums already mentioned have old schoolrooms. A day spent in such a schoolroom provides children with valuable knowledge and exerience as well as a great deal of fun. The ones described here are the ones we ourselves have used.

St. John's Museum, Warwick CV34 4NF. Costumes are provided for both children and adults and a Victorian education teaching pack is available from the museum. The room used is late Stuart rather than Victorian which we feel is a slight disadvantage, although, of course, Victorian schools were sometimes housed in much older buildings.

The Hereford and Worcester County Museum, Hartlebury Castle, near Kidderminster DY11 7XZ. This, again, offers children and adults the opportunity to dress up as Victorians and enjoy a day's Victorian schooling. The building (part of which is the Bishop of Worcester's palace) has some Victorian parts and the atmosphere is certainly very Victorian.

Toy museums

Bethnal Green Museum of Childhood, Cambridge Heath Road, London E2 9PA (which is part of the Victoria and Albert Museum).

The Museum of Childhood, 42 High Street, Royal Mile, Edinburgh EH1 1TG.

The Museum of Childhood, 1 Castle Street, Beaumaris, Gwynedd LLS8 8AP.

The Precinct Toy Collection, Harnert Street, Sandwich, Kent.

Military museums

The Imperial War Museum, Lambeth Road, London SE1 6HZ.

Imperial War Museum, Duxford, Cambridgeshire CB2 4QR.

Sites

In this section we felt we should include some of the excellent houses and castles (National Trust and otherwise) which provide historical experiences for children as well as some of the Roman sites in various parts of the country.

Berrington Hall, near Leominster HR6 0DW (National Trust). This large country house gives a good idea of how a big house was run in the Victorian era. It has a very good laundry.

Coughton Court, near Alcester, Warwickshire B49 5JA (National Trust). This is an Elizabethan House which has strong connections with the Gunpowder Plot.

Aston Hall, Trinity Road, Aston, Birmingham B6 6JD (a branch of the Birmingham Museums and Art Gallery). This is one of the last great Jacobean houses to be built in England. It was lived in by James Watt in the nineteenth century.

Blakesly Hall, Yardley, Birmingham B25 8RN (a branch of the Birmingham Museums and Art Gallery). This is an Elizabethan farmhouse with an interesting herb garden. The house has been furnished and equipped as it was in Elizabethan times, using the original house inventory as a guide.

Sarehole Mill, Cole Bank Road, Hall Green, Birmingham B13 0BD (a branch of the Birmingham Museums and Art Gallery). This is a working corn mill.

Cogges Farm, near Witney, Oxfordshire. This is a farm museum as well as being a working farm.

Roman Baths Museum, Pump Room, Stall Street, Bath, Avon BA1 1LZ.

Wroxeter Roman City (Virconium), Wroxeter, Shropshire SY5 6PH.

Fishbourne Roman Palace, Salthill Road, Chichester, West Sussex PO19 3QR.

Chedworth Roman Villa, Yanworth, Gloucestershire GL54 3LJ.

Hadrian's Wall, the Roman fortification stretching across the north of England.

Warwick Castle. This is one of the finest examples of a castle that is still standing. The staff have produced a new package for teachers allowing one teacher to be admitted free with every 20 children charged. A teacher's book is available. Contact the marketing manager, Warwick Castle, Warwick, CV34 4QU.

Associations and organisations

The Primary History Association, c/o Karen Svansoe, St. John's Wood CP School, Knutsford, Cheshire.

GEM (Group for Education in Museums) c/o Gail Durbin, Keysign House, 429 Oxford Street, London W1R 2HD.

The Historical Association, 59a Kensington Park Road, London SE11 4JH.

The National Trust, 36 Queen Anne's Gate, London SW1H 9AS.

English Heritage Education Service, Keysign House, 429 Oxford Street, London W1R 2HD.

Other resources

Buildings

- Cathedrals and parish churches.
- Old public buildings such as market halls, swimming baths, schools, civic halls and museum and library buildings.
- Old industrial buildings, shops and houses.

Television

How We Used to Live, Yorkshire Television.

Photographs

The Benjamin Stone Collection of Photographs, Birmingham Reference Library. There are other collections of old photographs available both locally and nationally. Consult your local library or museum.

Human resources

As well as the many possibilities for using human resources already mentioned on page 179, every teacher should be fully aware of the advantages of consulting the local adviser responsible for history.

Acknowledgements

The authors and publishers wish to thank the following for their help in the preparation of this book: Joan Alexander, Rita Smith and the children of Acocks Green Infant School, Birmingham; the children and staff of George Dixon Primary School, Birmingham; Dr Simon Penn and Avoncroft Museum of Buildings, Bromsgrove.

Other Scholastic books

Bright Ideas
The Bright Ideas books provide a wealth of resources for busy primary school teachers. There are now more than 20 titles published, providing clearly explained and illustrated ideas on topics ranging from *Word Games* and *Science* to *Display* and *Classroom Management*. Each book contains material which can be photocopied for use in the classroom.

Bright Ideas for Early Years
The *Bright Ideas for Early Years* series has been written specially for nursery and reception teachers, playgroup leaders and all those who work with 3- to 6-year-olds. The books provide sound practical advice on all areas of learning. The ideas and activities are easy to follow and clearly illustrated.

Inspirations
The *Inspirations* series provides a wide range of practical activities supported by essential background information. The books all offer strategies for the delivery of the National Curriculum and guidance on assessment and record-keeping. Photocopiable material is included.

Management Books
The Management Books are designed to help teachers to organise their time, classroom and teaching more efficiently. The books deal with topical issues, such as *Parents and Schools*, and organising and planning, *Project Teaching*, and are written by authors with lots of practical advice and experiences to share.

Let's Investigate
Let's Investigate is an exciting range of photocopiable activity books giving open-ended investigative tasks. Designed to cover the 6- to 12 year-old range these books are ideal for small group or individual work. Each book presents progressively more difficult concepts and many of the activities can be adapted for use throughout the primary school. Detailed teacher's notes outlining the objectives of each photocopiable sheet and suggesting follow-up activities have been included.